Praise for the TLV

"The Tree of Life Version is a miracle in motion."

Jack Hayford

"The TLV is the fulfillment of a long-awaited dream to have a complete translation by biblical scholars sensitive to the Hebraic character of both Testaments. The church has known since its earliest days that it has a spiritual indebtedness to the Jewish people (Rom. 15:27), since everything it holds dear came through Jewish hands. Unfortunately, this vital knowledge of the Jewish roots of Christianity is sorely lacking in the modern church. Fortunately, the TLV is now here to restore what has been lost at a time in history when it is needed most."

Randall Price, PhD, distinguished research professor; executive director of the Center for Judaic Studies, Liberty University

"This Bible is the collective work of this renewed Messianic Jewish community and the first and only of its kind. Translated directly from the original Greek and Hebrew texts and vetted by some of our best and brightest Messianic theologians and scholars, the translation is true to its original Hebraic roots and idiom. More than a historically important work, it represents the fulfillment of this prophetic, last days' restoration and the reestablishment of the Jewish Remnant to their unique and important leadership role in the body of the Messiah."

Jonathan Bernis, Jewish Voice Ministries International

"I wholeheartedly endorse the TLV and encourage everyone to read it."

Wayne Wilks Jr., PhD, executive pastor of Jewish Ministries, Gateway Church; president, Messianic Jewish Bible Institute

"I am so excited about this innovative new translation of the Bible. The Tree of Life Version is unlike any other Bible you've ever read. This Bible focuses on the Jewish roots that are so foundational to our Christian faith. With its relatable Hebrew language and authentic cultural context, you'll gain a new appreciation for how the Bible was originally meant to be read and understood."

Robert Morris, founding senior pastor, Gateway Church; bestselling author of *The Blessed Life*, *From Dream to Destiny*, and *Truly Free*

SHALOM
in PSALMS

A Devotional *from* the Jewish Heart *of* the Christian Faith

JEFFREY SEIF, GLENN BLANK,
AND PAUL WILBUR

BakerBooks

a division of Baker Publishing Group
Grand Rapids, Michigan

Published by Baker Books
a division of Baker Publishing Group
P.O. Box 6287, Grand Rapids, MI 49516-6287
www.bakerbooks.com

Printed in the United States of America

Library of Congress Cataloging-in-Publication Data
Names: Seif, Jeffrey L., 1955– author. | Blank, Glenn, author. | Wilbur, Paul (Worship leader), author.
Title: Shalom in Psalms : a devotional from the Jewish heart of the Christian faith / Jeffrey Seif, Glenn Blank, and Paul Wilbur.
   Other titles: Bible. Psalms. English. Tree of Life Version. 2017.
Description: Grand Rapids : Baker Books, 2017.
Identifiers: LCCN 2016036482 | ISBN 9780801019470 (pbk.)
Subjects: LCSH: Bible. Psalms—Devotional literature.
Classification: LCC BS1430.54 .S45 2017 | DDC 242/.5—dc23
LC record available at https://lccn.loc.gov/2016036482

17 18 19 20 21 22 23   7 6 5 4 3 2 1

SHALOM
in PSALMS

The Vision and How It Came Together

The book you have in hand is part of a larger, joint-venture translation project, a collaborative effort of a number of Messianic Jewish scholars, rabbis, and friends.

Messianic Rabbi Mark Greenberg and his wife, Daniah Greenberg, conceived the visionary idea of gathering Messianic scholars from across the broad spectrum of Messianic experience to see if they could work together on a translation. Mark and Daniah wanted it to be Jewish friendly, punctuated with Messianic Jewish nuances, accentuated with Messianic artwork, accurate, readable, and accessible to children—in short, a Messianic Family Bible.

This is no small vision!

The image of a shepherd leading sheep is the task and challenge of pastoral leadership. When it comes to getting scholars together—and Messianic Jewish scholars at that—it might have been more like a shepherd chasing a herd of cats! As they say, two Jews, three opinions!

Could we really do it—assemble a vetted translation representative of the whole Messianic Jewish movement? Yes, because everyone on this project loves the Bible and loves *Yeshua*.

Guided principally, though not exclusively, by the able hands of Rabbi Dr. Jeffrey Feinberg, the New Covenant Scriptures came to life under the title of *The Tree of Life Bible—The New Covenant*. That attended to, and with the first run nearly exhausted not long after it came off the press, we began working on the Older Covenant (*Tanakh*), at which time I was brought on by Rabbi Mark and Daniah Greenberg to serve as the project manager and vice president.

A team of text managers came together (Rabbi Jeffrey Adler, Rabbi Barney Kasdan, and Dr. Vered Hillel) and, along with several new translators with expertise in ancient Semitic languages, began work on renderings of the Hebrew Bible.

The Tree of Life Version (TLV) translation of the Psalms you have in hand was built on the Jewish Publication Society's 1917 version of the Hebrew Bible, now in the public domain. It had been guided by the able hands of our literary editor, Rabbi Dr. Glenn Blank, developed by a principal translator, Dr. Ihab Griess, double-checked by Dr. Patrice Fischer, and tweaked and approved by our theology committee (constituted then by Dr. Ray Gannon, Dr. Rich Robinson, and Rabbi Jeffrey Adler, and chaired by Rabbi Eric Tokajer). It was then sent to another language expert, Dr. Mordecai Cohen (in Israel), sent back to Dr. Blank, and then sent to Fred Edelstein for a final readability review—all with a mind to leave as good an impression on your mind's eye as possible.

Meanwhile, we also started a Messianic Jewish commentary on the Psalms. I had just recently finished shooting a television series in Israel on the Psalms of Ascent with Zola Levitt Presents and was geared up for psalms as a result. Given the popularity that the Psalms enjoy in the broader culture, often turned to by folk looking for biblical medicine for life's assorted hurts, developing a book to go hand in hand with the new rendering of the Psalms seemed a natural. But just as the translation itself represents the breadth of the Messianic Jewish movement, I didn't want to do the commentary alone.

Who would help me?

Spirited along by the vision of this project, I asked longtime good friend Paul Wilbur if he'd be willing to come alongside me and assist with commentary on the Psalms. He's a well-known artist—surely everyone in the Messianic movement and much of the Christian world knows and loves his music and gift for worship. I figured some might want to know more of his mind on the Psalms too. In this volume you will hear Paul the scholar as well as Paul the worshiper.

Messianic Rabbi Dr. Glenn Blank is less known to the broader world, yet he faithfully serves the Lord behind the scenes. He is one of the longest-running team members in the translation project and arguably the hardest working. He brings to the project valuable expertise in linguistics and literary theory. Given all the hard work he has done to make us all look good, I wanted readers to experience Glenn speaking in his own voice, as well as cleaning up all of ours.

In sum, though I conceived the idea of writing a Psalms devotional commentary, the book you have in hand was a team effort of talented people who give all the praise back to the Lord. My hope is that what has come from our hearts and minds will go to your minds and hearts—that you will find it useful for study and even more so for prayer. Above all, I hope that you'll hear God's heart for you, not only as you open up God's Word but also as you open yourself to it. My prayer is that you will hear Him speak to you in ways that make a difference for you.

Thank you for trusting us with the task of translating and commenting on God's Word for you.

Blessings,
Jeffrey Seif, DMin

A Worship Leader's Introduction to the Psalms

The book of Psalms has long been a source of encouragement and comfort for all who journey into its pages. The songs of the psalmists (not all are written by David) reveal many aspects not only of the writers but of the Author of all Scripture as well. As a teacher/songwriter/worship leader, I often refer to these verses for much more than just writing material—they are words of life to all who find them. There are psalms of healing and deliverance, prophetic songs that found their ultimate fulfillment in Israel's Messiah, songs of His presence and protection, and so much more.

Psalm 22:4 declares that ADONAI inhabits and is enthroned upon the praises of His people; Psalm 16:11 tells us that in His presence there is fullness of joy with pleasure at His right hand; and Nehemiah adds that the joy of the Lord is our strength (8:10). So I would like to encourage you with this spiritual truth—those who begin in praise will continue in joy and most certainly will finish strong. This book of meditations on the Psalms has been compiled not only for your edification but with the sincere desire for you to receive revelation that will inspire and provoke you to love and good deeds.

I pray that the Holy One of Israel who breathed these words into the psalmists so many years ago will revive them in your heart with insight and revelation so that you may finish strong!

Blessings and shalom,
Paul Wilbur

A Literary Editor's Introduction to the Psalms

The word *psalm* comes from a Greek word meaning a song to the accompaniment of a stringed instrument. Many of the psalms do refer to harp and lyre. It came to mean a song of praise, from which comes the Hebrew name of the book, *Tehillim*. Praise is indeed a major theme, though many psalms sing other notes, such as intercessory cries, laments, complaints, vows, sacrifices, and repentance. Yet even the songs of anguish or sorrow or questioning almost always return to God's praise.

The collection of psalms developed over hundreds of years. In the tenth century BCE, David and his court composed a core collection, likely including Psalms 3–16, 51–71, and 130–145. Levitical musicians who led Temple worship added more, notably Asaph contributing 73–83 and the sons of Korah providing 42–49 and 84–88. Royal psalms celebrated important public events during the reigns of David's descendants, such as a coronation (2), wedding (45), and Temple petitions on his behalf (20, 72, 89, 132, 144). Also scattered through the collection are hymns exalting the wisdom of *Torah* (1, 15, 19, 34, 37, 53, 73, 78, 94, 111, 112, 119, 139), possibly first inspired by the discovery of the scroll of Deuteronomy during the reign of Josiah. Other psalms (74, 79, 126, 137) mourn the destruction of the first Temple in 586 BCE. Sometime after the exile and the building of the Second Temple, the book of Psalms took its present form of five divisions or books (1–41, 42–72, 73–89, 90–106, and 107–150), each ending with a brief doxology or exaltation of God. One possible explanation for the five books is to parallel the five books of the *Torah*.

Psalms are poems sung or chanted in the Temple. We encourage you to read them aloud or make up new melodies to chant them, as the *Ruach HaKodesh* leads. Enjoy the vivid imagery, the emotional pathos, the building up of ideas, and the ebb and flow of feelings. Rather than rhymes, Hebrew poetry uses parallelism, where two lines of a verse build on the same meaning as in, for example, Psalm 27:1:

> ADONAI is my light and my salvation:
>> whom should I fear?
> ADONAI is the stronghold of my life:
>> whom should I dread?

Or two lines of a verse may contrast in meaning as in, for example, Psalm 27:10:

> Though my father and my mother forsake me,
>> ADONAI will take me in.

The poets are not rigid about it, however: the second line may develop the idea in the first, or the first line may illustrate an idea in the second as in, for example, Psalm 42:2:

> As the deer pants for streams of water,
>> so my soul pants for You, O God.

The psalms teach us many different ways to pray. Many prayers are deeply personal, reflecting circumstances in the lives of David and other ancient *kedoshim*, to which we can still relate today. Others are corporate, calling us to honor our God as a community. The Levites sang psalms designated for services in the morning, evening, or the watches of night, as well as for festivals and appointed times. Thanksgiving ushers us through the gates of His sanctuary. Praise affirms our trust in His promises and His power to protect us. Worship urges all people and all creation to exalt Him with all our being. Petitions raise our voice in times of trouble or trial, sickness or slander, persecution or poverty. Wisdom urges us to trust in God's ways, confess sin and do good, seek answers to difficult questions such as why evil people prosper while good people suffer in this life, and reaffirm God's faithfulness to those who wait patiently on Him.

There are a few technical terms in the Psalms that are difficult to translate. Some appear in the introductory verses, such as *miktam* and *shiggaion*. These terms may indicate musical instruments or poetic genres. In some cases, we provide translations that we believe are plausible though not definitive. The word *Selah*, which appears in the body of many psalms, is untranslatable; it may indicate a musical interlude or a poetic break in a song.

The psalms are a tremendous source of hope and consolation. Again and again they assure us that the God of Israel prizes His people, forgives the sinful, and will ultimately deliver the faithful, culminating in a confidence that God will give eternal joy to His *kedoshim*. The ancient kingdoms of Israel and Judah were but a foretaste of the glorious kingdom of God. Most wonderfully, the psalms contain many prophetic hints about the coming Messiah, the promised seed of David, the priest according to the order of Melchizedek, the suffering servant, and the triumphant savior and Lord.

Glenn David Blank, PhD

PSALM 1

Torah Is a Tree of Wisdom

¹ Happy is the one who has not walked in the advice of the wicked,
  nor stood in the way of sinners,
  nor sat in the seat of scoffers.
² But his delight is in the *Torah* of ADONAI,
  and on His *Torah* he meditates day and night.
³ He will be like a planted tree over streams of water,
  producing its fruit during its season.
  Its leaf never droops—
but in all he does, he succeeds.

⁴ The wicked are not so.
  For they are like chaff that the wind blows away.
⁵ Therefore the wicked will not stand during the judgment,
  nor sinners in the congregation of the righteous.
⁶ For ADONAI knows the way of the righteous,
  but the way of the wicked leads to ruin.

Jeffrey Seif and Glenn Blank

Though the first word is often translated "blessed," our preference for "happy" derives from the core meaning of this Hebrew word, אַשְׁרֵי, *ashrei*. "Blessed" sounds more religious than need be. Everyone wants to be happy—the religious and nonreligious alike—yet not everyone abides religious language or even believes in a personal God who is willing to help people be happy. *Ashrei* is not a giddy or jolly feeling but a calm contentment. The "delight" that one feels from meditating on the *Torah* (2) is a satisfying *shalom*, secure in one's relationship with *HaShem*. Israel's ancient and inspired songbook attests to a gracious God, predisposed to shine His favor upon those who live value-centered and virtuous lives, who follow the counsel of the wise rather than "the advice of the wicked" (1). Because God knows their ways (6), the righteous will be rewarded accordingly (3). Is that good news for you? Are you looking beyond the present for better things in *olam haba*, the world to come? Godly wisdom (for this is the first of many wisdom poems in the Psalter) knows about a happiness that comes with trusting faithfulness, drawing life from the Spirit of God and "producing its fruit during its season" (3)—which looks and tastes like His Spirit, with the sap of patience, kindness, and faithful love. On the other hand, manipulative and perverse scoffers are promised no such abiding happiness, their futures blown away in the wind (4). In the Hebrew Bible, a kindly disposed and just God dispenses His grace in accordance with how we "walk" or live our lives, step-by-step (1). If you share in the righteousness of Messiah, you can take heart, even in difficult times. For a righteous person is "like a tree planted by the waters," so firmly rooted that "its leaves will be green" even in a time of drought (see Jer. 17:8). That's something better and more enduring than whatever is trendy or "hot" today. That's good news from the Hebrew Bible, which is God's news for all.

PSALM 2

Coronation of Messianic King

¹ Why are the nations in an uproar,
   and the peoples mutter vanity?
² The kings of earth set themselves up[a]
   and rulers conspire together[b] against ADONAI
   and against His Anointed One[c]:
³ "Let's rip their chains apart,
   and throw their ropes off us!"

a. 2:2. Hebraically, *usurping power*.
b. 2:2. cf. Mark 3:6.
c. 2:2. Heb. *Mashiach*, or *Messiah*. cf. John 1:41.

[4] He who sits in heaven laughs!
    ADONAI mocks them.
[5] So He will speak to them in His anger,
    and terrify them in His fury:
[6] "I have set up My king
    upon Zion, My holy mountain."

[7] I will declare the decree of ADONAI.
    He said to me: "You are My Son—
    today I have become Your Father.[d]
[8] Ask Me, and I will give the nations as Your inheritance,
    and the far reaches of the earth as Your possession.
[9] You shall break the nations with an iron scepter.[e]
    You shall dash them in pieces like a potter's jar."[f]

[10] So now, O kings, be wise,
    take warning, O judges of the earth!
[11] Serve ADONAI with fear,
    and rejoice with trembling.
[12] Kiss the Son, lest He become angry,
    and you perish along your way—
    since His wrath may flare up suddenly.
    Happy is everyone taking refuge in Him!

Glenn Blank

In America, after all the campaigns and elections are over, the succession from one president to another is peaceful and orderly. For that and more, we must thank God for George Washington. But it was not so for ancient kings. We need only look at the plotting and scheming among David's sons and their supporters (1 Kings 1:5–53). It could have ended up in bitter and bloody war had not the prophet Nathan and wise old King David intervened to arrange the coronation of the young Solomon. After Solomon, though, things got worse, with Rehoboam and Jeroboam splitting the kingdom of Israel in two (1 Kings 12).

If much was at stake then, how much more so when we consider the crowning of David's greater Son, the Anointed One (מָשִׁיחַ, *Mashiach*)? Much was

d. 2:7. cf. Matt. 3:17.
e. 2:9. cf. Rev. 12:5; 19:15.
f. 2:9. cf. Rev. 2:27.

at stake then for everyone in the kingdom, and much is at stake for us as we look for Messiah to establish His kingdom on earth. The power brokers of this world are in a raucous tumult (1), rallying supporters and conspiring for one of their own choosing against the choice of the royal Father (2), and complaining about conditions left by the past regime (3). Suddenly the scene soars to heaven, where *HaShem* scoffs at the rabble-rousers (4) and makes it clear that He alone will determine the new king (6).

Then He turns His attention to address His chosen One, the Son (7). In ancient times, it was common to think of a king as a son of the gods. But something more is happening here: as the Father proclaimed at His immersion, *Yeshua* is His one and only beloved Son. If David could promise the surrounding nations as an inheritance to Solomon, God alone can promise all nations as the inheritance of *Mashiach*. A time is coming when the power brokers of this world will finally "be wise" (10), serve with fear and trembling (11), and kiss the royal Son in humble homage (12).

Whose side are you on? If you have not put your trust in the royal Son, fear the wrath of His coming judgment! But if you have, rejoice, for His kingdom and His grace will endure forever!

PSALM 3

Magen David

¹ A Psalm of David, when he fled from his son Absalom.
² ADONAI, how many are my foes!
　　Many are rising up against me!
³ Many are saying to my soul:
　　"There is no deliverance for him in God." *Selah*
⁴ But You, ADONAI, are a shield around me,
　　my glory and the lifter of my head.
⁵ I cry out to ADONAI with my voice,
　　and He answers me from His holy mountain. *Selah*
⁶ I lie down and sleep.
　　I awake—for ADONAI sustains me.
⁷ I will not be afraid of ten thousands of people all around
　　who have taken their stand against me.

[8] Arise, *ADONAI*! Deliver me, my God!
>> For You strike all my enemies on the cheek.
>> You shatter the teeth of the wicked.
[9] Deliverance belongs to *ADONAI*.[a]
>> Let Your blessing be on Your people. *Selah*

Glenn Blank

Have you ever been in a tight spot? Have you ever felt like someone was giving you a tough time, way beyond anything you deserve? You cry out to God for help, and you wonder if He hears you? David was in such a situation when he was fleeing from the rebellion of Absalom his son (1)—not to mention when he was fleeing from Saul earlier in his life. Yet David doesn't focus on Absalom or Saul or any other human adversary in his cry to God. His foes rising up against him loom larger than the particular humans who were chasing him. These foes were challenging God Himself. If "there is no deliverance for him in God" (3), to whom can he turn? David seemed to understand, as he saw "ten thousands . . . who have taken their stand against me" (7), that "our struggle is not against flesh and blood, but . . . against the spiritual forces of wickedness in the heavenly places" (Eph. 6:12). In such a struggle, you can only cry out to *HaShem* and take your stand in Him, taking up the shield of faith (Eph. 6:16). Then you will know that He alone is "a shield [מָגֵן, *magen*] around me, my glory and the lifter of my head" (4). He alone is your security, when you lie down and when you rise up. He alone is your "deliverance" (3, 9) or salvation—יְשׁוּעָה, *yeshuah*. (This word—which became the Name of Salvation in person—appears over sixty times in Psalms alone.) Remember that your tight spot is a temporary trial, but your יְשׁוּעָה is from the holy mountain and your glory is from the Eternal One.

a. 3:9. cf. Rev. 7:10.

21

PSALM 4

Prayer for Sleep in *Shalom*

[1] For the music director, on stringed instruments, a psalm of David.

[2] Answer me when I call,

God of my righteousness!

You set me free when I am in distress.

Be gracious to me and hear my prayer.

[3] O sons of men, how long will you turn my glory into my shame?

How long will you love worthlessness and pursue falsehood? *Selah*

[4] But know that ADONAI has set apart the godly for His own.

ADONAI will hear when I call to Him.

[5] Tremble, but do not sin![a]

Search your heart while on your bed, and be silent. *Selah*

[6] Offer righteous sacrifices

and put your trust in ADONAI.

[7] Many are asking, "Who will show us some good?"

May the light of Your face shine upon us, ADONAI!

[8] You have put joy in my heart—

more joy than when their grain and new wine overflow.

[9] I will lie down and sleep in *shalom*.

For You alone, ADONAI, make me live securely.

Jeffrey Seif

"Answer me when I call" and "be gracious to me [חָנֵּנִי, *chanayni*] and hear [שְׁמַע, *sh'ma*] my prayer" (2) have been heart cries of countless women and men since the dawn of creation. In so many ways, it's what we all want from God, is it not? Yet He responds with His own question: "How long will you love worthlessness and pursue falsehood?" (3). Alas, it's all too easy to love empty things. People who pursue futility and practice deceit suffer tragic ends, do they not? But "prayer changes things," as the saying goes, so every human being, though guilty, is but a single prayer away from a changed life—from experiencing God's graciousness. This psalm assures us that God is particularly predisposed to

a. 4:5. cf. Eph. 4:26.

reach down and help those who reach up and pursue Him. We read in verse 4, "ADONAI has set apart the godly for His own. ADONAI will hear when I call to Him." What a promise! If you are feeling alone, consider that God may want you for Himself. Those troubled by sin and circumstances can happily get the better of both. Getting right with God and offering "righteous sacrifices" to the Lord (6) holds out the promise that God will put "joy" in our hearts (8). It is all there for the asking. So, if you are willing, ask—and you shall receive.

⋇⋇⋇⋇⋇⋇⋇⋇⋇⋇ PSALM 5 ⋇⋇⋇⋇⋇⋇⋇⋇⋇⋇

Morning Prayer for Justice

¹ For the music director, on the wind instruments, a psalm of David.
² Hear my words, ADONAI,
    consider my groaning.
³ Listen to the sound of my cry for help,
    my King and my God, for I pray to You.
⁴ ADONAI, in the morning You hear my voice.
    In the morning I order my prayer before You and watch expectantly.
⁵ For You are not a God who rejoices in evil.
    No wickedness dwells with You.
⁶ Braggarts will not stand before Your eyes.
    You hate all wrongdoers.
⁷ You destroy those who speak falsehood.
    A person of bloodshed and deceit ADONAI detests.

⁸ But because of Your great lovingkindness, I will enter Your House.
    I will bow toward Your holy Temple, in awe of You.
⁹ Lead me, ADONAI, in Your righteousness, because of my enemies.
    Make Your path straight before me.
¹⁰ For nothing upright is in their mouth.
    Inside them is a ruin—their throat an open grave.
    They flatter with their tongue.[b]
¹¹ Declare them guilty, O God!
    Let them fall by their own schemes.

b. 5:10. cf. Rom. 3:13.

> Banish them because of their many transgressions—
> for they have rebelled against You.
> ¹² But let all who take refuge in You rejoice!
> Let them always shout for joy!
> You will shelter them and they exult—those who love Your Name.
> ¹³ For You bless the righteous, ADONAI.
> You surround him with favor as a shield.

Glenn Blank

From this psalm we can learn several important lessons about personal prayer. First, it's helpful to pray aloud. Note how the speech of earnest prayer builds up in verses 2–4—"my words," "my groaning," "the sound of my cry," "my voice," "my prayer." With spoken prayer comes confidence that *HaShem* will hear. (See if you can find all the words the psalmist uses for *hearing* in these verses.) You may think, doesn't *HaShem* already know the thoughts of my heart? Indeed He does, before you utter a word (Matt. 6:8). Nevertheless, a prayer spoken aloud with passion and perseverance gets His special attention (Luke 18:13–14).

Second, there is value in prayer in the morning—as David repeats twice (4), and so did the righteous Job (1:5), the historian Ezra (2 Chron. 2:20–21), and the Messiah *Yeshua* (Mark 1:35). Are you willing to set your prayer before the Lord each morning, watching and trusting *HaShem* to hear your cry?

Third, a prayer of faith exalts the goodness of God above wickedness and evil (5). Have you ever struggled with others who were deceitfully scheming against you? If so, you're in good company. David experienced great opposition—as did his descendant *Yeshua*—from boasters and workers of iniquity who speak falsehood (6–7). Yet his enemies are not his focus. God is. Instead of fretting, David enters the House of God, trusting in His loving-kindness and righteousness (8–9). He is not intimidated but confident that God will deal with his enemies justly (10–11) and provide a place of shelter for all who trust in His name (12–13).

Do you want to have this assurance? Then pray out of your heart each morning, with conviction. Then watch God our Father lead you out of trial and deliver you from evil.

PSALM 6

Prayer for Mercy

¹ For the music director, on the eight-string lyre, a psalm of David.
² *Adonai*, do not rebuke me in Your anger!
    Do not discipline me in Your wrath.
³ Be gracious to me, *Adonai*, for I am weak.
    Heal me, *Adonai*—for my bones are shuddering with fear,
⁴ as is my soul—
    and You, *Adonai*—how long?
⁵ Turn toward me, *Adonai*, deliver my soul!
    Save me—because of Your mercy.
⁶ For there is no memory of You in death,
    in *Sheol* who will praise You?
⁷ I am worn out with my groaning.
    Every night I make my bed swim,
    drenching my pillow with my tears.
⁸ My eyes are weakened with grief—
    they age because of my enemies.

⁹ Away from me, all you evildoers!
    For *Adonai* heard the sound of my weeping.
¹⁰ *Adonai* has heard my cry for mercy.
    Adonai accepts my prayer:
¹¹ "May all my enemies be ashamed, and stricken with terror.
    May they turn back in sudden disgrace."

Jeffrey Seif

People are what they are, and life is what it is. It is not going to change, and not everyone around you is going to change. Imperfect as it all is and as imperfect as we all are, we are sometimes confronted by our imperfections and forced to cry out with the psalmist, "*Adonai*, do not rebuke me in Your anger! Do not discipline me in Your wrath!" (2). Instead, "be gracious to me [חָנֵּנִי, *chanayni*], *Adonai*" (3). This last expression says it all in so many ways. "Heal me" is another appeal for mercy—especially when "my bones are shuddering with fear" (3). How much we need His grace and mercy—both to get it and to give it. Incessant aggravations can and do cause us to feel "worn out" (7), and as a result our eyes (and our perspective) are "weakened" (8). Finally the psalmist acknowledges, "Adonai heard the sound of my weeping" (9).

Let me ask a pointed question: In your heart of hearts, do you really believe that Adonai does hear? Do you trust that He is full of mercy? Does God hear your heart cry? The psalmist assures you that He does—"Adonai has heard" and He "accepts my prayer" (10). Do you trust the gracious One to hear and accept you? Irrespective of past sins and circumstances, Scripture holds out the promise that Adonai is near to all who call upon Him (Ps. 145:18). If you pick up the phone and call, you will be included in the "all." Those uncertain how to dial up God's number would do well to consider what one of *Yeshua's* disciples committed to writing many years ago: "I am the way, the truth, and the life" (John 14:6). Go His way. See His truth. Find His life. People may not change—those "evildoers" (9) who seem to be your enemies may never "be ashamed" (11) on this side of judgment day—but you can change. In the process of so doing, you will discover that the change that comes through trusting Him makes all the difference.

PSALM 7

Adonai Magen

¹ A passionate song of David, which he sang to Adonai concerning Cush,
   a Benjamite.
² Adonai my God, in You I have taken refuge.
      Save me from each of my persecutors, and deliver me.
³ Otherwise he will rip me apart like a lion,
      with no one to rescue me.
⁴ Adonai my God, if I have done this—
      if there is guilt on my hands,
⁵ if I have paid back evil to anyone at peace with me,
      or unjustly attacked my adversary,
⁶ then let the enemy chase me,
      overtake me, and trample me into the ground,
      leaving my honor in the dirt! *Selah*

⁷ Arise, Adonai, in Your anger,
   arise against the fury of my enemies!

Awake for me!

You decreed justice.

[8] Let an assembly of peoples gather around You

and return on high, above them.

[9] ADONAI judges the peoples.

Vindicate me, ADONAI,

according to my righteousness and integrity in me. ·

[10] Please, end the evil of the wicked

and sustain the righteous.

A just God examines hearts and minds.

[11] My shield is God—

Savior of the upright in heart.

[12] God is a righteous judge,

a God who is indignant every day.

[13] If He does not relent,

He will sharpen His sword.

He has bent His bow and made it ready.

[14] He prepares His own deadly weapons.

He makes His fiery arrows.

[15] Look! The one pregnant with trouble conceives mischief

and brings forth deceit.[a]

[16] He digs a pit, scrapes it out,

and then falls into the hole he has made.

[17] His mischief will turn on his own head.

His violence will boomerang on his crown.

[18] I will praise ADONAI for His justice.

I sing praise to the Name of ADONAI *Elyon*!

Glenn Blank

David was passionate about justice. Surely he was treated unjustly—adversaries were persecuting him (2) and threatening to rip him apart (3); they were accusing him of evil (4)—when in fact it is they who do so to him! First Samuel 24 tells of Saul and his army chasing David in the wilderness. Yet, when David had a chance to kill Saul and thus defend and avenge himself, he didn't. Instead, he trusts *HaShem* to be his refuge and rescue him (2).

a. 7:15. cf. Jacob 1:15.

Similarly *Yeshua* teaches us to turn the other cheek (Matt. 5:39), and Paul tells us to leave vengeance to *HaShem* (Rom. 12:19).

David is passionate about trusting in God to do justice, swearing, if he has ever taken matters into his own hands, then let his own life and honor be trampled into the dirt (4–6)! Because of his faith, David is able to see *HaShem* arising to decree justice before the assembly of the peoples (7–8). Vindication will surely come from the heavenly judge (9). God's justice is greatest because He alone is able to examine hearts (10), He alone is perfectly righteous at all times (12), and He alone can bring ultimate vindication with His sword and fiery arrows (13–14).

Yet the weapons of God are not carnal—God does not literally wield a sword and bow—but spiritual, though divinely powerful (2 Cor. 10:4). For that matter, justice is not a physical thing—you cannot actually see it, yet you know when things are right or not. "It's not fair!" From the time we were little children, we all have a sense of fairness. Just as we have a sense of physical balance that helps us keep physically upright, we also have a sense of moral balance that helps us keep morally upright—sensing what is right or wrong, just or unjust. Because justice is fundamentally spiritual, David recognizes that only God can bring it about. David recognizes that left to themselves, people usually just make things worse—conceiving mischief and giving birth to deceit (15), digging a hole and then falling into it (16). Only God can set things right again. Sometimes He does it by letting people experience the consequences of their actions falling upon their own heads. Sometimes He does it by authorizing human agents with the decree of His word—who are well equipped with fearsome weapons (Jer. 51:20; Rom. 13:4). However He does it, let us be confident that God is our refuge (2) and our shield (11, מָגֵן, *magen*). Since He is our righteous judge (12), let us always sing praises to Him for His justice (18).

 # PSALM 8

Humanity Is God's Splendor

[1] For the music director, upon the Gittite lyre: a psalm of David.
[2] ADONAI our Lord,
   how excellent is Your Name over all the earth!
      You set Your splendor above the heavens.

[3] Out of the mouths of babies and toddlers
    You established power,[a] because of Your enemies,
    to silence the foe and the avenger.
[4] When I consider Your heavens, the work of Your fingers,
    the moon and the stars, which You established—
[5] what is man, that You are mindful of him?
    And the son of man, that You care for him?[b]
[6] Yet You made him a little lower than the angels,
    and crowned him with glory and majesty!
[7] You gave him dominion over the works of Your hands.
    You put all things under their feet:[c]
[8] all sheep and oxen,
    and also beasts of the field,
[9] birds in the air, and fish in the ocean—
    all passing through the paths of the seas.

[10] ADONAI our Lord, how excellent is Your Name over all the earth!

Paul Wilbur

King David begins and ends this beloved psalm with the same words: "ADONAI our Lord, how excellent is Your Name over all the earth! [*ADONAI Adoneinoo, ma-adir shimcha b'chol ha-aretz!*]" (2, 10). And with good reason! The *Name* (*HaShem*) of the Lord fills the earth with majesty and glory! Consider this: the Name of the Lord is to be praised forever (Ps. 145:21); the Name of the Lord is a strong tower of safety, a refuge in times of trouble (Prov. 18:10); the Name of *Yeshua* is above every other name (Phil. 2:9–11). Moreover, He has given us authority to use His glorious Name against the power of the enemy, sickness, disease, and destruction (Matt. 10:1; Luke 9:1). Do believers really have this power to change things, to change circumstances? After all, as David recognizes, "What is man, that You are mindful of him?" (5). You too might wonder, what does God see in measly me? Yet the Spirit of God has revealed to all who trust in His Name, "You . . . crowned him with glory and majesty" (6). So gracious and full of love is our God, who has made us in His image, and who has shared His Name—the Name *Yeshua*—with us!

a. 8:3(2). cf. Matt. 21:16.
b. 8:5. cf. Heb. 2:6.
c. 8:7. cf. 1 Cor. 15:27; Heb. 2:8.

So sing the Name, declare the Name, rejoice in the Name! And don't forget that you can pray in the authority of His Name.

Another weapon of our warfare is disclosed in verse 3, when David declares that the Lord has established power, even in the mouths of babies, to silence the foe and the avenger. How much more powerful can *praise* be in the mouth of a believer—wielding that two-edged sword with skill and anointing? How can our praise be so powerful? David reveals that truth to us in Psalm 22:4, when he declares that it is none other than the Holy One of Israel who is enthroned upon our praises. Also in Psalm 16:11, he reveals that in the presence of the Holy One there are "eternal pleasures at Your right hand." We can say with confidence that our praise provokes His presence, and in His presence is joy, pleasure, and power to overcome the works of the enemy! Can you begin to see now why David encouraged us to keep the praise of *HaShem* continually in our mouths (Ps. 34:2)?

PSALM 9

Our Righteous Judge

1 For the music director, to the tune of "The Death of the Son," a psalm of
  David.
2 I will praise ADONAI with my whole heart.
  I will tell about all Your wonders.
3 I will be glad and rejoice in You.
  I will sing praise to Your Name, *Elyon*!
4 When my enemies turn back,
  they stumble and perish before You.
5 For You upheld my right and my cause.
  You sat upon the throne, judging righteously.
6 You rebuked the nations,
  You destroyed the wicked—
  blotting out their name forever and ever.
7 The enemy is finished, in ruins forever.
  You overturned their cities—
  even the memory of them has perished.

⁸ But ADONAI reigns forever.
    He established His throne for judgment.
⁹ He judges the world in righteousness
    and governs the peoples justly.
¹⁰ ADONAI is a stronghold for the oppressed,
    a high tower in times of trouble.
¹¹ Those who know Your Name trust You—
    for You, ADONAI, never have forsaken those who seek You.
¹² Sing praises to ADONAI, who dwells in Zion.
    Declare His deeds among the peoples.
¹³ He who avenges blood remembers.
    He will not forget the cry of the afflicted.
¹⁴ Be compassionate to me, ADONAI.
    See my affliction from those hating me.
    Lift me up from the gates of death.
¹⁵ Then I will tell all Your praises
    in the gates of the daughter of Zion,
    rejoicing in Your salvation.
¹⁶ The nations sank into the pit they made.
    The net they hid caught their own foot.
¹⁷ ADONAI is known for executing judgment.
    The wicked one is trapped in the work of his own hands. *Selah*
¹⁸ The wicked will turn to *Sheol*,
    as will all the nations that forget God.
¹⁹ For the needy will not forever be forgotten,
    nor the hope of the poor perish forever.
²⁰ Arise, ADONAI, do not let man triumph.
    Let the nations be judged before You.
²¹ Strike them with terror, ADONAI.
    Let the nations know they are only human. *Selah*

Jeffrey Seif

God came through for the psalmist, and He will come through for you. The psalmist's enthusiasm is not contrived or forced—consider the circumstances. He declares, "I will praise ADONAI with my whole heart" (2), and "I will be glad and rejoice in You" (3). Worship leaders are forever trying to get us to lift our voices—each of us "with [our] whole heart" (בְּכָל-לִבִּי, *b'chol leebee*)—in the hope that it will lift our spirits.

The source of the psalmist's enthusiasm was seeing God's hand in his own life. He says, "For You upheld my right and my cause" (5). Yes, God has proved Himself to be "a stronghold for the oppressed, a high tower in times of trouble" (10). When we experience and reflect on how God has come through for us in life, worship becomes a lot easier. Worship begins when we turn to Him and say, "Thanks!" So the psalmist leads us, by remembering a God who will "not forget the cry of the afflicted" (13) and acknowledging that God does "lift me up from the gates of death" (14).

Perhaps you have been assailed by circumstances, for we all live out less than perfect lives. Why not take a moment to think about God's goodness and ways that He has personally lifted you up from the gates of death? Sometimes we can feel all alone, betrayed by people and abandoned by circumstance. Let's put our faith in God and remember "the needy will not forever be forgotten" (19).

PSALM 10

Freedom from Terror

> [1] Why, ADONAI, are You standing far off?
>> Why hide Yourself in times of trouble?
> [2] In pride the wicked hotly hunts the poor.
>> Let them be caught in the plots they have planned.
> [3] For the wicked one boasts about his soul's desire.
>> The greedy one curses, reviling ADONAI.
> [4] The wicked one, with his nose in the air, never seeks Him.
>> All his thoughts are: "There is no God."
> [5] His ways are secure at all times.
>> He haughtily disregards Your judgments.
>> He snorts at all his adversaries.
> [6] He says in his heart: "I'll never be shaken!
>> From generation to generation nothing bad will happen."
> [7] His mouth is full of cursing, lies and oppression.
>> On his tongue are trouble and iniquity.[a]

a. 10:7. cf. Job 20:12; Rom. 3:14.

[8] He lies in ambush near villages.

> In hidden places he slays the innocent.
> His eyes watch in secret for the helpless.

[9] He lurks in a hiding place like a lion in a thicket.

> He lies in wait to catch the helpless.
> He catches the unfortunate one, dragging him away in his net.

[10] The victim is crushed, brought down,

> and falls into his mighty claws.

[11] He says in his heart: "God has forgotten.

> He hides His face—He will never see it."

[12] Arise, ADONAI! O God, lift up Your hand.

> Do not forget the afflicted.

[13] Why does the wicked one revile God?

> He says in his heart:
> "You will never require anything."

[14] You saw—for You see trouble and grief,

to take it in Your hand.

> The victim puts his trust in You—
> You are the helper of the orphan.

[15] Break the arm of the wicked, evil one!

> Call him to account for his wickedness—

until no more is found.

[16] ADONAI is King forever and ever!

> Nations will be wiped off His land.

[17] You hear, ADONAI, the desire of the meek.

> You encourage them and incline Your ear.

[18] You vindicate the orphan and oppressed,

> so that man, who is earthly, may terrify no more.

Jeffrey Seif

Does God play hide-and-seek with His people? So it may seem sometimes: "Why hide Yourself in times of trouble?" (1). It's a question many of us have asked, is it not? *HaShem* already knows the question in our hearts. Such a question, expressing a feeling of abandonment, naturally leads to complaints in the following verses. (You wouldn't know anybody who complains to God, would you?) The lowly are afflicted by the haughty (2) and the greedy seem to fare better than the needy (3). Those who never seek God and say, "There is no God" (4), seem to find success in life, while the righteous who seek Him too often languish and fall victim to the wicked one's intrigue—lurking like a beast catching the helpless in his "mighty claws" (10).

What can the righteous say, then or now? The righteous can say, "Arise [קוּמָה, *kumah*], ADONAI!" (12). They can remember that, however far off He may seem every now and again, God still is "the helper of the orphan" (14)—and all the needy. God really is "King forever and ever" (16). Mindful of the heart cry of the humble, God will be their helper. His help will arise for you too. If you keep seeking Him, you will find Him.

PSALM 11

Judgment from Heaven

¹ For the music director, a psalm of David.
　　In ADONAI I have taken shelter.
　　How can you say to my soul:
　　"Fly like a bird to your mountain?
² For look, the wicked bend the bow.
　　They fix their arrow on the bowstring
　　so they can shoot from the shadows
　　at those who are upright in heart.
³ If our foundations are destroyed,
　　what should the righteous do?"

⁴ ADONAI is in His holy Temple.
　　ADONAI's throne is in heaven.ᵃ
　　His eyes are watching.
　　His eyelids observe the children of men.
⁵ ADONAI examines the righteous.
　　But the wicked and one loving violence His soul hates.
⁶ On the wicked He will rain down fire, brimstone
　　and scorching wind as the portion of their cup!
⁷ For ADONAI is righteous—He loves justice.
　　The upright will see His face.

a. 11:4. cf. Matt. 5:34; Acts 7:49; Rev. 4:2.

Glenn Blank

If you like drama, this one draws you in. After a quick assertion of *HaShem* as his shelter, the psalmist immediately responds to an accusation from *you* (1). You, gentle reader, might feel a bit on the defensive, objecting, "I didn't say that!" But apparently someone did. You look around for the accuser. Was it one of David's adversaries—Saul or Absalom? Or were other foes firing a fiery arrow— a metaphor for a wicked word—which they "shoot from the shadows" (2)? Apparently they want to remain anonymous. Or was it the spirit of the ageless accuser, *satan*? Have *you* ever heard his wily voice whispering woes into your soul? "Run away!" "Fly like a bird to your mountain!" (1). The Hebrew for the pronoun attached to "fly" and "your" is in the plural. Is the psalmist hinting that this voice speaks to all of us, that we all must seek shelter from *HaShem*? But only the word of *HaShem* is a sure foundation (3; Luke 6:48).

Then the drama shifts, suddenly, to the throne room of heaven (4). There the mutterings of accusers fall silent. There it is only *HaShem* examining the children of men, both the righteous (צַדִּיק, *tzadeek*) and the wicked (5). It is not a passive examination but an ongoing test of righteousness. *HaShem* has a "soul" that "hates" (5)—not with the impure motive of man that strikes with cruel violence but the pure motive of God that works justice. Sulfurous brimstone and fire hotter than what destroyed Sodom fall on the wicked (6), but a gaze of the face of love awaits the upright (7). Whose word are you trusting in now?

PSALM 12

Silence the Flattering Lips

¹ For the music director, on the eight-string lyre, a psalm of David.
² Help, ADONAI! For no one godly exists.
　For the faithful have vanished from the children of men.
³ Everyone tells a lie to his neighbor,
　talking with flattering lips and a divided heart.
⁴ May ADONAI cut off all flattering lips—
　a tongue bragging big things.

⁵ They say: "With our tongue we'll prevail.
　　We own our lips—who can master us?"

⁶ "Because of the oppression of the poor,
　　because of the groaning of the needy,
　　now will I arise," says ADONAI.
　　"I will put him in the safe place—he pants for it."

⁷ The words of ADONAI are pure words—
　　like silver refined in an earthly crucible,
　purified seven times.

⁸ You will keep us safe, ADONAI.
　　You will protect us from this generation forever.

⁹ The wicked strut all around,
　　while vileness is exalted by mankind.

Glenn Blank

There are times when the lover of God feels all alone, "for the faithful have vanished" (2). Consider Elijah running away and moaning that of all the prophets, "I alone am left," or Paul in prison writing about friends who betrayed him, or *Yeshua* sweating blood while His disciples kept falling asleep. You can also feel alone even when plenty of people are around, especially when all you hear are lies, flattery, and double-talk (3). So you cry out to *HaShem*, "Help!" and ask Him to intercede and silence the empty "bragging" of proud tongues (4–5). If the boasting in the courts of Israel was upsetting, how much more so the prattle of talk shows and news analysts, the babble in school hallways and shopping malls?

What does *HaShem* say? Instead of the jabbering, He hears "the groaning of the needy" (6). Therefore He arises, providing a safe place (or salvation) for which the oppressed pants (6). Not responding to the blather, the words of *HaShem* are pure, like silver refined in a crucible seven times (7). God holds His people in the hottest part of the fire of suffering in order to completely purify us. The godly take heart in the eternal assurance of salvation that protects them from this generation (8).

Yet the psalmist still sees the wicked strutting about (9). His poem ends where it began, wondering when God will put an end to the worldly vileness exalting itself.

How about you? Will you give all your attention to the noise and duplicity all around you? Will you complain about the heat of the fire? Or, in the midst of the fire, will you be safe, trusting in the pure words from heaven?

PSALM 13

Trust in His *Chesed*

¹ For the music director, a psalm of David.
² How long, ADONAI? Will You forget me forever?
How long will You hide Your face from me?
³ How long must I have cares in my soul
and daily sorrow in my heart?
How long will my enemy triumph over me?
⁴ Look at me and answer, ADONAI my God.
Light up my eyes, or I will sleep in death.
⁵ Or else my enemy will say: "I have overcome him!"
and my foes will rejoice because I am shaken.

⁶ But I trust in Your lovingkindness,
my heart rejoices in Your salvation.
I will sing to ADONAI,
because He has been good to me.

Jeffrey Seif

"Until when?" (עַד-אָנָה, *ad anah?*). It's the question of the ages—and the psalmist doesn't hesitate to ask it. "How long, ADONAI?" he asks in verse 2, and in verse 3, where he expands it further: "How long must I have cares in my soul and daily sorrow in my heart? How long will my enemy triumph over me?" Pushed as he is, he feels that he'll die if God doesn't show up on his behalf (4). Absent an answer, won't his adversaries have reason to rejoice? He's in a tough spot—one we all find ourselves in from time to time. Unlike many of us, though, the psalmist is able to look beyond the moment to the Mover, who can not only get him beyond the moment but also out of the tough spot. You can too, if you take to heart what he says: "But I trust in Your lovingkindness, my heart rejoices in Your salvation. I will sing to ADONAI, because He has been good to me" (6). One who starts off with the honest question, "How long?," can still finish by affirming his trust in God's goodness and His ultimate victory—however long it is in coming. As Habakkuk 2:3–4 says, "It will surely come—it will not delay. . . . The righteous will live by his trust." May our hearts truly learn this lesson of trusting faith.

✳✳✳✳✳✳✳✳✳ PSALM 14 ✳✳✳✳✳✳✳✳✳

There Is No God?

[1] For the music director, of David.
    The fool said in his heart:
"There is no God."
    They are corrupt; their deeds are vile;
there is no one who does good.[a]
[2] ADONAI looked down from heaven on the children of men,
    to see if there are any who understand,
who seek after God.
[3] They all turned aside, became corrupt.
    There is no one who does good
    —not even one.
[4] "Will evildoers never understand—
    those who consume My people as they eat bread—
    and never call on ADONAI?"
[5] There they are, in great dread.
    For God is with the righteous generation.
[6] You would frustrate the plan of the lowly.
    Surely ADONAI is his refuge!
[7] O may He give Israel's salvation out of Zion!
    When ADONAI restores His captive people,
    Jacob will rejoice, Israel will be glad!

a. 14:1. cf. Rom. 3:10–12.

Jeffrey Seif

God knows what people are thinking. He reveals their thoughts: "The fool said in his heart: 'There is no God'" (1). Does the fool (נָבָל, *naval*) walk around saying that to himself or herself—"There is no God . . . There is no God . . . There is no God"? For that matter, what does it mean to say something "in the heart"? Does the heart have a tongue? Of course not—it's a figure of speech. Yet from *HaShem*'s point of view, it might as well be true, since He hears the "corrupt" (3) murmuring such things all the time—as surely as He heard the children of Israel murmuring their discontent in their tents, and *Yeshua* heard the Pharisees and scribes murmuring their resentment in their secret councils. They have "turned aside" (3) to "consume" the righteous (4). So, who are the righteous people? They are the ones who "seek after God" (2) and "call on ADONAI" (4). Is that you? Though the mocker disdains the lowly or afflicted one, the latter has a refuge in *HaShem* (6). For salvation will come "out of Zion" (7). You can count on this promise. When *HaShem* "restores His captive people . . . Israel will be glad" (7). The Hebrew word for "salvation" is יְשׁוּעָה, *yeshuah*. *Yeshua* has come out of Zion and will come again (Isa. 59:20; Rom. 11:26)—for all who put their trust in the יְשׁוּעָה of Israel.

 # PSALM 15

Walking with Integrity

¹ A psalm of David.
    ADONAI, who may dwell in Your tent?
    Who may live on Your holy mountain?
² The one who walks with integrity,
    who does what is right,
    and speaks truth in his heart,
³ who does not slander with his tongue,
    does not wrong his neighbor,
    and does not disgrace his friend,

⁴ who despises a vile person in his eyes,
  but honors those who fear A_DONAI_,
    who keeps his oath even when it hurts,
  and does not change,
⁵ who lends his money without usury,
    and takes no bribe against the innocent.
    One who does these things will never be shaken.

Glenn Blank

After tasting the surpassing goodness of God, can a mere mortal stay there? Apparently that's what David was wondering, after he had brought the ark of the covenant into a tent that he pitched on a hill in Jerusalem (1), with much dancing and fanfare (2 Sam. 6:12–17). David concludes that the answer goes beyond exuberance to ethics. If you want to abide in His presence, you must walk "with integrity" (2). *Yeshua* also promised his disciples, "If you keep My commandments, you will abide in My love" (John 15:10). The way to remain in His presence is to become like Him—in character. The one who may dwell with Him does what is right and speaks truth in his heart, because that's what He would do. The next three verses of this psalm work out some of the details of walking in integrity: loving your neighbor in what you say (3), keeping your word even when it costs (4), trading money to help rather than to hurt (5). So, can a mere mortal walk with integrity consistently enough to abide in His tent, in His presence? Only if he stays close to the One who is already there, and so becomes more and more like Him.

 # PSALM 16

The Path of Eternal Life

¹ A Michtam of David.
    Keep me safe, O God, for in You I have found shelter.
² I said to A_DONAI_: "You are my Lord—
    I have no good apart from You."
³ As for the *kedoshim* who are in the land,
    they are noble—in them is all my delight.

[4] As for those who run after another god,
   may their sorrows multiply.
      I will not pour out their drink offerings of blood,
   nor lift up their names with my lips.

[5] ADONAI is my portion and my cup.
      You cast my lot.
[6] My boundary lines fall in pleasant places
      —surely my heritage is beautiful.
[7] I will bless ADONAI, who counsels me.
      Even at night my heart instructs me.
[8] I have set ADONAI always before me.
      Since He is at my right hand, I will not be shaken.
[9] So my heart is glad and my soul rejoices.
      My body also rests secure.
[10] For You will not abandon my soul to *Sheol*
      nor let Your faithful one see the Pit.[a]
[11] You make known to me the path of life.
      Abundance of joys are in Your presence,
   eternal pleasures at Your right hand.[b]

Glenn Blank

Though I am no Paul Wilbur, this psalm sings in my soul, a song of security
and fullness of joy in God's presence, in this life and forever. David opens
with a petition—for safety and shelter (1)—and then proceeds to rejoice in
all the ways his request is answered. Security is found first and foremost in
relationship with "my Lord" (אֲדֹנָי, ADONAI). The path of eternal life begins
by putting your trust completely in Him alone as Lord of your life, and set-
tling it completely within your soul that "I have no good apart from You" (2).
Have you settled within your soul that He alone is Lord of everything? When
I did that, as a young man in Brussels after a long search, it changed everything, starting with the company I kept. People I never would have associated
with—the *kedoshim* (קְדוֹשִׁים, saints)—became my delight (3) rather than
those "who run after another god" (4). Do you delight in the *kedoshim* who
love the Lord faithfully?

a. 16:10. cf. Acts 13:35.
b. 16:8–11. cf. Acts 2:25–28.

Before I knew Him, I was chasing after vanities, things of no lasting value or significance. But now I know that He is my portion, within boundary lines that He alone can and will maintain. Moreover, He is my cup of joy, sharing with me a heritage that endures from generation to generation (5–6). Even more wonderful is my intimate relationship with my Lord. When I thank and bless Him, His presence is there to guide and teach me, from within my own heart (7). How awesome that He is always "before me" and also "at my right hand" (8)—brushing my face with His unshakable presence. When you are near Him, your soul rejoices—even your body, though frail and fickle, rejoices! I think of my father- and mother-in-law—they each died of cancer, yet lived their last days with a serenity that comes only from knowing God deeply. Scholars debate about whether David understood the details of the resurrection and eternal life, but it doesn't need to be that complicated. The *kedoshim* settle their hearts totally on ADONAI and come to know Him in a deep and abiding way. They just know He will not abandon His faithful ones to *Sheol* (10). And He has *already* made known to me the fullness of joy in His path of life. That is why *Yeshua* could say, "I am the resurrection and the life! Whoever believes in Me, even if he dies, shall live. And whoever lives and believes in Me shall never die" (John 11:25–26). Because He has made known to me this fullness of joy, I know that my eternal destiny is secure in אֲדֹנָי.

 PSALM 17

A Plea for Vindication

¹ A prayer of David.
　　Hear, ADONAI, a just plea, listen to my cry!
　　Give ear to my prayer—from lips with no deceit.
² From Your presence comes my vindication.
　　Your eyes see what is right.
³ You have examined my heart.
　　You searched me at night.
　　Though You test me, You find nothing.
　　I resolved that my mouth will not sin.

42

⁴ As for the deeds of mankind—
    by the word of Your lips
    I have kept out of the ways of the violent.
⁵ My steps have kept on Your paths.
    My feet have not slipped.
⁶ I called upon You, O God,
  for You will answer me.
    Incline Your ear to me,
  hear my speech.
⁷ Be wonderful with Your lovingkindness,
    O Savior of those taking refuge at Your right hand
    from those rising up against them.
⁸ Protect me like the pupil of the eye.
    Hide me in the shadow of Your wings,
⁹ from the wicked who attack me—
  my enemies, who surround me.
¹⁰ Their callous heart they shut tight.
    With their mouth they speak proudly.
¹¹ Our steps are now surrounded.
    They set their eyes to throw us down to the ground,
¹² like a lion eager to tear to pieces,
    like a young lion crouching in cover.
¹³ Arise, ADONAI! Confront him!
  Make him bow down!
    Deliver my soul from the wicked with Your sword,
¹⁴ from men, with Your hand, ADONAI,
    from men of the world whose portion is in this life.
    You fill their belly with Your treasure
    —with plenty of children—
    and leave their surplus to their babes.
¹⁵ I in righteousness will behold Your face!
    When I awake,
  I will be satisfied with Your likeness.

Jeffrey Seif and Glenn Blank

Have you ever prayed to the Lord, "Listen to my cry"? More than once, probably! Like the psalmist, though, can you go on to say that your request comes from "lips with no deceit" (1)? It's a question you might want to ask yourself, because when you find yourself in a bind, the natural inclination is to try to untie the knots. For some of us, this may involve fudging on the truth every now and again. Just a little lie, a white lie . . . but when you're asking God to listen to you, it helps if you can approach Him, as the psalmist does, with integrity. God's eyes "see what is right" (2). Just to make sure, He examines your heart and tests your character. Wouldn't it be great if you could say, "I resolved that my mouth will not sin" (3)? Or at least, "I have kept out of the ways of the violent" (4)? Life has a way of testing us, does it not? Not everyone passes. Yet it would seem to be possible to do so. "My steps have kept on Your paths. My feet have not slipped" (5). This walk is not mere luck. You don't just happen to stumble onto the right paths. You must determine that you are going to do so, mindful that God does save those who call upon Him and take refuge in Him (7). God protects the righteous in the shadow of His wings, as surely as an eyelid protects the pupil of the eye (8). Though wicked foes surround and attack (9), to cast the righteous down (11) and tear them to pieces (12), the righteous one can still call on *HaShem*: "Arise, ADONAI!" (13). Surely He will deliver him from the callous with his proud mouth (10), from the crafty whose "portion is in this life" and of this world (14).

Does the psalmist expect deliverance from his distress, or is he just venting? Do you? If you call on Him, you will know what it is to hide in the shadow of His wings and what it is to "be satisfied with" His likeness (15). The psalmist expects good from God—in this life and in the life to come. How about you? If this last verse and Psalms 16:11; 49:16; Job 19:25–26; John 11:25; and Revelation 22:4 are all true, then all who trust in *Yeshua* will surely awaken to His presence in a resurrection that represents the ultimate fulfillment of righteousness and goodness.

PSALM 18

ADONAI Lives! Blessed Be My Rock

¹ For the music director: a psalm of David the servant of ADONAI. He chanted the words of this song to ADONAI on the day ADONAI delivered him from the hand of all his enemies, and from the hand of Saul.

² He said, I love You, ADONAI my strength!
³ ADONAI is my rock, my fortress and my deliverer.
      My God is my rock, in Him I take refuge,
   my shield, my horn of salvation, my stronghold.
⁴ I called upon ADONAI, worthy of praise,
      and I was rescued from my enemies.
⁵ Cords of death entangled me.
      Torrents of Belial overwhelmed me.
⁶ Cords of *Sheol* coiled around me.
      Snares of death came before me.
⁷ In my distress I called on ADONAI,
   and cried to my God for help.
      From His Temple He heard my voice,
   my cry before Him came into His ears.
⁸ Then the earth rocked and quaked.
      The foundations of mountains trembled.
      They reeled because He was angry.
⁹ Smoke rose from His nostrils
   and consuming fire from His mouth.
      Coals blazed from Him.
¹⁰ He parted the heavens and came down,
   with thick darkness under His feet.
¹¹ He rode upon a *cheruv* and flew.
      He soared on the wings of the wind.
¹² He made darkness His cover,
      His *sukkah* all around Him—
      dark waters, thick clouds.
¹³ Out of the brilliance before Him
      passed His thick clouds, hail and fiery coals.
¹⁴ ADONAI also thundered in the heavens,
      and *Elyon* gave forth His voice, hail and fiery coals.
¹⁵ He shot His arrows and scattered them,
      hurled lightning bolts and routed them.
¹⁶ Then ravines of water appeared.
      The foundations of earth were exposed,
   at Your rebuke, ADONAI,
   at a blast of breath from Your nostrils.
¹⁷ He reached down from on high
   and took hold of me.
      He drew me out of mighty waters.

¹⁸ He saved me from my powerful enemy,
　　　from those who hated me—
　　　for they were much stronger than me.
¹⁹ They came against me in my day of calamity,
　　　but ADONAI was my support.
²⁰ He brought me out to a wide-open place.
　　　He rescued me since He delighted in me.
²¹ ADONAI rewarded me for my righteousness.
　　　For the cleanness of my hands He repaid me.
²² For I kept the ways of ADONAI,
　　　and did not turn wickedly from my God.
²³ For all His judgments are before me.
　　　I do not put His rulings away from me.
²⁴ I also had integrity with Him,
　　　and kept myself from my sin.
²⁵ So ADONAI rewarded me for my righteousness,
　　　for the cleanness of my hands in His eyes.

²⁶ With the loyal You deal loyally.
　　　With the blameless You are blameless.
²⁷ With the pure You are pure,
　　　and with the crooked You are shrewd.
²⁸ For You save lowly people,
　　　but haughty eyes You humble.
²⁹ For You light up my lamp.
　　　ADONAI my God shines in my darkness.
³⁰ For with You I rush on a troop,
　　　with my God I scale a wall.
³¹ As for God, His way is perfect.
　　　The word of ADONAI is pure.
　　　He is a shield to all who take refuge in Him.
³² For who is God, except ADONAI?
　　　And who is a Rock, except our God?
³³ God girds me with strength
　　　and makes my way straight.
³⁴ He makes my feet like those of deer
　　　and makes me stand on my heights.
³⁵ He trains my hands for battle,
　　　so my arms can bend a bronze bow.

[36] You gave me the shield of Your salvation.

Your right hand upholds me,

Your gentleness makes me great.

[37] You broaden my steps beneath me,

so my ankles have not slipped.

[38] I pursue my enemies and overtake them,

and will not return till they are wiped out.

[39] I will crush them till they cannot rise,

till they fall beneath my feet.

[40] For You girded me with strength for battle.

You made those who rose up against me bow down before me.

[41] You also made my enemies turn their backs to me.

I cut off those who hate me.

[42] They cry out, but there is none to save

—even to ADONAI, but He did not answer them.

[43] Then I beat them as fine as dust before the wind.

I pour them out like mud in the streets.

[44] You free me from strifes of the people.

You set me as head of the nations—

people I did not know are serving me.

[45] As soon as they hear, they obey me.

Children of foreigners cringe before me.

[46] Children of foreigners lose heart

and come trembling from their hideouts.

[47] ADONAI lives! And blessed be my Rock!

Exalted be God my salvation!

[48] God—He gives me vengeance

and subdues peoples under me.

[49] He delivers me from my enemies.

Indeed You lift me up above those who rise up against me.

You deliver me from the violent man.

[50] Therefore I praise You among the nations,

ADONAI, and sing praises to Your Name.[a]

[51] Great victories He gives to His king.

He shows loyal love to His anointed—

to David and his seed, forever.

a. 18:50. cf. Rom. 15:9.

Jeffrey Seif and Glenn Blank

Are you a "servant" (עֶבֶד, *eved*) of the Lord (1)? A believer? Maybe. Or a pew-sitter? Perhaps. But are you a "servant of ADONAI"? Do we even think in these terms anymore? Isn't a servant something like a slave? Some people I know think religion exists to serve us. It's all about getting our needs met and finding which congregation does it the best, which minister feeds us what we need. *Oy.* We need help. Where can we find people and places to deliver what we need?

How about from God Himself? This psalmist describes God as his "strength" (2), a "rock," a "refuge," a "shield," and a "stronghold" (3). Is that what you need? When you're in dire straits, when it seems like you're being "entangled" by "cords of death" (5) or some other "distress" (7), you can call on God. From His Temple, God, who cares for you, "parted the heavens and came down" (10). He has "thundered" (14) about the unjust way you've been treated. He has "shot His arrows" against the wicked (15). He has "reached down" and "took hold" of you and "saved" you from a "powerful enemy" (17–18). Why would God care for you like that? Simple: "He rescued" you because "He delighted in" you (20).

Isn't that what we want out of religion—God's gracious, powerful hand and saving help? It's less about what congregation delivers the most uplifting service and more about God Himself acting on our behalf. He wants you to go to a congregation not to receive but to give. Though counterintuitive in so many ways, biblical religion beckons us to care and share, to help others and then wait patiently for the help that comes from God. The way we get it is to give it. That's what *Yeshua* recommends (Acts 20:35). Then you will be a servant (עֶבֶד, *eved*) of the Lord. To the natural mind, it makes no sense. Still, it works. It's better to have single-hearted integrity with Him (24) and watch how God rewards you for your righteousness (25). It's true. If you are loyal to God, He personally promises to be loyal to you (26). He will shine in your darkness (29). *Yeshua* is the light (John 8:12), and He will give His light to you. With God at your side (or within you), you can "scale a wall" (30), you can gird yourself with strength (33), you can stand on heights (34), and you can train your hands for battle (35). Trusting in the Almighty will inspire you with such confidence. You will be able to "pursue" and "overtake" your enemies (38), knowing that you will get the better of them (39–46). God Himself is thus your deliverer, the One who will "lift" you up above those who "rise up against" the righteous (49). Isn't this victorious life what we need—and want? Experiencing God in this way is not just for the Bible writers of yesteryear, for the blessing comes to anyone who believes that "ADONAI lives!" and exalts Him as "God my salvation" (47). He is God who delivers (49). He is God who shows "loyal love to His anointed—to David and his seed, forever" (51).

In Hebrew, the ultimate Anointed One is מָשִׁיחַ, *Mashiach*—the Messiah. Though each king of Judah was a "son of David," they all point to the great "Son of David," the Messiah. And "his seed" refers to the promise He made to our ancestors—Abraham, Isaac, and Jacob—the promise of a unique, treasured people who will experience the blessing of God through King Messiah, forever. Forever is a long, long time. It extends to our time and beyond. You can believe it—God's mercies extend to you at this time—even to you, now.

❉❉❉❉❉❉❉ PSALM 19 ❉❉❉❉❉❉❉

Glory from Heaven and *Torah*

¹ For the music director, a psalm of David.

² The heavens declare the glory of God,
  and the sky shows His handiwork.
³ Day to day they speak,
  night to night they reveal knowledge.
⁴ There is no speech, no words,
  where their voice goes unheard.
⁵ Their voice has gone out to all the earth
  and their words to the end of the world.ᵃ
  In the heavens He pitched a tent for the sun.
⁶ It is like a bridegroom coming out of his bridal chamber.
  It is like a strong man rejoicing to run his course.
⁷ It rises at one end of the heavens
 and makes its circuit to the other end.
  Nothing is hidden from its heat.

a. 19:5. cf. Rom. 10:18.

⁸ The *Torah* of ADONAI is perfect,
　　restoring the soul.
　　　　The testimony of ADONAI is trustworthy,
　　making the simple wise.
⁹ The precepts of ADONAI are right,
　　giving joy to the heart.
　　　　The *mitzvot* of ADONAI are pure,
　　giving light to the eyes.
¹⁰ The fear of ADONAI is clean,
　　enduring forever.
　　　　The judgments of ADONAI are true
　　and altogether righteous.

¹¹ They are more desirable than gold,
　　yes, more than much pure gold!
　　　　They are sweeter than honey
　　and drippings of the honeycomb.
¹² Moreover by them Your servant is warned.
　　　　In keeping them there is great reward.
¹³ Who can discern his errors?
　　　　Cleanse me of hidden faults.
¹⁴ Also keep Your servant from willful sins.
　　　　May they not have dominion over me.
　　　　Then I will be blameless,
　　free from great transgression.
¹⁵ May the words of my mouth
　　and the meditation of my heart
　　be acceptable before You,
　　　　ADONAI, my Rock and my Redeemer.

Glenn Blank

The tripartite structure of this psalm is so striking that some scholars have wondered if it was originally three different poems. Yet the magnificence of all three parts seems to demand one inspired poet. After enjoying the dramatic grandeur of each part, I urge you, dear reader, to meditate on what unifies them—before you peek at my own offerings below.

The first part (2–7) offers the testimony of the heavens. If David could be in awe of the spectacle of clouds by day and the expanse of stars by night (2–3),

SHALOM in PSALMS

how much more so can we wonder at the glory of galaxies and nebulae sent down to us by Hubble and Spitzer? If David could compare the sun to a bridegroom on his wedding day or an athlete running his race (6), to what could we compare the furnace-fusing trillions of protons that excite the aurora borealis in our northern skies? Yet as heroic as the sun may appear, it is the Creator, not creation (as in Egypt or other pagan countries neighboring ancient Israel), who is to be worshiped. Creation points only to the One who "pitched a tent for the sun" (5), the One who spoke time and space into existence.

The second part (8–10) offers the testimony of *Torah*. Here David makes his tribute to Moses, or rather, to the One who spoke into the mind of Moses. Suddenly the dynamic sweeping movement of the first seven verses stops— confronting us with firm, vertical architecture and drawing our thoughts heavenward. Each perfectly straight line begins with a powerful noun—"testimony," "precepts," "fear"—continues with "ADONAI," and concludes with a phrase of potent impact—"restoring the soul," "giving joy to the heart." How can you not stand up and notice? How can you not pay attention to what these words are declaring? How can you not understand that beyond the truth of these words is the Truth of the Word?

The third part (11–15) offers the testimony of a human servant. What can mere man say after the universe and the *Torah* have uttered their praises? Yet someone has to see and hear. Physicists posit the *anthropic* principle— somehow the universe has been constructed so that conscious life *must* emerge to observe it. Yet the servant does more than observe—he must taste the sweetness of His truth (11), must be warned by His judgments or rewarded by His righteousness (12), must be cleansed by His purity (13), must be freed from the domination of sin by His perfection (14), must meditate on His glory. Would the creation, let alone this poem, be complete without the servant meditating on "my Rock and my Redeemer" (15)?

Have you figured out the unity yet? Here are just a few possibilities. The whole psalm is a testimony—heavens, *Torah*, humanity—all exalting the One who made them. The whole psalm speaks—day to day uttering (3) precepts (9) and judgments (10), the words of my mouth (15). The whole psalm celebrates the glory and the purity and the shining light of ADONAI. The whole psalm is a poetic speech and a meditation.

Now go back to the beginning and read the whole psalm aloud, celebrating each ray of light, tasting each word, and meditating on the freedom that your Redeemer has given back to you.

PSALM 20

ADONAI-*Nissi*

¹ For the music director, a psalm of David.
² May ADONAI answer you in the day of trouble!
    May the Name of the God of Jacob set you up securely on high.
³ May He send you help from the Sanctuary
    and support you from Zion.
⁴ May He remember all your meal offerings
    and accept the fat of your burnt offering. *Selah*
⁵ May He grant you your heart's desire
    and fulfill all your plans.
⁶ We will shout for joy in your victory
  and lift up our banners in the Name of our God!
    May ADONAI fulfill all your petitions.

⁷ Now I know that ADONAI saves His anointed.
    He answers him from His holy heaven with saving strength of His
        right hand.
⁸ Some have chariots, some have horses,
    but we remember the Name of ADONAI our God.
⁹ They have collapsed and fallen,
    but we rise up and support each other.
¹⁰ ADONAI, save the king!
    Answer us on the day we call!

Paul Wilbur

When I recorded this psalm of David live in San Antonio, Texas, back in 2005 for the *Watchman* project, I sensed that there was a particular anointing on these verses. David begins and ends this psalm with prayer for the righteous, and intercession is certainly a theme throughout. I would encourage you to pray these powerful verses over yourself and receive the blessing that they bring. Don't miss the continuing theme of *Melech David*—put your trust in the only sure Rock—that is, the Name of the Lord. What's in a name? Answers and protection for one (2), help and support (3), the desires of your heart and plans that succeed (5), all your requests (6), salvation (7), and power over your enemies (8). That's what! This would be a good place to shout "Halleluyah!" for the Name (*HaShem*) of the Lord! (See the comments on Ps. 8.)

One other thing that I love about this song of David is the sense of community and encouragement. David plays the role of a father and a shepherd for all Israel when he prays and intercedes for our well-being. I am always encouraged when I consider that David's voice was always heard in heaven, and here he is praying for me! Take heart that this prayer is for you; say *Amen* with every blessing spoken. Receive the promise that *HaShem* answers from His holy heaven with saving power (7) for you, and remember—when you are victorious, we will shout for joy!

PSALM 21

The Victorious King

¹ For the music director, a psalm of David.
² *ADONAI*, the king rejoices in Your strength!
  How greatly he delights in Your salvation.
³ You granted him his heart's desire,
  and You did not withhold the request of his lips. *Selah*
⁴ For You met him with the best blessings.
  You set on his head a crown of pure gold.
⁵ He asked You for life, You gave it to him,
  length of days forever and ever.
⁶ His glory is great through Your salvation.
  Honor and majesty You bestow on him.
⁷ For You bestow on him eternal blessings,
  gladden him with joy in Your presence.
⁸ For the king trusts in *ADONAI*,
  and in the lovingkindness of *Elyon*
  he will not be shaken.
⁹ Your hand will find all Your enemies.
  Your right hand will overtake those who hate You.

¹⁰ You will make them like a fiery furnace
   at the time of Your appearing.
      In His wrath ADONAI will swallow them up
   and fire will consume them.
¹¹ You destroy their offspring from earth,
      their seed from the children of men.
¹² Though they intended evil against You
      and devised a plot, they cannot succeed.
¹³ For You make them turn their backs.
      You aim Your bowstrings at their faces.
¹⁴ Be exalted, ADONAI, in Your strength!
      We will sing and praise Your might.

Glenn Blank

Psalms 20 and 21 form a pair of royal psalms, exalting the king of Israel. Psalm 20 prepares a king to overcome a time of trouble by seeking help from the Sanctuary, lifting up banners for victory, trusting in *HaShem* rather than in chariots and horses (7–8), and ending with an appeal to "save the king!"

Psalm 21 celebrates the victory—the king delights in salvation (2), for he has received his heart's desire (3) to overcome his enemies (9), with bowstrings aimed at their faces (13). The second and last verses frame the whole with a mighty word: בְּעֻזֶּךָ, *b'ozekha*, "in Your strength." The king's victory reveals the glorious favor of *HaShem* on him. The trouble through which this king gained the victory may have been a battle or a coronation (5), or both. As noted with Psalm 2, the succession of kings was often an occasion of conniving (12) and bloodshed. So it was important that the king consolidate his position—which in Israel happened only with the "best blessings" (4) of *HaShem*, displayed through length of days, glory, honor, majesty, and joy (5–7).

So exalted is the king in the favor of *HaShem*, that we cannot help but see in him a foreshadowing of the Messiah, the King of kings. The Messiah is the one King who has received eternal life, upon whom *HaShem* does bestow salvation (*yeshuah*)—for His Name is salvation—and eternal blessings (5–7). Though believers tend to see *Yeshua* meek and mild, He also comes as a warrior, swallowing up His enemies with wrath and fire (10), destroying the wicked from the earth (11). When this King appears, will you sing and praise His might? The victory of salvation is His! Now is the time to exalt the King!

PSALM 22

Suffering Servant

¹ For the music director, on "The Doe of the Dawn," a psalm of David.

² My God, my God,
    why have You forsaken me?
        Distant from my salvation
    are the words of my groaning.ᵃ

³ O my God, I cried out by day, but You did not answer,
    by night, but there was no rest for me.

⁴ Yet You are holy,
    enthroned on the praises of Israel.

⁵ In You our fathers put their trust.
    They trusted, and You delivered them.

⁶ They cried to You and were delivered.
    In You they trusted, and were not disappointed.

⁷ Am I a worm, and not a man?
    Am I a scorn of men, despised by people?

⁸ All who see me mock me.
    They curl their lips, shaking their heads:

⁹ "Rely on ADONAI! Let Him deliver him!
    Let Him rescue him—since he delights in Him!"ᵇ

¹⁰ Yet You brought me out of the womb,
    made me secure at my mother's breasts.

¹¹ From the womb I was cast on You—
    from my mother's womb You have been my God.

¹² Be not far from me!
    For trouble is near—
    there is no one to help.

¹³ Many bulls have surrounded me.
    Strong bulls of Bashan encircled me.

¹⁴ They open wide their mouths against me,
    like a tearing, roaring lion.

¹⁵ I am poured out like water,
    and all my bones are disjointed.

a. 22:2(1). cf. Matt. 27:46; Mark 15:34.
b. 22:9. cf. Matt. 27:43.

My heart is like wax—
melting within my innards.

¹⁶ My strength is dried up like a clay pot,
my tongue clings to my jaws.
You lay me in the dust of death.

¹⁷ For dogs have surrounded me.
A band of evildoers has closed in on me.
They pierced[a] my hands and my feet.

¹⁸ I can count all my bones.
They stare, they gape at me.

¹⁹ They divide my clothes among them,
and cast lots for my garment.[b]

²⁰ But You, ADONAI, be not far off!
O my strength! Come quickly to my aid!

²¹ Deliver my soul from the sword—
my only one from the power of the dog.

²² Save me from the lion's mouth.
From the horns of the wild oxen rescue me.

²³ I will declare Your Name to my brothers.
I will praise You amid the congregation.[c]

²⁴ You who fear ADONAI, praise Him!
All Jacob's descendants, glorify Him!
Revere Him, all you seed of Israel.

²⁵ For He has not despised or disdained the suffering of the lowly one.
Nor has He hidden His face from him,
but when he cried to Him, He heard.

²⁶ From You is my praise in the great assembly.
I will fulfill my vows before those who fear Him.

²⁷ Let the poor eat and be satisfied.
Let them who seek after Him praise ADONAI.
May your hearts live forever!

²⁸ All the ends of the earth will remember and turn to ADONAI.
All the families of the nations will bow down before You.

²⁹ For the kingdom belongs to ADONAI,
and He rules over the nations.

a. 22:17. Or, *like a lion.*
b. 22:19. cf. Matt. 27:35; Mark 15:24; Luke 23:34; John 19:24.
c. 22:23. cf. Heb. 2:12.

³⁰ All the rich of the earth will feast and worship.
> Everyone who goes down to the dust will kneel before Him—
> even the one who could not keep his own soul alive.
³¹ His posterity will serve him, telling
> the next generation about my Lord.
³² They will come and declare His righteousness
> to a people yet to be born—
> because He has done it!

Glenn Blank

Who exploded this piercing roar: "My God, my God, why have You forsaken me?" (2). Was it David running for his life, or Hezekiah on his near death-bed, or Jeremiah in a miry cistern? Or do all the suffering saints unite in the earthshaking moan of Messiah? Barely able to breathe, *Yeshua* groaned these words—and undoubtedly meditated on the whole psalm as He agonized for us.

What wild swings of extreme emotions the sufferer expresses! From despair (2–3) to worshipful trust (4–6), from wormy depression and rejection (7–9) to manic memories of mama's breast and mama's womb (10–11), from the terror of bulls and lions and dogs circling, roaring, gnashing, gashing (12–17) to the prospect of deliverance from the beasts—in reverse order, the dog's paw, the lion's mouth, and the wild oxen's horns (20–22). And that's just the first half! While the first part (1–22) keeps falling into despair, the second part (23–32) keeps proclaiming praise. Though the first sinks into the absolute humiliation of public nakedness (18–19), the second exalts in the congregation (23, 26, 32). Though once despised and mocked (7–8), the lowliness of the lowly is no longer despised or disdained (25). While at first complaining, "You did not answer" (3), the second part insists, "when he cried out to Him, He heard" (25). Surely this sufferer has experienced all our emotions—all our excruciating aches and all our yearning hopes.

Recognizing the sufferer is crucial to unraveling the mystery of his pain. Jewish and Christian scholars debate whether verse 17 should read "they pierced my hands and my feet" or "like a lion at my hands and my feet" (while others have suggested, they "dug" or "disfigured" or "bound" my feet). The difference is a stroke in one ancient Hebrew letter. However we read it, it wasn't pleasant. But let us step back and see this man feeling like a worm, despised by the people, with the crowds curling their lips and shaking their heads at the sufferer (8), sneering at his hope of deliverance (9), beholding his disjointed, though unbroken, bones

(15, 18), while others are casting lots for his garment (19). From the mystery of His agony, can you discern the image of the Sufferer? Because of what He has endured, not only will "all Jacob's descendants" glorify *HaShem* (24), but also "all the families of the nations will bow down before You" (28). Not only will all the living—"the rich of the earth"—worship Him, but also all the dead—"who goes down to the dust"—will kneel before Him (30). (Never mind that other psalms complain that the dead cannot praise Him! Can you decipher this mystery?) Not only His generation but also all the generations to come will tell about Him (31). They will declare "to a people yet to be born—because He has done it!" (32). What has He done? Once and for all, listen to the Sufferer's final word—for you and for me—"Finished!"

PSALM 23

ADONAI-Ro-eh

¹ A psalm of David.
  ADONAI is my shepherd, I shall not want.
² He makes me lie down in green pastures.
  He leads me beside still waters.
³ He restores my soul.
  He guides me in paths of righteousness
for His Name's sake.

⁴ Even though I walk through the valley of the shadow of death,
  I will fear no evil, for You are with me:
  Your rod and Your staff comfort me.
⁵ You prepare a table before me in the presence of my enemies.
  You have anointed my head with oil, my cup overflows.
⁶ Surely goodness and mercy will follow me all the days of my life,
  and I will dwell in the House of *ADONAI* forever.

Paul Wilbur

The Hebrew title for the book of Psalms is *Tehillim*, which means "songs of praise." These few lines are among the best known, beloved, and cherished of all Scripture verses. David begins, "*ADONAI* is my shepherd, I shall not want" (1). The Name translated as *ADONAI* is the holy Name by which *HaShem* responded to Moses: "Suppose I go . . . and they ask me, 'What is His Name?' What should I say to them?" (see Exod. 3:13–14). This Name is so holy that religious Jews will not even pronounce it. Some believers have translated it as *Yahweh* or *Jehovah*, but the truth is, no one really knows exactly how to pronounce it. It may be best to treat it as Orthodox Jews do and simply say *HaShem* (the Name) or Lord. David clearly identifies that He alone is his shepherd, provider, and protector—the One who revealed Himself to Moses on Mount Sinai is his shepherd. It is worth noting here that the word רֹעִי, *ro'i*, my shepherd (Gen. 49:24) is also thought to be derived from the word רֵעַ, *re'a*, friend. What a comforting revelation from David: the God of Abraham and Moses is also our shepherd and friend. Messiah *Yeshua* calls us His friends in John 15:15. With *HaShem* as our shepherd and friend, we both are well provided for now and have assurance that we "will dwell in the House of *ADONAI* forever" (6).

This shepherd makes us lie down in green pastures and leads us beside still waters (2). Then He does something that no ordinary shepherd can do—"He restores my soul" (3). My mind, my will, and my emotions are restored when I submit to the leading of this shepherd and friend. When the shepherd/friend of my soul leads me into righteousness, He does it for the sake of His own Name. Yet I am the one who benefits from His grace and goodness—truly the work of a shepherd who is unlike any other. Even if I must walk through times of great danger and darkness, I can do so without fear because the shepherd's rod and staff are there to comfort me and remind me of His presence (4). And surely goodness and mercy will chase me down, search me out, and follow after me *all* the days of my life, and I will dwell in the House of the Lord forever.

Every sheep knows his shepherd's voice, but a stranger's voice he will not follow (see John 10). Do you know *HaShem* as your shepherd and friend?

 # PSALM 24

The King of Glory

¹ A psalm of David.
   The earth is *ADONAI*'s and all that fills it—ᵃ
   the world, and those dwelling on it.

a. 24:1. cf. Deut. 10:24; Ps. 89:11; 1 Cor. 10:26.

² For He founded it upon the seas,
and established it upon the rivers.
³ Who may go up on the mountain of ADONAI?
Who may stand in His holy place?
⁴ One with clean hands and a pure heart,
who has not lifted his soul in vain,
nor sworn deceitfully.
⁵ He will receive a blessing from ADONAI,
righteousness from God his salvation.
⁶ Such is the generation seeking Him,
seeking Your face, even Jacob! *Selah*
⁷ Lift up your heads, O gates,
and be lifted up, you everlasting doors:
that the King of glory may come in.
⁸ "Who is this King of glory?"
ADONAI strong and mighty,
ADONAI mighty in battle!
⁹ Lift up your heads, O gates,
and lift them up, you everlasting doors:
that the King of glory may come in.
¹⁰ "Who is this King of glory?"
ADONAI-*Tzva'ot*—He is the King of glory! *Selah*

Paul Wilbur

Have you ever heard it said that the earth is the devil's playground? Well, David sets the record straight from the opening verse, declaring that the earth and all that fills it—its abundance—is ADONAI's. Even all who live on the earth are His possession. He is the One who gathered all the waters in one place (Gen. 1:9) to create the seas and the rivers (2). Because He created it all, it all belongs to Him. Though *satan* has been prowling the earth ever since he was cast out of heaven, he is not the creator nor the owner of anything. He comes only to steal, kill, and destroy (John 10:10).

So, who may appear before the Lord on His mountain, in His holy place (3)? Only "one with clean hands and a pure heart" (4). In biblical times there were strict regulations of ceremonial purity and rules for service before the presence of the Lord. There were washings for the body, special garments for the priests, anointing with oil, and preparations to be made before going in to minister before ADONAI. But for those whose heart is set on the face of the Lord, there is favor, blessing, and righteousness, because God has provided His *yeshuah*, His salvation. David finishes his thought by saying, "Such is the generation seeking Him"—those who desire and long for His face (6).

As I travel around the world, I am observing a new generation of worshipers—those who are unashamed and unafraid. They speak many different languages and come from many different cultures and backgrounds, yet they are a righteous generation that will not be denied the presence of God. I have heard them shout for joy and felt their passionate worship, which goes up to the very throne of the Lord. The "clean hands" that David speaks of may refer to our deeds. Those who approach the presence of ADONAI should examine their deeds, to see that there is no evil intent. A "pure heart," now that is a little more elusive, to say the least! In Psalm 51:12, King David cries out, "Create in me a clean heart, O God, and renew a steadfast spirit within me." The Scriptures indicate that the heart of man is desperately in need of a supernatural touch by the *Ruach* or breath of God. *Yeshua* taught that the heart or spirit of each person needs to be reborn; it needs a transformation that only the hand of ADONAI can bring (John 3:3). There are two parts of a person that are immaterial—the soul, which connects us to the earth, and the *lev* (לֵב) or heart of man, which connects us to heaven. This *lev* needs to be "born from above" or "born anew."

Now that we have settled the prerequisites, the gates and doors of eternity are ready to open—so that *Melech ha-Kavod* (מֶלֶךְ הַכָּבוֹד), the King of glory, may come in! It is an obvious reference to the King Messiah who is also ADONAI-*Tzva'ot*, the Lord of Hosts, or armies of ADONAI. Verses 7–10 are often set in song because of the power and majesty they ascribe to the coming of the King of Israel. And if you'd like an even more graphic description of this coming King, check out Revelation 19:11–16. Yes, He is *Melech Hamlachim*, King of all kings!

PSALM 25

Teach Me Your Paths

¹ Of David.

To You, ADONAI, I lift up my soul.

² O my God, in You I trust,

    so I will not be ashamed,

    and my enemies will not gloat over me.

³ Surely no one who waits for You will be ashamed.

    But the treacherous without cause will be ashamed.

⁴ Show me Your ways, ADONAI.

    Teach me Your paths.

⁵ Guide me in Your truth, and teach me,

    for You are God, my salvation,

    for You I wait all day.

⁶ Remember, ADONAI,

    Your compassions and Your mercies—

    for they are from eternity.

⁷ Remember not the sins of my youth, nor my rebellion.

    According to Your mercy remember me,

  for the sake of Your goodness, ADONAI.

⁸ Good and upright is ADONAI.

    Therefore He directs sinners in the way.

⁹ He guides the humble in what is right,

    and teaches the humble His way.

¹⁰ All ADONAI's ways are lovingkindness and truth

  to those who keep His covenant and His testimonies.

¹¹ For Your Name's sake, ADONAI,

    pardon my guilt, for it is great.

¹² Who is this man who fears ADONAI?

    He will instruct him in the way he should choose.

¹³ His soul abides in goodness,

    and his offspring will inherit the land.

¹⁴ The secret of ADONAI is for those who fear Him.

    He makes His covenant known to them.

¹⁵ My eyes are always looking to ADONAI,

    for He will pull my feet out of the net.

¹⁶ Turn to me and be gracious to me,

    for I am lonely and afflicted.

¹⁷ The troubles of my heart increase.

    Bring me out of my distress.

¹⁸ See my affliction and my suffering,

    and take away all my sins.

¹⁹ See my enemies, how many they are—
   they hate me with violent hatred.
²⁰ Guard my soul and deliver me.
   Let me not be ashamed, for I take refuge in You.
²¹ May integrity and uprightness protect me—
   for I wait for You.
²² Redeem Israel, O God,
   from all their troubles.

Jeffrey Seif and Glenn Blank

What does it mean to lift up "my soul" (נַפְשִׁי, *nafshi*) to God (1)? What does it mean to "trust" in God (2)? Expressions like these are thrown around, but what do they mean street-level? Now? Today? For us? For that matter, what does it mean to hope in or "wait" (קִוִּתִי, *kiviti*) for God (3, 5)? And what are the longed-for "ways" of God (4)? Though many are hard-pressed to answer these questions personally, let alone theologically, who among us doesn't need help acknowledging the "sins of my youth" (7)—and since? Anyone with a conscience comprehends our human condition. Sadly, too many just live with it and accept sinful living to be the norm. If that's you, it's particularly tragic, because there is a God who "directs sinners in the way" (8)—the way of a clean conscience in His sight.

Here are some clues to this "way" God wants to teach us: humility (9) and covenant keeping (10). He gives grace to those who are humble, who are teachable, who are faithful. To experience His pardon, one must accept responsibility for one's actions (11) and "fear ADONAI"—then He will "instruct him in the way" (12). The fear of ADONAI is not a panic but an abiding trust in His goodness (13), confident in His promise of an inheritance. Faith is a precious secret to those who know His covenant (14); those who don't and haven't received His covenant still live in ignorance and uncertainty. Yet those who keep seeking *HaShem* experience His deliverance "out of the net" of unseen adversaries (15). When you feel lonely, you can cry out, "turn to me and be gracious to me" (16). It resounds now as it did then because troubles abound now as then. God abides with us still. Who will turn to Him and abide with Him? The psalmist answered that question for himself: "May integrity and uprightness protect me—for I wait for You" (21). Would that we all were like-minded.

Now might be a good time to pray through this psalm, with faith in God's covenant faithfulness: O Lord, help me to humble myself before You.

I acknowledge my sins and shortcomings. Turn to me in my weakness. Renew in my soul knowledge of Your goodness and grace, and teach me how to walk in Your way of faithfulness and integrity. I will wait for You. Amen.

✳✳✳✳✳✳✳✳ PSALM 26 ✳✳✳✳✳✳✳✳

Walking with Integrity

¹ Of David.
    Vindicate me, ADONAI,
    for I have walked in my integrity,
    and trusted in ADONAI without wavering.
² Probe me, ADONAI, and test me,
    refine my mind and my heart.
³ For Your love is before my eyes
    and I have walked in Your truth.
⁴ I have not sat with men of falsehood,
    nor do I consort with hypocrites.
⁵ I detest the company of evildoers,
    and do not sit with the wicked.
⁶ I will wash my hands in innocence,
    so I can walk around Your altar, ADONAI,
⁷ hearing the voice of thanksgiving
    while proclaiming all Your wonders.
⁸ ADONAI, I love the House where You live,
    the place where Your glory dwells.
⁹ Do not take my soul away with sinners,
    nor my life with people of bloodshed—
¹⁰ in whose hands are wicked schemes,
    whose right hand is full of bribes.
¹¹ But I—I will walk in my integrity.
    Redeem me and be gracious to me.
¹² My feet stand on level ground.
    In congregations I will bless ADONAI.

Jeffrey Seif and Glenn Blank

Does faithfulness pay off and steadfastness pay dividends now and in the future? The psalmist says he has "walked" in his integrity "without wavering" (1). How many of us can make that claim? He asks God to "probe" him (2). Don't trials come without asking? He walks (3) in God's truth (אֱמֶת, *emet*). How many of us can speak of truth with such integrity? Nowadays the world says, "Everything is relative," so steadfast faithfulness and truthfulness can be in high demand yet short supply. The psalmist is confident that these virtues are why God should take him seriously. Walking in God's truth requires some distance from those who live lies. Therefore he disdains "men of falsehood" (4), refuses to sit with them (5), and pledges to "wash my hands in innocence" (6). He wants distance from those who make a lifestyle out of deceit. How about you?

One way to determine where someone is going in life is to take note of the people they are traveling with. Good people build up; bad people tear down. Righteous people trend upward, the wicked downward. The results may not be instantaneous—the book of Job as well as other psalms and biblical passages wrestle with this issue. But to the psalmist, the principle is straightforward and simple. Sooner or later, God *will* vindicate the righteous. Therefore he loves the House where the Lord lives (8) and does not want his soul taken away with sinners (9). By walking through life with integrity (11), he is confident that his feet "stand on level ground" (12).

How about you? The wrong kind of people can too easily divert any of us from the right kind of living. We all hear that "crime doesn't pay" or "drugs make you stupid," yet the allure of short-term benefits or pleasure entice many a soul. Would that include any you know personally? What is called for is resolve—and integrity. But face it, it's hard to muster resolve, let alone integrity, all by yourself. That's why we recommend a genuine relationship with Israel's Messiah. There has never been anyone who lived a more blameless life than the One who "walked the walk" all the way to the cross. Alcoholics Anonymous and similar groups have demonstrated the power of confessing your weakness and relying on a "higher power." There is no one higher, more reliable, with more integrity, than *Yeshua*! In John 1:12, He goes on record that all who receive Him have "the right to become children of God." In other words, He will let you walk in *His* integrity (not just your own). He will "redeem" you and "be gracious" to you (11). He will also connect you with congregations that "bless ADONAI" (12). The choice is yours—as is your future. Right choices will ultimately bear good fruit; poor choices won't. It's that straightforward and simple.

❋❋❋❋❋❋❋❋❋ # PSALM 27 ❋❋❋❋❋❋❋❋❋

Let Your Heart Take Courage

¹ Of David.
  ADONAI is my light and my salvation:
whom should I fear?
  ADONAI is the stronghold of my life:
whom should I dread?
² When evildoers approached me to devour my flesh
  —my adversaries and my foes—they stumbled and fell.
³ Though an army camp besieges me, my heart will not fear.
  Though war breaks out against me, even then will I be confident.
⁴ One thing have I asked of ADONAI,
    that will I seek:
    to dwell in the House of ADONAI
all the days of my life,
    to behold the beauty of ADONAI,
and to meditate in His Temple.
⁵ For in the day of trouble He will hide me in His *sukkah*,
    conceal me in the shelter of His tent,
    and set me high upon a rock.
⁶ Then will my head be high above my enemies around me.
    In His Tabernacle I will offer sacrifices with shouts of joy.
    I will sing, yes, sing praises to ADONAI.

⁷ Hear, ADONAI, when I call with my voice,
    be gracious to me and answer me.
⁸ To You my heart says: "Seek My face."
    Your face, ADONAI, I seek.
⁹ Do not hide Your face from me.
    Do not turn Your servant away in anger.
    You have been my help.
    Do not abandon me or forsake me,
O God my salvation.

¹⁰ Though my father and my mother
>   forsake me, ADONAI will take me in.
¹¹ Teach me Your way, ADONAI,
>   and lead me on a level path—
>   because of my enemies.
¹² Do not turn me over to the desire of my foes.
>   For false witnesses rise up against me,
>   breathing out violence.
¹³ Surely I trust that I will see the goodness
>   of ADONAI in the land of the living.
¹⁴ Wait for ADONAI.
>   Be strong, let your heart take courage,
>   and wait for ADONAI.

Paul Wilbur

Ah, Psalm 27, another song of David and another of my favorites! I was sitting with friends in Nashville, Tennessee, writing new songs for my project called *Desert Rain*, and suggested we write a song with strength and power that believers could sing with confidence and that would encourage faith . . . no problem! As I strummed a chord pattern, one of my friends sang, "The Lord is my light and my salvation, why should I be afraid?" He was simply quoting directly from the source of strength, power, and faith, and as we looked further at this psalm, we found an entire new song just waiting to be discovered.

There is so much to say about this incredible word of encouragement! David begins, "ADONAI *ori*"—"The LORD is my light." The word אוֹר, *'or*, usually speaks about heavenly lights like the sun, moon, and stars, but also includes fire, lamps, and lightning. Sometimes in Israel you will hear people greet each other in the morning with "*Boker or!*"—literally, "Morning light!" in reply to someone who says "*Boker tov*," meaning "Good morning."

Consider all the applications of just these first two Hebrew words: the sun gives warmth, life, sight; the moon and stars mark time, the seasons, and true direction for navigators; a lamp gives sight and direction; his *Torah* or Word is a lamp unto our feet and a light for our path (Ps. 119:105); wisdom lights a person's face (Eccles. 8:1); may the light of His face shine on us (Num. 6:25); and one day, when He replaces the sun with His glory (Rev. 21:23), the Lamb of God, King Messiah, will be our eternal lamp (*ner tamid*) in the new Jerusalem!

David boldly declares that ADONAI is his warmth, direction, sight, wisdom, splendor, glory, life, and guidance; therefore . . . why should I be afraid of anything, or anyone? He then proclaims, "ADONAI yishee," the Lord is "my salvation," meaning deliverance, hope, liberty, victory, welfare, and shelter, from the Hebrew word yesha—from whence comes the Name of Messiah, our salvation, Yeshua HaMashiach (the Messiah). So in these few words, David confesses his faith in ADONAI who is all these and more to him; therefore, he will not be afraid of anything or anyone. Well, sure, you might say, if I had a palace, an army, and great wealth, I wouldn't be afraid either! Don't forget that David's life was filled with struggles and strife. As a young boy he protected his father's flocks from lions and bears with sticks and stones; he stood against the giant Goliath with a few smooth stones and a strap of leather; his best friend's father, King Saul, chased him with an army to take his life; his wife mocked his worship; his own son Absalom raised an army to kill him—he had more reasons than the average man to be afraid. What David teaches us in these opening words is a profound life lesson.

When learning to ride a motorcycle, they teach you *not* to focus your attention on the obstacle in the road you wish to avoid. Why? Because wherever you focus your eyes is exactly where your motorcycle will take you! Rather, you should look for a pathway *around* the obstruction that will keep you safe from harm and disaster. Similarly, David is teaching us not to focus our attention on the lions, bears, and Goliaths of life, or the adversary come to devour us, or the army come to besiege us (2–3), but to fix our gaze on the author and finisher of our faith, who will hide us in His sanctuary and keep us from harm (5). For David, ADONAI was his path, his light, and his strong tower of safety in every situation. Some writers have suggested that this psalm of David reveals a conflicted man: a man of confident faith in verses 1–6 who utters a "welcome to my life" cry for help in verses 7–12. I would suggest that it is because of David's confident faith in verses 1–6 that he knows where to go when times get tough. Evidence is submitted in the closing two verses. He declares to himself—and to us—in spite of all the challenges he faces in life, his confidence of a good end, which lies securely in the hands of the Lord —"let your heart take courage, and wait for ADONAI" (14). He is always faithful, and He will strengthen your heart!

PSALM 28

Hoshia-na!

[1] Of David.
　To You, ADONAI, I call—
my Rock, do not be deaf to me.
　If You were silent to me,
I would become like those going down to the Pit.
[2] Hear the sound of my pleas,
　　when I cry to You for help,
　　when I lift up my hands toward Your holy Sanctuary.
[3] Do not drag me away with the wicked and with doers of iniquity,
　　who speak peace with their neighbors,
　　while evil is in their hearts.
[4] Repay them for their deeds, their evil acts.
　　Repay them for the deeds of their hands.
　　Bring back on them what they deserve.
[5] Since they show no regard for the deeds of ADONAI
　　nor the work of His hands,
　　He will tear them down
and never build them up.
[6] Blessed be ADONAI, because He has heard
　　the sound of my supplications.
[7] ADONAI is my strength and my shield.[a]
　　My heart trusts in Him, and I was helped.
　　Therefore my heart leaps for joy,
　　and I will praise Him with my song.
[8] ADONAI is their strength—
　　a stronghold of salvation for His anointed.
[9] Save Your people, bless Your inheritance,
　　shepherd them and carry them forever.

a. 28:7. cf. Eph. 6:16.

Glenn Blank

David offers us, by example, four valuable lessons about prayer. First, if you are having some *tsouris* (trouble), you can call on *HaShem*, your "Rock" (1). With earnestness, pour out your pleadings to Him, even lifting up your hands to express how much you need to have His answer (2). Second, you can be sure that *HaShem* makes a distinction between the righteous (who call on Him with trust) and the wicked (who "show no regard" for His works)—the former He will build up and the latter tear down (4–5). Some would prefer to smooth over the harsh consequences of this distinction, not liking the idea that *HaShem* might drag him "away with the wicked" (3). Yet the prophets and *Yeshua* Himself agree that life has been set up with consequences for iniquity, and ultimately there will be a day of reckoning before the true Judge. Third, once you have poured out your supplications, be confident that He has heard you (6). When you trust in Him with all your heart, you will experience His protection, and you will sing joyful praises to Him (7). Fourth, it is good to move from supplication to intercession, from praying for your own needs to praying for others. Especially pray for their salvation, which is found in His Anointed One (8). You can be sure that *HaShem* will answer these prayers, for He is the shepherd of Israel (9). Many *kedoshim* have followed this pattern of prayer: moving from heartfelt request to trust, then from praise to intercession.

PSALM 29

God Thunders throughout Creation

¹ A psalm of David.
　　Ascribe to ADONAI, O sons of God,
　　　ascribe to ADONAI glory and strength.
² Ascribe to ADONAI the glory of His Name.
　　Bow down to ADONAI in the beauty of holiness.
³ The voice of ADONAI is over the waters.
　　The God of glory thunders—
　　ADONAI is over mighty waters.

⁴ The voice of ADONAI is powerful.
> The voice of ADONAI is full of majesty.

⁵ The voice of ADONAI breaks the cedars.
> Yes, ADONAI shatters cedars of Lebanon.

⁶ He makes Lebanon skip like a calf,
> Sirion like a young wild ox.

⁷ The voice of ADONAI hews out flames of fire.

⁸ The voice of ADONAI shakes the desert.
> ADONAI shakes the wilderness of Kadesh.

⁹ The voice of ADONAI makes the deer writhe in birth
> and strips forests bare,
> and in His Temple all are saying, "Glory!"

¹⁰ ADONAI sits enthroned over the flood.
> Yes, ADONAI sits as King forever.

¹¹ ADONAI gives strength to His people.
> ADONAI blesses His people with *shalom*.

Jeffrey Seif and Glenn Blank

"I scratch your back; you scratch mine." We know people play by this rule. Does God? Repeatedly the psalmist speaks of ascribing (הָבוּ, *havu*, as in giving an offering) to God awesome attributes of "glory" (כָּבוֹד, *kavod*) and "strength" (עֹז, *oz*), and of bowing down to Him in worship (1–2). Following a flood of poetic images about His rather intimidating voice (3–9), he speaks of God who, in turn, "gives strength to His people" and "blesses His people with *shalom*" (11).

Feeling cursed in so many ways, people long for blessings—from others or at least from God. Could it be that the way to get blessings is to be a blessing? The psalmist gives blessing to God and then, in return, goes on record saying that it is ADONAI who in turn gives blessings to the psalmist, and God is able to give in far greater measure than you or me. This deal isn't just for dead writers: it's for living readers. God lives on for scores of generations and the principle lives on in every generation: "Give, and it will be given to you" (Luke 6:38)—so promised Israel's "Prince of Peace" (Isa. 9:6). This principle works. Experiment with it, and experience it. There are many blessings, many different things to ascribe to *HaShem*. Like the psalmist, you too can go on record extolling God's ways—as well as the Savior who elucidated them—and be ever so thankful that you embraced God's ways.

✳✳✳✳✳✳✳✳ PSALM 30 ✳✳✳✳✳✳✳✳

Joy Comes in the Morning

¹ A psalm, a song for the dedication of the Temple, of David.

² I will exalt You, ADONAI,
for You have lifted me up,
and did not let my enemies gloat over me.

³ ADONAI my God, I cried to You for help,
and You healed me.

⁴ ADONAI, You brought my soul up from *Sheol*.
You kept me alive, so I would not go down to the Pit.

⁵ Sing praise to ADONAI, His faithful ones,
and praise His holy name.

⁶ For His anger lasts for only a moment,
His favor is for a lifetime.
Weeping may stay for the night,
but joy comes in the morning.

⁷ When I felt secure, I said:
"I will never be shaken."

⁸ ADONAI, in Your favor
You made my mountain stand strong.
When You hid Your face,
I was terrified.

⁹ To You, ADONAI, I called,
and to my Lord I made my plea:

¹⁰ "What gain is there in my blood,
in my going down to the Pit?
Will the dust praise You?
Will it declare Your truth?

¹¹ Hear, ADONAI, and be gracious to me.
ADONAI, be my help."

¹² You turned my mourning into dancing.
You removed my sackcloth and clothed me with joy.

¹³ So my glory will sing to You and not be silent.
ADONAI my God, I will praise You forever.

Jeffrey Seif and Glenn Blank

The wishes associated with verse 12 are proverbial no-brainers. Who among us wouldn't like God to turn our "mourning into dancing"? Who wouldn't like God to remove our sackcloth and clothe us with joy? If this transformation is something you could use, here's a question: Are you willing to pay the dues—or rather, put forth the effort to truly lean on *HaShem* and call out to Him for help? Each time David cries out to God for help (3, 9, 11), he finds that God has brought his "soul up from *Sheol*" (4), sent His gracious help (11), and turned his mourning into dancing (12). Redemption works this way. His "faithful ones" are urged to keep singing praise to God (5) and to be mindful that "weeping may stay for the night, but joy comes in the morning" (6). When you're weeping about your troubles, and your enemies (real, spiritual, or imagined) are gloating over you (2), you might not believe it at the moment, or for all that long night of weeping, but morning will surely come—and just as surely God will give grace. If you put your trust in Him, you need not fear "going down to the Pit" (10), let alone anything less permanently traumatic.

Now that you've seen how David finds his help, one question remains: Are you willing to seek God the way David did? If you want joy in the morning, you may need to cry out to Him in the night.

PSALM 31

Refuge, *Sukkah*, Shelter

¹ For the music director, a psalm of David.
² In You, ADONAI, have I taken refuge:
    Let me never be put to shame.
    In Your righteousness, deliver me.
³ Turn Your ear to me, rescue me quickly.
    Be a rock of refuge for me, a stronghold for my deliverance.
⁴ Since You are my rock and my fortress,
    You lead me and guide me for Your Name's sake.
⁵ Free me from the net they hid for me,
    for You are my refuge.

⁶ Into Your hand I commit my spirit.ᵃ
     You have redeemed me, ADONAI, God of truth.
⁷ I detest those who continue to watch worthless idols,
     but I trust in ADONAI.
⁸ I will be glad and rejoice in Your lovingkindness,
     for You saw my affliction.
     You knew the troubles of my soul.
⁹ You did not hand me over to the enemy.
     You set my feet in a wide-open place.
¹⁰ Be gracious to me, ADONAI,
  for I am in distress.
     My eyes waste away with grief,
  my soul and my body as well.
¹¹ For my life is consumed in sorrow
  and my years in sighing.
     My strength fails because of my anguish
  and my bones waste away.
¹² Because of all my adversaries
     I am the contempt of my neighbors
  and a dread to my acquaintances.
     Seeing me on the street, they flee from me.
¹³ I am as forgotten as a dead man.
     I have become like a broken vessel.
¹⁴ For I have heard the whispering of many.
     There is terror on every side
  as they conspire against me
  and plot to take my life.
¹⁵ But I have trusted in You, ADONAI.
     I said: "You are my God."
¹⁶ My times are in Your hands.
     Deliver me from the hands of my foes and from those who pursue me.
¹⁷ Make Your face shine on Your servant.
     Save me in Your lovingkindness.
¹⁸ ADONAI, let me not be ashamed,
     for I have called upon You.
     Let the wicked be ashamed—
     let them be silent in *Sheol*.

a. 31:6(5). cf. Luke 23:46; Acts 7:59.

74

[19] Let the lying lips be mute.
  For they speak arrogantly against the righteous,
  with pride and contempt.
[20] How great is Your goodness,
  which You have stored up for those who fear You,
  which You have given to those who take refuge in You,
  before the children of men.
[21] In the shelter of Your presence
  You hide them from people's plots.
  You conceal them in a *sukkah*
  from the strife of tongues.
[22] Blessed be ADONAI,
  for He has shown me His wonderful love
  in a besieged city.
[23] I said in my alarm,
  "I have been cut off from Your sight!"
  But You heard the sound of my pleas
  when I cried out to You.
[24] Love ADONAI, all His *kedoshim*!
  ADONAI preserves all the faithful,
  but the proud He pays back in full.
[25] *Chazak!* Let your heart take courage,[b]
  all you who wait for ADONAI.

Glenn Blank and Jeffrey Seif

From his many experiences in dire circumstances, David cries out in prayer, "let me never be put to shame" (2, 18). He expresses much confidence in *HaShem* as his refuge (2, 3, 5, 20), fortress (4), shelter and *sukkah* (21). Yet in the end he is still urging himself (and us) to "let your heart take courage, all you who wait for ADONAI" (25). So, what does it mean to "wait for ADONAI"? What does it mean after you've said in your alarm, "I have been cut off from Your sight!" (23)? Is this poem a prayer of desperation? Is the psalmist still waiting for God's presence to return to him (or at least the feeling of His presence), along with whatever presents He might bring with Him? He admits that *HaShem* "knew the troubles of my soul" (8). He confesses his "distress" and the toll of grief on his body (10), "consumed in sorrow" (11). He beseeches God, "Deliver

b. 31:25. cf. 1 Cor. 16:13; Eph. 6:10.

me from the hands of my foes" (16). He petitions, "Make Your face shine on Your servant" (17), echoing the Aaronic blessing of Numbers 6:25. Life doesn't always seem fair, does it? So David admits. Difficulties notwithstanding, he keeps hanging in there, rejoicing in the Lord's lovingkindness (8), resolutely trusting in Him (15), and affirming, "How great is Your goodness, which You have stored up for those who fear You" (20). He does expect victory, sooner or later, even if he is experiencing setbacks at the moment. Do you find yourself in a similar situation? Have you been crying out in alarm? Take heart in *HaShem*: "*Chazak!* [Be strong!] Let your heart take courage" (25).

At just such a crisis of soul, a descendant of David cries out as David does (6), "Into Your hands I entrust My spirit" (Luke 23:46). *Yeshua* fully understands those who experience affliction (8), whose "strength fails" (11) because of iniquity (though not His but ours), who feel the "contempt of my neighbors" (12), or who feel "forgotten as a dead man" (13). *Yeshua* heard the "whispering of many" conspiring to take his life (14). Through it all, He never stopped trusting in the Father. Though He experienced much shame outwardly, within His soul He still declared, "You are My God." If you are going through a trial, remember that He went through a trial, for you—so that your spirit might not be with the unrepentant wicked in *Sheol* (18), cut off from His sight (23), but brought by His hand into a wide-open place (9). Remember that even in the midst of the ordeal, He still says—together with all the faithful *kedoshim* (24)—"Blessed be ADONAI, for He has shown me His wonderful love" (22).

PSALM 32

Confess, Return, and Learn

¹ Of David, a contemplative song.
> Blessed is the one whose transgression is forgiven, whose sin is pardoned.
² Blessed is the one whose guilt ADONAI does not count, and in whose spirit there is no deceit.ᵃ

a. 32:1–2. cf. Rom. 4:7–8.

[3] When I kept silent,
>   my bones became brittle
>   through my groaning all day long.
[4] For day and night Your hand was heavy upon me.
>   My strength was drained as in the droughts of summer. *Selah*
[5] Then I acknowledged my sin to You
>   and did not hide my iniquity. I said:
>   "I confess my transgressions to ADONAI,"
>   and You forgave the guilt of my sin.[b] *Selah*

[6] So let everyone who is godly pray to You
in a time when You may be found.
>   When great floodwaters rise,
they will not reach him.
[7] You are my hiding place—
>   You will protect me from distress.
>   You surround me with songs of deliverance. *Selah*

[8] "I will instruct you and teach you in the way you should go.
I will give counsel—My eye is on you.
[9] Do not be like the horse or the mule,
>   which have no understanding,
>   and must be held in with bit and bridle
>   or they will not come to you."
[10] Many are the sorrows of the wicked,
>   but lovingkindness surrounds the one who trusts in ADONAI.
[11] Be glad in ADONAI and rejoice,
>   you righteous, and shout for joy,
>   all who are upright in heart.

Glenn Blank

God knows our hearts, often better than we do ourselves. The first five verses reveal the struggle that we sometimes go through to confess our sins; the last four deal with how hard it can be for us to receive counsel. What's the connection? Hmm ... we may not want to admit it, but sometimes we want to bury things rather than deal with them. Please pay attention: God in His wisdom has some good counsel for you.

b. 32:5. cf. 1 John 1:9.

A good illustration (and possible inspiration) for this psalm is from the annals of David (2 Sam. 11–12). The hero-king committed a double crime trying to cover up his adultery with Bathsheba, first by bringing Uriah home to his wife, then conniving his death and a quick wedding before the baby was born. *Oy!* When the prophet Nathan confronted him, David practically exploded in repentance, fasting and lying on the ground. But when the child died, David arose, washed, and worshiped in the House of *HaShem*. His behavior was puzzling to people around him but perfectly obvious to God. David understood that instead of covering up, it is much better to let the Lord do the covering, with His atonement (1). People sometimes think that God wants to clobber us. Actually, because His very nature is love (*chesed*), *HaShem* delights to show mercy—and then bless us! See Hosea 3:1 for the mercy Hosea offered to his adulterous wife, Gomer—in order to illustrate what God keeps offering to Israel. Or consider the mercy *Yeshua* showed to those who crucified Him (really, all of us) by praying, "Father, forgive them, for they do not know what they are doing" (Luke 23:34).

God designed guilt as a signal—you just did something wrong! Confess it and God will "not count" it against you (2)—because Messiah *Yeshua* has already made atonement for you. Keeping silent drives guilt inward, where it does damage to your body (3). Repressed guilt can feel "heavy" and sap your strength (4). So stop trying to hide from God—after all, He already sees everything! Confess your transgression to Him, and He will forgive your guilt (5). As Romans 8:1 promises, "There is now no condemnation for those who are in Messiah *Yeshua*." Confession and forgiveness restore your relationship with God so that you can be confident again that God will protect you from distress (6–7).

It works! God wants to "instruct you" in this way. You may as well be transparent with God—His "eye" is already on you (8). Yet some people refuse to listen to this lesson. God doesn't want to treat you like a stubborn mule. That's why He warned Cain, "Sin is crouching at the doorway" (Gen. 4:7). He created us in His image, with freedom of action and conscience. The "sorrows of the wicked" (10) start when they separate themselves from God by sin and then, in shame, refuse to acknowledge it. But the joys of the righteous abide in the mercy (חֶסֶד, *chesed*) of *HaShem* (10–11).

God called David "a man after His own heart" (1 Sam. 13:14) not because David was perfect but because he was transparent. You can be like David—if you trust completely in the mercy of Messiah.

 # PSALM 33

All Creation Praise the Creator

¹ Sing for joy to ADONAI, you righteous.
  Praise is fitting for the upright.
² Praise ADONAI with the harp.
  Sing praises to Him with a ten-string lyre.
³ Sing to Him a new song!ª
  Play skillfully amid shouts of joy.

⁴ For the word of ADONAI is upright
  and all His work is done in faithfulness.
⁵ He loves righteousness and justice.
  The earth is full of the love of ADONAI.
⁶ By ADONAI's word were the heavens made,
  and all their host by the breath of His mouth.
⁷ He gathers the waters of the sea together in a heap.
  He lays up deep waters in storehouses.
⁸ Let all the earth fear ADONAI.
  Let all the inhabitants of the world stand in awe of Him.
⁹ For He spoke, and it came to be.
  He commanded, and it stood firm.
¹⁰ ADONAI foils the purpose of the nations.
  He thwarts the plans of the peoples.
¹¹ The plan of ADONAI stands forever,
  the purposes of His heart from generation to generation.
¹² Blessed is the nation whose God is ADONAI,
  the people He chose for His own inheritance.
¹³ ADONAI looks down from heaven.
  He observes all humanity.

a. 33:3. cf. Rev. 5:9.

[14] From His dwelling place He gazes
 on all the inhabitants of the earth—
[15] He who fashions the hearts of all,
 who discerns all their deeds.
[16] No king is saved by his great army,
 no warrior is delivered by great strength.
[17] A horse is a false hope for victory,
 nor can its great strength save.
[18] Behold, the eyes of ADONAI are on those who fear Him,
 waiting for His love,
[19] to deliver their souls from death,
 and to keep them alive in famine.
[20] Our soul waits for ADONAI—
 He is our help and our shield.
[21] Our heart rejoices in Him,
 because we trusted in His holy Name.
[22] Let Your lovingkindness, ADONAI,
 be upon us, as we have waited for You.

Paul Wilbur

The psalmist begins with an exhortation to "sing for joy to ADONAI, you righteous," then tells us that "praise is fitting for the upright" (1). Let's break this down a little bit. First of all, רַנְּנוּ, *ra-n'noo*, actually means to give a shrill, ringing cry of joy. A righteous person, or *tzaddik*, is usually someone admired for conforming to a legal or moral code, but what does the Bible say? Psalms 14:3; 53:4; and Romans 3:10 all agree that no one is righteous, not even one. But Romans 3 tells us the Good News that righteousness is a free gift of ADONAI to all who believe or put their trust in His salvation through *Yeshua*, Israel's Messiah!

This joyful shout is fitting or comely for the upright. My friend Don Moen wrote a song restating this verse in a more contemporary fashion: "Praise looks good on you!" It is a line that not only brings a smile to my face but also carries a revelation: praise in our mouths casts a reflection on our countenance. If we will surrender a joyful shout to the Lord, our face and our attitude will surely follow suit! Let the righteous praise ADONAI with instruments "skillfully amid shouts of joy" (3)—in other words, not loud for loud's sake, but with skill and anointing. If we are singing and playing as part of a worship team, it should be done with skill as well as with heart!

The next few verses (4–9) extol the power of the word of Adonai, for by His word the heavens, the seas, and the earth were formed. Recall how Hebrews 1:3 says that all things are sustained and upheld by the power of His word and Colossians 1:17 says that in Him all things exist and are held together. Because of the greatness of Adonai and His word, the psalmist rightly declares that any nation that chooses Him is a blessed nation (12). I couldn't agree more! When righteous kings like David or Hezekiah turned their nation to God, they overcame all their enemies. Likewise, I believe the greatness of our own nation depends on leaders like Washington and Lincoln acknowledging the greatness of the God we serve. Victory won't come merely from our own strength (16)—warhorses and other technological weapons may be awesome assets in battle, but deliverance comes only from the Lord. Remember how Gideon with his tiny army of 300 chased away 125,000 Midianites? Or how about Jehoshaphat's victory against three armies with a praise and worship team?

Because "the eyes of Adonai are on those who fear Him" (18), we have hope. We wait for Him (18, 22)—we depend on His grace and mercy to sustain us, to deliver us from death (19), to be our help and shield (20), and to give us a future and a hope. Because we do trust in Him, "our heart rejoices in Him" (21). So give the Lord a joyful shout, you righteous, because He is worthy, and praise looks good on you!

PSALM 34

Taste and See

¹ Of David, when he feigned insanity before Abimelech, who drove him
    away, and he left.
² I will bless Adonai at all times.
    His praise is continually in my mouth.
³ My soul boasts in Adonai.
    The humble ones hear of it and rejoice.
⁴ Magnify Adonai with me
    and let us exalt His Name together.

⁵ I sought *ADONAI*, and He answered me,
  and delivered me from all my fears.
⁶ They who looked to Him were radiant,
  and their faces will never be ashamed.
⁷ This poor man cried, and *ADONAI* heard,
  and saved him out of all his troubles.
⁸ The angel of *ADONAI* encamps around those who fear Him,
  and delivers them.
⁹ Taste and see how good *ADONAI* is.
  Blessed is the one who takes refuge in Him.
¹⁰ Fear *ADONAI*, His *kedoshim*,
  for those who fear Him lack nothing.
¹¹ Young lions may lack, and go hungry,
  but those who seek *ADONAI* want for no good thing.

¹² Come, children, listen to me:
  I will teach you the fear of *ADONAI*.
¹³ Who is the one who delights in life,
  and loves to see good days?
¹⁴ Keep your tongue from evil,
  and your lips from speaking treachery.
¹⁵ Depart from evil and do good.
  Seek *shalom* and pursue it.ᵃ
¹⁶ The eyes of *ADONAI* are on the righteous,
  and His ears are attentive to their cry.
¹⁷ The face of *ADONAI* is against evildoers,
  to cut off the memory of them from the earth.
¹⁸ The righteous cry out and *ADONAI* hears,
  and delivers them from all their troubles.
¹⁹ *ADONAI* is close to the brokenhearted,
  and saves those crushed in spirit.
²⁰ Many are the distresses of the righteous,
  but *ADONAI* delivers him out of them all.
²¹ He keeps all his bones—
  not one of them is broken.ᵇ
²² Evil kills the wicked—
  those who hate the righteous will be held guilty.

a. 34:12–15. cf. 1 Pet. 3:10–12.
b. 34:21. cf. John 19:33–36.

²³ *ADONAI* redeems the soul of His servants
   —no one who takes refuge in Him will be held guilty.

Jeffrey Seif and Glenn Blank

Bad things can happen to good people. Consider David (v. 1 refers to his story in 1 Sam. 21:10–15). Though previously anointed and appointed, the hero-warrior David had many days on the run from the wicked Saul, when he had to play the fool with the foolish just to preserve his precarious life. Reflecting on it all, and God's deliverance, he says: "I will bless *ADONAI* at all times" (2), even "boasts in *ADONAI*" (3) and beckons others to "magnify *ADONAI*" with him (4). Why is this man so happy?

The answer is that God answers prayer: "I sought *ADONAI*, and He answered me, and delivered me from all my fears" (5). David certainly had his tough times, but he also knew that God "saved him out of all his troubles" (7). Leaving behind his precarious circumstances, he is able to leap to a visionary theological promise: "The angel of *ADONAI* encamps around those who fear Him" (8). If you fear your circumstances, you'll live in a panic. But if you fear *ADONAI*, you'll abide in His presence. These are very different kinds of fear, aren't they? When the *kedoshim* fear God rather than circumstances, they "lack nothing" (10)—perhaps because all we really need is God's love.

David then offers some valuable advice to "children" about the "fear of *ADO-NAI*" (12). Children need to learn about this fear—and so do many adults. If you want to "delight in life" and "see good" (13), then watch your tongue, so restless to inspire evil (14); also "depart from evil" and "seek *shalom*" (15). What you fear and what you pursue reveal what kind of person you are. God's "eyes" are on the righteous to hear their cry and deliver them (16, 18, 20). But his "face" is against evildoers, to annihilate even the memory of them (17). Though David and other *kedoshim* may at times feel brokenhearted, *HaShem* comes with saving grace and deliverance (19–20). *Yeshua* suffered distresses for us, yet none of His bones were broken (21; John 19:33, 36). Be patient: ultimately *HaShem* will judge the wicked guilty (22) and will redeem "the soul of His servants" (23). If you bless Him at all times, He will deliver you for all time. David learned that and was and is forever grateful. When you have the perspective of a godly fear, then you will "taste and see" (9) how good God really is.

PSALM 35

Justice for the Oppressed

¹ A psalm of David.
    ADONAI, oppose those who oppose me.
    Fight those who fight me.
² Take hold of shield and buckler,
    and rise up to my help.
³ Draw out also a spear and battle-axe.
    Stop those who pursue me.
    Say to my soul: "I am your salvation."
⁴ May those who seek my life
    be ashamed and disgraced.
    May they be turned back and humiliated
    —those who plot evil against me.
⁵ May they be like chaff before the wind,
    with the angel of ADONAI driving them off.
⁶ May their way be dark and slippery,
    with the angel of ADONAI pursuing them.
⁷ For without cause they hid their net for me,
    and without cause they dug a pit for my soul.
⁸ Let ruin come upon him by surprise.
    Let the net he hid entangle himself
    —into that same pit let him fall.
⁹ Then my soul will rejoice in ADONAI
    and delight in His salvation.
¹⁰ All my bones will say:
    "ADONAI, who is like You,
    rescuing the poor from one too strong for him,
    the poor and needy from one who robs him?"
¹¹ Violent witnesses rise up.
    They question me about things I know nothing about.
¹² They repay me evil for good—
    my soul is forlorn.
¹³ But as for me, when they were sick,
    my clothing was sackcloth.
    I afflicted my soul with fasting,
    my prayer kept returning to my heart.

[14] I went about mourning as though for my own friend or brother.
    I bowed down dressed in black as though for my own mother.
[15] But at my stumbling they gathered in glee.
    Wretches gathered against me whom I did not know,
tearing at me without ceasing.
[16] They mocked profanely, as if at a feast,
    they gnashed at me with their teeth.

[17] My Lord, how long will You look on?
    Rescue my soul from their ravages—
    my solitary existence from the lions.
[18] I praise You in the great assembly,
    acclaiming You among a throng of people.
[19] Do not let my deceitful enemies gloat over me without cause,
    nor let those who hate me for nothing wink an eye.[a]
[20] For they never speak *shalom*,
    but devise deceitful words against the quiet ones in the land.
[21] Yes, they open their mouth wide against me, saying:
    "Aha! Aha! Our own eyes have seen it!"
[22] You have seen it, ADONAI—be not silent!
    ADONAI, be not far from me.
[23] Arise, awaken to my defense,
    to my cause—my God and my Lord!
[24] Vindicate me, ADONAI my God,
    according to Your justice,
    and do not let them gloat over me.
[25] Don't let them say in their heart:
"Aha! Just what we wanted!"
    Don't let them say:
"We swallowed him up!"
[26] May they be ashamed and humiliated,
those who rejoice over my misery.
    May they who exalt themselves over me
    be clothed with shame and disgrace.
[27] May they shout for joy and be glad,
    those who delight in my righteous cause.
    May they always say:
"Exalted be ADONAI, who delights in His servant's *shalom*."

a. 35:19. cf. John 15:25.

²⁸ Then my tongue will declare aloud
    Your justice and Your praises all day.

Jeffrey Seif and Glenn Blank

David doesn't hold back. "ADONAI, oppose . . . fight those who fight me" (1). If he is to be taken seriously, God will do just that—not just meddle in human affairs, but fight on his side. David can seem pretty radical in his insistence that God take up military paraphernalia such as a shield and a spear (2–3) in order to get the better of his foes. He even enlists the aid of the fearsome "angel of ADONAI" (5). Nowadays, some folks sheepishly refuse to think of God offering such a spirited defense—wouldn't He prefer us just to "turn the other cheek"? While bearing insult for His Name's sake is commendable, do we really need to let the world simply roll over us like a Mack truck? David has precedent: *HaShem* stood up for the children of Israel when He overthrew the Egyptian chariots (Exod. 14:25). Nor is He done yet. *Yeshua* in His glory declares: "I will come to you soon and make war against them with the sword of My mouth" (Rev. 2:16).

There are circumstances when defense against violent foes is appropriate. On the one hand, individuals should generally not take matters into their own hands, for "vengeance is Mine," says the Lord (Deut. 32:35; Rom. 12:19). On the other hand, in a just society, police and military forces must bear arms to enforce laws, and courts should provide redress for grievances. The God of Sinai is the same as the God of Revelation—the One who values justice and executes it, preferably through people to whom He has delegated authority, but if not, intervening Himself.

The psalmist knows—indeed, "all my bones will say"—that the righteous One will deliver "the poor from one too strong for him" (10). So he piles it on a bit, just to make sure *HaShem* knows the justice of his cause, making sure He knows how "my soul is forlorn" (12), "my clothing was sackcloth" (13), and "I bowed down dressed in black as though for my own mother" (14). Wow, talk about Jewish guilt! Could it really work with the Holy One? Probably not, but it does keep the psalmist focused in his prayer. He apparently understands that even when it looks bad, even when his enemies gather "in glee" at his stumbling (15), he should keep persevering in prayer. He may wonder aloud, "My Lord, how long will You look on?" Yet at the right time, He will "rescue my soul" (17). *HaShem* will surely "vindicate me . . . according to Your justice" (24). Though he does not or cannot defend himself from those "who exalt themselves over me" (26), he turns to God to turn things around. Then those who "delight in my righteous cause"—and presumably agree with him in his prayer—will "shout for joy and be glad" (27). Yes, may it be! *Shalom* is more than an emotional state of mind. *Shalom* also means that the abused will get justice, wrongs will be made right, menacing foes will be refuted. Amen?

It is right, and biblical, to pray for justice to be done to those who exalt in their wickedness, as well as for justice to be done for those who trust in God's righteousness. Isn't that what happened when those who conspired against David were defeated, and he was restored as king in Jerusalem? Isn't that what happened when those who conspired against *Yeshua* were frustrated, when He rose from the dead, and His disciples were empowered to spread the Good News in Jerusalem? Isn't that what happened when Hitler and his henchmen were defeated, and Israel rose from the ashes of the Holocaust? Yes, justice keeps happening, working its way steadily through our history. Though it may seem like we are waiting and waiting, rest assured, the testimony of the whole Bible is clear: God is just, and justice will prevail. When it happens, shouldn't we respond like David, "Then my tongue will declare aloud Your justice and Your praises all day" (28)? Since *Yeshua* has already won the victory over sin and death, how about declaring aloud His justice and His praise today, now?

PSALM 36

With God Is the Fountain of Life

> [1] For the music director, of David the servant of ADONAI.
> [2] An oracle of Transgression—within my heart, to the wicked one:
>   "There is no fear of God before his eyes.[a]
> [3] For he flatters himself in his own eyes,
>   too much to notice his iniquity—or hate it.
> [4] His mouth's words are iniquity and deceit.
>   He has ceased to be wise and do good.

a. 36:2(1). cf. Rom. 3:18.

⁵ Even on his bed he plans sin.
He puts himself on a path that is no good, never refusing evil."

⁶ Your love, ADONAI, is in the heavens,
Your faithfulness up to the skies.
⁷ Your righteousness is like the mountains of God.
Your judgments are like the great deep.
You preserve man and beast, ADONAI.
⁸ How precious is Your love, O God!
The children of men find refuge in the shadow of Your wings.
⁹ They drink their fill from the abundance of Your House.
You give them drink from the river of Your delights.
¹⁰ For with You is the fountain of life—
in Your light we see light.
¹¹ Continue Your lovingkindness to those who know You,
and Your justice to the upright in heart.
¹² May the foot of pride never tread on me,
nor the hand of the wicked drive me away.
¹³ There the evildoers lie fallen—
thrown down, not able to rise!

Glenn Blank

Have you seen images of a man with a devil on one shoulder and an angel on the other? This psalm is an ancient version of that. It opens with a mysterious "oracle," which turns out to be an utterance of "Transgression" (or Rebellion) personified. First, this voice tempts the wicked to ignore the "fear of God" (2). Not good, for elsewhere we know that this fear is "the beginning of wisdom" (Ps. 111:10; Prov. 1:7) and it leads the wise to "hate evil" (Prov. 8:13). Without this fear, the voice of Rebellion makes one too foolish to notice his own iniquity, let alone hate it (3). Things get worse: sin and deceit fill his mouth, and then he overtly starts planning sin—he's up to "no good" (4–5).

On the other hand, there is the angel singing praise to *HaShem*, exalting His lovingkindness (חֶסֶד, *chesed*) and faithfulness (אֱמוּנָה, *emunah*) "up to the skies" (6), an exaltation also found in Psalms 57:10 and 104:4. More high praise follows for His judgments and preservation (7), His precious love and the refuge of His wings (8), His abundance and delights (9), and finally the climax in the "fountain of life" and light (10). You can easily imagine angels singing these verses of high praise to the Almighty.

So, whose voice are you listening to? You certainly can't take it for granted. These voices continually compete for our attention—all the more through our HDTV sets and i-devices. The psalmist turns to prayer for more love and justice (11), so that "the foot" of pride and "the hand" of wickedness would not drag him away (12). Shouldn't we also be praying about the voices we listen to? The psalm ends with a warning, reminding us of the fate of the wicked who indulge the voice of Transgression: they will be "thrown down, not able to rise!" (13). So again, should you be praying about the voices whispering to you?

PSALM 37

Inheritance of the *Kedoshim*

¹ Of David.
> Do not fret because of evildoers,
>> nor be envious of them who do wrong.
² For like the grass they soon wither
>> and fade like a green herb.
³ Trust in ADONAI and do good.
>> Dwell in the land, feed on faithfulness.
⁴ Delight yourself in ADONAI,
>> and He will give you the requests of your heart.
⁵ Commit your way to ADONAI.
>> Trust in Him, and He will do it.
⁶ He will bring out your vindication as light,
>> and your cause will shine as noonday.
⁷ Be still before ADONAI and wait patiently for Him.
>> Do not fret over one prospering in his way,
>> over one carrying out wicked schemes.
⁸ Put away anger and turn from wrath.
>> Do not fret—it only leads to doing evil.
⁹ For evildoers will be cut off,
>> but those who wait for ADONAI—
> they will inherit the land.

¹⁰ Yet a little while,
>> and the wicked will be no more.
>> Yes, you will look at his place,
> but he will not be there.
¹¹ But the meek will inherit the land,
>> and delight in abundant *shalom*.
¹² The wicked plots against the righteous
>> and gnashes at him with his teeth.
¹³ The Lord laughs at him—
>> for He sees his day is coming.
¹⁴ The wicked have unsheathed their sword and have bent their bow
> to bring down the poor and needy,
> to slay those whose conduct is upright.
¹⁵ Their sword will pierce their own hearts,
>> and their bows will be broken.
¹⁶ Better a little that the righteous have
>> than the wealth of many wicked.
¹⁷ For the arms of the wicked will be broken,
>> while ADONAI upholds the righteous.
¹⁸ ADONAI knows the days of the blameless—
>> their inheritance endures forever.
¹⁹ They will not be ashamed in an evil time
>> and in days of famine they will be satisfied.
²⁰ For the wicked will perish,
>> and the enemies of ADONAI will be like the beauty of the fields—
> they will vanish—vanish like smoke.
²¹ The wicked borrows and does not repay,
>> but the righteous is a gracious giver.
²² For His blessed ones inherit the land.
>> But those He curses will be cut off.

²³ From ADONAI a man's steps are made firm,
>> when He delights in his way.
²⁴ Though he stumble,
>> he will not fall headlong,
>> for ADONAI is holding his hand.
²⁵ I was young and now I am old,
>> yet I have never seen the righteous one forsaken,
>> nor his children begging for bread.
²⁶ All day long he is gracious and lends.
>> So his offspring will be a blessing.

²⁷ Turn from evil and do good,
  so you may live forever.
²⁸ For *Adonai* loves justice
 and does not abandon His godly ones.
  They will be preserved forever,
 but the seed of the wicked will be cut off.
²⁹ The righteous will inherit the land
  and dwell in it forever.
³⁰ The mouth of the righteous utters wisdom
  and his tongue speaks justice.
³¹ The *Torah* of his God is in his heart.
  His steps do not slip.
³² The wicked lies in wait for the righteous,
  seeking to slay him.
³³ But *Adonai* will not leave him in his hand,
  or let him be condemned when judged.
³⁴ Wait for *Adonai* and keep His way,
  and He will exalt you to inherit the land.
  When the wicked are cut off, you will see it.
³⁵ I have seen a wicked, ruthless man
  flourishing like a leafy tree in native soil.
³⁶ But once he passed by, he was no more.
  Though I looked for him, he could not be found.
³⁷ Notice the man of integrity and watch the upright—
  for the man of *shalom* has a future.
³⁸ But transgressors will be destroyed altogether.
  The future of the wicked will be cut off.
³⁹ Yet the salvation of the righteous is from *Adonai*.
  He is their stronghold in time of trouble.
⁴⁰ *Adonai* helps them and delivers them.
  He rescues them from the wicked and saves them—
 because they take refuge in Him.

Glenn Blank

This psalm is an acrostic poem—every other verse begins with a letter of the Hebrew alphabet—verse 1 begins with an *aleph* (א), verse 3 with a *bet* (ב), and so on. Acrostic order tends to be fairly static—rather than moving or wrestling with a dilemma to a conclusion, the psalm presents a stable order.

(This acrostic pattern is found in many other psalms, such as 34, 119, 145, which are also similar in their praises of God's order.) Indeed, that's the point this poem makes from the get-go. There's no need to fret about evildoers (1), for they will wither away soon enough (2). On the other hand, there is safe pasture for those who trust in *HaShem* (3). In other words, though things may look bad or out of order temporarily, the long view is that justice and goodness will prevail and stabilize. This counterbalancing of temporary evil and long-run good recurs again and again, for example, in the advice "do not fret" (8), "for evildoers will be cut off" (9), "yet a little while, and the wicked will be no more" (10), and instead "the meek will inherit the land" and "abundant shalom" (11).

A modern reader (or even an ancient one) may wonder, how can we be so sure? You may even wonder, how can this "old" man be so sure he has "never seen the righteous one forsaken, nor his children begging for bread" (25)? Doesn't this view of ultimate order run aground on the second law of thermodynamics, which insists that everything tends to disorder? And all the more so when human beings muck things up! Indeed, the certainty of this stable worldview comes in for a challenge elsewhere in Scripture, such as in Job, where a saint suffers horribly and challenges his friends to explain why, or when we consider the suffering of Jeremiah in an evil generation, or wonder at the misery of Paul in a cold prison in 2 Timothy. Sometimes *kedoshim* (saints) never seem to get the promised satisfaction or even release from their suffering.

Wisdom still says: wait. Order and justice ultimately will prevail, not merely because of the strength of good people but because of the power of a good God. "Commit your way" to Him, for "He will do it" (5). "Be still . . . and wait patiently for Him" (7), because those who wait "will inherit the land" (9). A "little while" may be a few years or may be a little longer, but the wicked will surely be "no more" (10, 36). Entropy and evil will run their course on earth. Ultimate justice and goodness are certain from the perspective of heaven, the perspective of eternity. The wicked "plots against the righteous," but the Lord "sees his day is coming" (12–13). Indeed, the wicked often bring their downfall upon themselves—"their sword will pierce their own hearts" (15). If they do not self-destruct or simply "vanish like smoke" (20), *HaShem* will condemn them (33) and cut them off (34, 38).

The idea of inheritance recurs in verses 9, 11, 18, 22, 29, and 34. Those who "wait for" *HaShem* (7, 9, 34) will receive this inheritance. Inheritance reverses the decay of disorder. The *Torah* provides for the elimination of debts and freeing of Jewish slaves every seven years (Deut. 15:1, 12) and a complete restoration of all property to the original owners every fifty years in the Year of Jubilee. God's will is to restore all things, and ultimately, the Scriptures assure us, His will is done. Though Job has to endure much suffering and a bit of chastening from the mouth of God, in the end he receives a double inheritance. Though Paul suffered much for the sake of the Good News, to the end he was confident that the children of God are "heirs of God and joint-heirs with Messiah" (Rom. 8:17). Though many faithful *kedoshim* of Hebrews 11 died without receiving the promises, they remained confident that God has prepared an inheritance, "a city" and a "better resurrection." Though *Yeshua* suffered on the tree, He was raised up to everlasting life, and now He waits for the day, which only the Father knows, when He will return to restore all things (Acts 3:21).

The Lord sees that day coming (13). In that day, "the righteous will inherit the land and dwell in it forever" (29). If not sooner, then in that day, "the man of *shalom* has a future" (37). Are you willing to trust Him and wait for that day? Until then, keep the *Torah* of our God in your heart (31), run to the stronghold of *HaShem* in time of trouble (39), and He will help you and deliver you.

PSALM 38

A Burden Too Heavy for Me

¹ A psalm of David, for a memorial.
² ADONAI, do not rebuke me in Your anger
   or discipline me in Your wrath.
³ For Your arrows have sunk deep into me
   and Your hand has pressed down on me.
⁴ There is no health in my flesh because of Your indignation.
   There is no wholeness in my bones because of my sin.
⁵ For my iniquities are on my head—
   like a burden too heavy for me.
⁶ My wounds are foul and festering
   because of my foolishness.

⁷ I am bent over, bowed down greatly.
    All day I walk about in mourning.
⁸ For my heart is filled with burning pain,
    and there is no health in my body.
⁹ I am numb and utterly crushed.
    I groan because of anguish in my heart.
¹⁰ My Lord, all my longing is before You,
    and my sighing is not hidden from You.
¹¹ My heart pounds, my strength fails me.
    The light of my eyes—also, not with me.

¹² My friends and my companions stay away from my wound,
    and my kinsmen stand far off.
¹³ They who seek my life set traps.
    Those who seek my hurt threaten destruction, uttering lies all day.
¹⁴ But I, like someone deaf, hear nothing,
    like a mute, not opening his mouth.
¹⁵ Yes, I am like one who cannot hear,
    whose mouth has no arguments.
¹⁶ But I wait for You, ADONAI—
    You will answer, O Lord my God.
¹⁷ For I said: "Don't let them gloat over me
    or exalt themselves over me, when my foot slips."
¹⁸ For I am about to fall,
    and my pain is before me constantly.
¹⁹ So I confess my guilt.
    I am troubled because of my sin.
²⁰ My lively enemies are numerous.
    Many hate me wrongfully.
²¹ Those who repay evil for good oppose me
    because I pursue what is good.
²² Do not forsake me, ADONAI.
    O my God, be not far from me.
²³ Hurry to my aid, my Lord, my salvation.

Jeffrey Seif and Glenn Blank

David felt utterly crushed. Imperfect as we all are, we can relate to someone who beseeches, Lord, "do not rebuke me in Your anger or discipline me in Your wrath" (2). People sin. If you're honest and sensitive enough, the pangs of guilt can feel like "arrows have sunk deep into" you (3). You might wonder if God's hand has anything to do with the pressure you feel (3), or if the source of your pain is His "indignation" (4). But is all this guilt something good or bad? While many a counselor may labor to help us see that we are not so bad, the Divine Counselor sometimes beckons us to see what we really are. David agonizes over his "sin" (4), his burdensome "iniquities" (5), and the "foul and festering" wounds of "foolishness" (6). The oppression of his conscience is so heavy that he is "bent over, bowed down" and walking in "mourning" (7). It affects his health: his heart burns (8), he feels "numb" and "crushed" (9), his heart "pounds" and his eyes are failing (11). It affects his relationships: his friends and companions "stay away from my wound" (12) as if he were a leper, afflicted with *tza'arat*, crying out "unclean, unclean!" to warn people away (Lev. 13:45). Meanwhile his enemies seek to hurt him through traps and lies (13).

What can the afflicted one do in such a pass? He waits for *HaShem*. While waiting, he can do some self-examination. Instead of rationalizing away his feelings or blaming them on people and circumstances, he realizes he must "confess" his guilt and own up to his sin (19). He comes to the end of blame-shifting and sanitizing and speaks the language of responsibility—which is the passageway to forgiveness, healing, and reorienting his life. He trusts God not to forsake him (22) and to hurry to his aid (23). Honest people give God something to work with. Transparent people are just the sort God is looking to work with and deliver.

How about you? Are you still blame-shifting, or are you willing to accept some responsibility? Are you moaning and groaning about your situation, or are you willing to wait for *HaShem* and listen for His answer? Rest assured that He understands your situation, because He has been there—in the brutal experience of Messiah *Yeshua* on the day of His suffering and death. All the symptoms—the wounds (from a Roman scourge), the bent-over experience (under the weight of an execution stake), the heart burning and pounding—He experienced them all, as well as friends abandoning him and foes uttering lies about him. Before Pilate, he was "like a mute, not opening his mouth" (14). Yet it was not guilt of His own that weighed Him down, but ours. If *Yeshua* was willing to bear such oppression for us, how can we but believe that He will deliver us? Once and for all, He has delivered us from the guilt of our sin! Even though I perish, I believe: He is "my Lord, my salvation [*yeshuah*]" (23).

PSALM 39

Make Me Know the Number of My Days

¹ For the music director, for Jeduthun, a psalm of David.
² I said:
> "I will guard my ways, so I will not sin with my tongue.
> I will muzzle my mouth while the wicked are before me."
³ So I became utterly speechless,
> kept silent even from good,
> but my anguish was stirred up.
⁴ My heart was hot within me,
> while I was musing, the fire burned.
> Then I spoke with my tongue:
⁵ "Let me know, ADONAI, my end
> and what the number of my days is.
> Let me know how short-lived I am.
⁶ Behold, You made my days mere hand-breadths,
> and my lifetime as nothing before You.
> Surely all humanity is but vapor. *Selah*
⁷ Everyone goes about as a mere phantom.
> Surely they are making an uproar in vain, heaping up stuff—
> yet not knowing who will gather it.[a]
⁸ And now, my Lord, what do I wait for?
> My hope is in You.
⁹ Deliver me from all my transgressions.
> Do not make me the scorn of a fool.
¹⁰ I am speechless, not opening my mouth
> —for You have done it.
¹¹ Remove Your scourge from me.
> I perish by the blow of Your hand.
¹² With rebukes You chasten one for iniquity
> and You consume like a moth what he finds pleasure in.
> Surely all humanity is but a vapor. *Selah*
¹³ Hear my prayer, ADONAI,
> and listen to my cry—

a. 39:7. cf. Luke 12:20.

do not keep silent at my tears.
For with You I am an outsider, a sojourner,
as all my fathers were.
¹⁴ Turn your gaze away from me, so I may smile again,
before I go, and am no more."

Jeffrey Seif

Our lives are both precarious and short. Precarious, because of the myriad weaknesses inherent both in ourselves and in others; short, because the journey we frail creatures make, from the womb to the tomb, plays out in a relatively short span of time. The psalmist says, "I will guard my ways" and "muzzle my mouth" (2). That apparently wasn't easy for him (some of us can relate). He admits that his "anguish was stirred up" and his "heart was hot" within him (3–4). To give himself some perspective, he asks *HaShem* to appreciate "the number of" his days—how short his life really is (5). From God's perspective, "all humanity is but vapor" (6, 12) and the all-too-human habit of "heaping up stuff" is pointless (7). What we do with time becomes manifest in time. The young act like they are going to be here forever and can get away with anything. Those of us who have accumulated some years feel like the pace is picking up! One day we will sail to the end of life's voyage and find ourselves on another shore. There is a reckoning for iniquity (12). When the psalmist considers that he is but a moth or vapor (12), an outsider or sojourner on this planet, as all his fathers were, he cries out to *HaShem* in prayer (13).

It has been said: "There is no such thing as reality, only perspective." Though I do believe there is *a* reality, I am nonetheless aware that people live in *their* realities—interior thought worlds that inform us and define us in so many ways. Would we not do well to be informed by the sobering realities noted here? Realizing that life is short, and that there's a judgment associated with how we live it, imposes a sobriety that perhaps we might not otherwise have. Before "I go, and am no more" (14), let's consider how we may guard our ways.

PSALM 40

Written about Me in the Scroll

¹ For the music director, a psalm of David.
² I waited patiently for ADONAI.
    He bent down to me and heard my cry.
³ He brought me up out of the slimy pit, out of the mud and mire.
    Then He set my feet on a rock.
    He made my steps firm.
⁴ He put a new song in my mouth—
a hymn of praise to our God.
    Many will see and fear,
and trust in ADONAI.
⁵ Blessed is the one
    who put his confidence in ADONAI,
    who has not turned to the arrogant,
    nor to those who fall into falsehood.
⁶ Many things You have done, ADONAI my God
    —Your plans for us are wonderful—
    there is none to be compared to You!
    If I were to speak and tell of them,
    they would be too many to count!
⁷ Sacrifice and offering You did not desire
    —my ears You have opened—
    burnt offering and sin offering You did not require.
⁸ Then I said: "Here I am, I have come—
    in the scroll of a book it is written about me.
⁹ I delight to do Your will, O my God.
    Yes, Your *Torah* is within my being."
¹⁰ I proclaim good news of righteousness in the great assembly.
    Behold, I am not shutting my lips—
    ADONAI, You know!
¹¹ I did not hide Your righteousness within my heart.
    Rather I declared Your faithfulness and Your salvation.
    I did not conceal Your lovingkindness
    and Your truth from the great assembly.

¹² ADONAI, do not withhold Your compassions from me.
    Let Your mercy and Your truth always protect me.

¹³ For evils beyond number surround me,
  my sins have overtaken me
  —I cannot see—
  they are more than the hairs of my head
  —and my heart fails me.
¹⁴ ADONAI, please deliver me!
  ADONAI, come quickly to help me!
¹⁵ Let those who seek my life to sweep it away
  be put to shame and humiliated.
    Let those who wish me evil
  be turned back in disgrace.
¹⁶ Let those who say to me, "Aha! Aha!"
  be appalled over their own shame.
¹⁷ Let all those who seek You rejoice and be glad in You.
  Let those who love Your salvation
  continually say: "ADONAI be magnified!"
¹⁸ But I—I am poor and needy—
  yet my Lord is mindful of me.
  You are my help and my deliverer—
  O my God, do not delay!

Glenn Blank

Some have puzzled over why this psalm starts out with thanksgiving for deliverance (1–11), then concludes with a petition for deliverance (12–18), most of which also appears as Psalm 70. Did the psalmist decide to just add the two parts together arbitrarily? Probably not—too many Hebrew words and ideas echo in the two halves. But then, shouldn't one give thanks *after* the prayer has been answered? True enough. But in general, thanksgiving is actually a better way to approach God. Psalm 100 recommends, "Enter His gates with thanksgiving." Even most mortals respond better to a request after you've thanked them. With God, something else is at stake: thanksgiving increases our trusting faith to approach Him with another request.

There are many other important lessons about prayer here. First, it is good to wait patiently for *HaShem* (2). Sometimes when you're in a desperate situation—suppose you find yourself in a slimy pit (3) or some other less murky but uncomfortable place—it can be tough to wait. But, as the saying goes, good things come to those who wait. Moreover, you're more likely to notice them. You might also notice what God has been doing in your life. If you forget to appreciate that He made your "steps firm" (3), if you haven't gotten around to singing that hymn of praise He wants to put in your mouth—then remember now. It's important that you do, so that "many will see . . . and trust in ADONAI" (4).

Second, *HaShem* blesses the one who trusts His truth rather than the falsehood of the arrogant (5). People too easily believe flattery or familiar lies, but the reality is, there is none to be compared with *HaShem* or to His deeds and plans for us (6).

Third, though *HaShem* has commanded sacrifices and offerings, He desires them less than hearing someone say, "I delight to do Your will, O my God" (7–9). The preference for heart intent (*kavanah*) and sincere obedience over outward yet insincere acts is a theme of the prophets (see Isa. 1:11; Jer. 6:20; 7:22, 23; Amos 5:22; Mic. 6:6–8). *Yeshua* critiqued those who pray and fast just so others may notice (Matt. 6). How much time are you spending in your prayer room with your ears open (7), saying to Him, "Here I am, I have come" (8)? Are you spending enough time in the Holy Book that you can truly say, "Your *Torah* is within my being" (9)? If you truly delight in Him, and truly follow *Yeshua* as Lord, you will.

Fourth, prayer speaks out in public (10–11). When *HaShem* has done a work within you, surely you cannot keep shutting your lips or hiding His righteousness from others. You must declare His salvation! Have you been sharing about the faithfulness of your Master with others? Why would you conceal His love? You must declare His salvation!

Fifth, the more you have experienced His compassion (רַחֲמִים, *rachameem*), the more you will be confident that His mercy always protects you (12). When evil surrounds you—even your own sins (13)—you will know that you can cry out to *HaShem* for deliverance (14).

Sixth, do not let your hearts be troubled or discouraged. Whether it happens quickly or not, those who wish you evil will be turned back in disgrace (15), while those "who love" His salvation will again magnify *HaShem* (17).

Seventh, rejoice and be glad in Him (17)!

The psalm ends where it began, with confidence that my Lord (אֲדֹנָי, *Adonai*) will be "my help and my deliverer." Do you have this confidence? Apply these ancient and effective lessons of prayer: wait patiently, trust in Him, spend time alone with Him and His *Torah*, proclaim His salvation, experience His compassion, do not be troubled, and rejoice!

PSALM 41

Even My Close Friend

[1] For the music director: a psalm of David.

[2] Blessed is the one who considers the wretched—
  ADONAI will deliver him in the evil day.

[3] ADONAI will protect him and keep him alive.
  He will be made blessed in the land.
  You will not give him over to the desire of his foes.

[4] ADONAI will strengthen him on his sickbed.
  May You restore him completely from his bed.

[5] I said: "ADONAI, have mercy on me.
  Heal my soul, for I have sinned against You."

[6] My enemies speak evil about me:
  "When will he die and his name perish?"

[7] And if someone of them comes to see me, he speaks falsely.
  He stores up evil in his heart,
  then he goes out and chatters.

[8] All who hate me whisper together about me.
  They imagine the worst about me:

[9] "Something evil was poured into him—
  he will not get up again from the place where he lies."

[10] Even my own close friend,
  whom I trusted, who ate my bread,
  has lifted up his heel against me.[a]

[11] But You, ADONAI, have mercy on me,
  and raise me up, so I may repay them.

[12] By this I know that You delight in me:
  that my enemy does not shout in triumph over me.

[13] You uphold me in my integrity
  and set me before Your face forever.

[14] Blessed be ADONAI, the God of Israel,
  from everlasting to everlasting.
  Amen and amen!

a. 41:10. cf. Matt. 26:23; Luke 22:21.

Glenn Blank

If there's one thing worse than the wretchedness of a sickbed, it would be when supposed friends are whispering lies against you when you are down. David might have experienced this when Absalom hatched his plot against him. Secomd Samuel 15 doesn't mention an illness, but it might explain why David was so sluggish in responding. In any case, *Yeshua* the Son of David surely can relate.

We can read this psalm as a prayer within a prayer within a prayer. The outermost one (1–4) is a prayer of petition: may ADONAI "deliver him" (2), may He "not give him over" (3), may ADONAI "strengthen" and "restore him completely" (4). Those who join in this prayer will be blessed (2) along with the suffering petitioner "in the land" (3)—in contrast to the evil enemies we will meet in the innermost prayer.

The next layer introduces the suffering psalmist, praying in the first person: "I said" (5), "uphold me in my integrity" (13). It's personal. It is on the basis of a personal relationship with *HaShem* that David can confidently expect mercy and forgiveness for his sin (5) and be restored to the intimate place "before Your face forever" (13). May this confident intimacy be an example for the rest of us!

The innermost layer (6–12) points out David's enemies—the word for "enemy" appears in verses 6 and 12. Their violence is not with weapons (yet) but with their hearts—storing up evil (7), imagining the worst (8)—and their tongues, chattering and whispering about him. The worst one was a "close friend, whom I trusted" (10). David had his Ahithophel, a close confidant turned traitor. Yet at this innermost level we also recognize *Yeshua*. It was bad enough that most of his disciples abandoned Him, but one of them betrayed Him for the price of a slave.

We can also recognize *Yeshua* when the prayer turns to a request to "raise me up" (11). By His resurrection we know that *HaShem* delights in Him— thus He has silenced the triumph of the enemy (12). Seeing *Yeshua* at this innermost layer is where we can all identify with the sufferer. No matter what we have experienced in life, we know that *Yeshua* has experienced it with us. In Him, we have mercy. In Him, we are raised up and healed. In Him, the enemy does not triumph. In Him, ADONAI delights.

PSALM 42

My Soul Thirsts for God

¹ For the music director, a contemplative song of the sons of Korah.

² As the deer pants for streams of water,
    so my soul pants for You, O God.

³ My soul thirsts for God, for the living God.
    When will I come and appear before God?

⁴ My tears have been my food day and night,
    while they say to me all day: "Where is your God?"

⁵ These things I remember as I pour out my soul within me.
    For I used to go along with the throng,
    walking with them to the House of God, with a voice of joy and
        praise,
  a multitude keeping a festival.

⁶ Why are you downcast, O my soul?
    Why are you murmuring within me?
    Hope in God, for I will yet praise Him,
  for the salvation of His presence.

⁷ My God, my soul is downcast within me!
    Therefore I remember You from the land of Jordan
    and from the peaks of Hermon, from Mount Mitzar.

⁸ Deep calls to deep in the roar of Your waterfalls.
    All Your waves and breakers have swept over me.

⁹ By day ADONAI commands His love,
    and at night His song is with me—
    a prayer to the God of my life.

¹⁰ I will say to God my Rock:
    "Why have You forgotten me?
    Why do I go about mourning, under the oppression of the enemy?"

¹¹ As with a crushing in my bones,
    my adversaries taunt me,
    by saying to me all day, "Where is your God?"

¹² Why are you downcast, O my soul?
    Why are you murmuring within me?
    Hope in God, for I will yet praise Him,
    the salvation of my countenance and my God.

Paul Wilbur

This song was written to the chief musician as a *maskil*, or contemplative poem of insight, by the sons of Korah (1). I'll get to the insight in a moment, but first to the heart of the matter. Verse 2 was made one of the most beloved worship choruses in modern times by my friend Marty Nystrom many years ago. I am certain that he had no idea what this one-verse song would do when he wrote, "As the deer panteth for the water so my soul longeth after thee; you alone are my heart's desire and I long to worship thee." I believe the whole Body of Messiah knows and still sings this song. It so captures the heart of a worshiper that it transcends all doctrinal lines and boundaries.

What about the wisdom or insight? These verses are crying for help while at the same time confessing faith in ADONAI. The psalmist cries, "My tears have been my food day and night" while his enemies taunt him with the question over and again, "Where is your God?" (4). His soul is downcast (6) and disquieted, perhaps confused or even angry—have you ever felt this way?—but he continually reminds himself that ADONAI is his salvation. "Deep calls to deep" (8)—another oft-quoted line—sounds like intimate prayer that assures and consoles. What a comfort it is to me to know that ADONAI sings over me during the night watches (9), like a loving mother who rocks her frightened child to sleep and chases the shadows away with her soothing voice. What does He sing, you may ask? Why, He sings songs of deliverance and protection! In Psalm 32:7, David declares, "You are my hiding place—You will protect me from distress. You surround me with songs of deliverance."

I believe this psalm also points to the agony and faithfulness of the Suffering Servant of Isaiah 53, Israel's Messiah. He was alone, rejected, mocked, covered by billows of pain and despair. Yet during the night watches deep called to deep, and *Ben-Elohim* heard *Abba* command His love, assuring Him of His destiny and treasured prize.

✳✳✳✳✳✳✳ PSALM 43 ✳✳✳✳✳✳✳

Send Forth Your Light

¹ Vindicate me, O God,
  and champion
my cause against an ungodly nation.
    From a deceitful and unjust man, deliver me!
² For You are my God, my stronghold.
    Why have You spurned me?
    Why do I go about gloomy because of the oppression of the enemy?
³ Send forth Your light and Your truth—
    let them guide me.
    Let them bring me to Your holy mountain
and to Your dwelling places.
⁴ Then I will come to the altar of God,
    to the God of my exceeding joy,
    and praise You upon the harp
    —O God, my God.
⁵ Why are You downcast, O my soul?
    Why are you murmuring within me?
    Hope in God, for I will yet praise Him,
the salvation of my countenance.

Paul Wilbur

This psalm might be the heart cry of anyone who has lived on planet Earth for any length of time. We have all experienced deceit and unfaithfulness on a number of levels, whether in romance, business, friendship—you name it. Life is full of people looking out for themselves. The psalmist cries out for deliverance "from a deceitful and unjust man" (1). Solomon makes a similar lament in Proverbs 20:6: "Many a man claims his loyalty, but a faithful man who can find?" It is bad enough when you are shunned or betrayed by another human being, but the writer even believes he has been "spurned" or cast aside by God, his "stronghold" (2), *HaShem* Himself! He's in a bad place for sure, but deliverance is only one verse away—in fact, it's waiting in his mouth.

He implores, "Send forth Your light and Your truth" (3). The word for light is אוֹר, *'or*, meaning righteousness, victory, guidance, justice, or even the favor of a countenance—because if you can see someone's countenance, they are right there with you in the midst of whatever you are going through! The word for truth is אֱמֶת, *emet*, which means the loving faithfulness of *HaShem* that leads us to walk in His ways. This psalmist is no ordinary man. Why do I say that? Because he asks for the very help he needs to get back to a place of worship, focusing on the solution to his woes rather than sitting and having a little pity party about his circumstances. Oh, how many of us need to learn this lesson well.

Since the psalmist understands that everything he needs for life and happiness is there in the presence of *HaShem*, his request is not for an army to deliver him or finances to aid him, but to be in His presence. "In Your presence, that's where I am strong!" Though once downcast (5), the attitude of his soul has turned around: he encourages himself in the Lord, and then he prophesies his future and a good resolution to his pressing problems. Once more he puts his hope and trust in the Lord, "the salvation of my countenance" (5). Could this interesting phrase be a way to "save face" (humorous thought!), or could he mean that our countenance is a barometer of the soul? He did tell us in Psalm 34:6 that those "who looked to Him were radiant, and their faces will never be ashamed."

✻✻✻✻✻✻✻✻ PSALM 44 ✻✻✻✻✻✻✻✻

Arise, O God of Our Fathers

¹ For the music director, a psalm of the sons of Korah, a contemplative
song.
² We have heard with our ears, O God
—our fathers have told us—
of a work You did in their days, in days of old.
³ With Your hand You displaced nations, but You planted them.
You afflicted peoples, and You drove them out.
⁴ For it was not by their own sword that they took possession of the land,
nor did their own arm save them.
But it was Your right hand, Your arm, and the light of Your face—
for You favored them.

5 You are my King, O God—
    command victories for Jacob!
6 Through You we push back our foes.
    Through Your Name we trample those rising up against us.
7 For I do not trust in my bow,
    nor can my sword save me.
8 For You saved us from our oppressors
    and put to shame those who hated us.
9 In God we make our boast all day
    and Your Name we praise forever. *Selah*
10 Yet You have spurned and humiliated us,
    and no longer go out with our armies.
11 You make us retreat before the enemy.
    Those who hate us have plundered us.
12 You gave us to be devoured like sheep[a]
    and have scattered us among the nations.
13 You are selling Your people cheaply—
    not even getting a great price for them.
14 You made us a taunt for our neighbors,
    a scorn and ridicule for those around us.
15 You have made us a byword among the nations,
    head-wagging among the peoples.
16 All day my disgrace is before me,
    and my face is covered with shame—
17 because of the sound of taunting and reviling
    from the face of a vengeful enemy.
18 All this came upon us, though we did not forget You,
    nor were we false to Your covenant.
19 Our heart did not turn back,
    nor did our steps stray from Your path.
20 Yet You crushed us in a place of jackals,
    covered us with the shadow of death.
21 If we had forgotten the Name of our God
    or stretched our hands to a foreign god,
22 would God not have discovered it?
    For He knows the secrets of the heart.
23 But for Your sake we are slain all day.
    We are counted as sheep for slaughter.[b]

a. 44:12. cf. Rom. 8:36.
b. 44:23. cf. Rom. 8:36.

²⁴ Awake! Why do You sleep, my Lord?
  Wake up! Do not cast us off forever.
²⁵ Why do You hide Your face
  and forget our misery and oppression?
²⁶ For our soul sinks down to the dust.
  Our belly cleaves to the earth.
²⁷ Arise, be our help,
  and redeem us
  for Your mercy's sake.

Glenn Blank and Jeffrey Seif

Here is a biblical poem that could speak for the generations after the *Shoah* (Holocaust). It begins with commendations of God from our ancestors:"Our fathers have told us . . . of a work You did in their days" (2). These days, when we gather around the Passover table, we also remember what God did "in days of old." But do most modern Jews believe the stories? Do our people believe"with Your hand You displaced nations" and"planted them" (3) when Israel came out of Egypt—let alone Europe? Today, only about 20 percent of American Jews believe in God,¹ so would they acknowledge that it was "Your right hand" and"the light of Your face" that saved us (4)? On the other hand, 80 percent of Israelis believe in God²—perhaps because they recognize that it is by a miracle of God that"we push back" and"trample those rising up against us" (6). With hardly any weapons and the United Nations imposing a weapons boycott at the beginning of the War of Independence, Israelis could not trust only in their swords (7).

In the Diaspora, most post-Holocaust Jews share the attitude of this psalm-ist. To him, it seems that God's redemptive acts occurred only in the days of old. He complains, You"no longer go out with our armies" (10). He frets, You"make us retreat before the enemy" (11). He moans, we are"devoured like sheep" (12). He even blames God for"selling Your people cheaply" (13). He accuses God of making Israel"a scorn and ridicule," a laughingstock"among the peoples," and a "disgrace" (14–16). Not many of us would be as blunt to God—unless we were really, really upset.

Though appreciative of what God did for previous generations, a cha-grined psalmist laments what seems like God's absence from his own life and circumstances. Things are not going well. Moreover, he doesn't see that his generation has done anything to deserve such a calamity. How were we "false to Your covenant" (18)? We "did not turn back, nor did our steps stray from Your path" (19). With stinging pain, he rebukes God for what has happened: "You crushed us . . . covered us with the shadow of death" (20). It doesn't seem fair to him. "Awake!" he demands. "Why do You sleep, my Lord?" (24). Today, many Jews wonder how God could sleep through all the cries from the death camps. Again the cry, "Arise, be our help" (27).

Have you ever felt this way? Have you ever said to yourself or to God: Why are these things happening to me? Why does everything seem to be going wrong? It's a reasonable question or complaint. Since it's in the Bible, it must be OK. Notice, though, that the psalmist assumes that God is still listening. Things may be going badly—Israel's back was to the wall then as it has often been since—but the psalmist hasn't given up. He hasn't lost faith. With just this much faith, you can be straight with God—and He will listen to your cry.

The truth is, *Am Israel Chai!* The people of Israel live! Nearly three thousand years have passed since the psalmist gave voice to his concerns over Israel's then-impending utter doom, yet Israel still lives. Israel's God must be doing something right. God's keeping power still watches over Israel and watches over all who gaze His way, mindful that He will "redeem us for Your mercy's sake" (27).

PSALM 45

A Royal Wedding Song

¹ For the music director, according to "Lilies." Of the sons of Korah, a contemplative song, a love song.
² My heart is stirred with a good word.
    I speak my verses to the king.
    My tongue is the pen of a skillful writer.
³ You are the most handsome of the sons of men.
    Grace pours from your lips.
    Therefore God has blessed you forever.
⁴ Gird your sword on your thigh, O mighty one,
    in your splendor and your majesty.

[5] In your majesty ride victoriously,
>   on behalf of truth, meekness and justice.
>   Let your right hand display awesome things.
[6] Your arrows are sharp.
>   Peoples fall beneath you—
>   into the heart of the king's enemies.
[7] Your throne, O God, is forever and ever,
>   and a scepter of justice is the scepter of Your kingdom.
[8] You have loved righteousness and hated wickedness.
>   Therefore, God, your God, anointed you with the oil of gladness
>   above your companions.[a]
[9] All your robes have myrrh, aloes, cassia.
>   From ivory palaces, stringed instruments
>   make you glad.
[10] Kings' daughters are among your honored women.
>   At your right hand stands the queen
>   in gold of Ophir.

[11] "Listen, O daughter, consider and incline your ear.
>   Forget your people and your father's house.
[12] Then the king will desire your beauty.
>   Honor him, for he is your lord.
[13] A daughter of Tyre comes with a gift.
>   The richest people will court your favor."
[14] All glorious is the king's daughter within the palace—
>   her gown is interwoven with gold.[b]
[15] She will be led to the king in embroidered garments.
>   Her virgins, her companions following her, are coming in to you.
[16] They are led in with joy and gladness—
>   they enter into the palace of the king.

[17] Your sons will take your fathers' place.
>   You will make them princes throughout the land.
[18] I will cause your name to be remembered in all generations.
>   Therefore the nations will praise you forever and ever.

---

a. 45:7–8. cf. Heb. 1:8–9.
b. 45:14. cf. Exod. 39:2–3; Rev. 19:7–8.

Jeffrey Seif and Glenn Blank

Not everyone knows how to speak to people in authority. Ancient Romans trained in rhetoric developed a style called "panegyric"—meaning to extol a person or thing—and were trained in how to politely address officers, magistrates, and kings. It seems this court poet was too. The occasion was a royal wedding—think of the spectacle of Prince William and Kate—only here we're talking about a sitting king and queen. He picks up his pen to magnify the king as "the most handsome," well-spoken, and "blessed . . . forever" of all (3). Even in peacetime, the royal commander in chief must "gird your sword . . . in your splendor and your majesty" (4). Because he rides "on behalf of truth, meekness and justice" (5), "peoples fall beneath you" (6).

The greatest glory of this king is that he represents God. For it is God's throne that "is forever and ever" (7). Identifying with the one true God, this king "loved righteousness" and "hated wickedness," and is "anointed" above all others (8). The fragrance of the king's robes catches the scent of the incense in the Temple (Exod. 30:34–35), and his "ivory palaces" (9) are almost a glimpse of the crystal city of God (Rev. 21:10–11).

Here comes the bride! Adorned in "gold of Ophir" (10), she is beckoned to "forget your people" and "honor" the king (11–12). Then she will share in his honor and glory, "her gown . . . interwoven with gold" (14), and led magnificently to the king with her train of virgins (15). Following her, future generations join the parade—as yet unborn "will take your fathers' place" as princes (17). Then the king's "name" will be "remembered in all generations" (18).

This poet knows how to glamorize the royalty, does he not? Now, who could be that spectacular? To be sure, ancients went all out to lionize their kings. But when we moderns read it, we have to wonder, who was this king? Maybe the greatest king in Israel—David, slayer of Goliath and his ten thousands? Still, can it be said that he "loved righteousness" and "hated wickedness"? Yes and no. David was known for his virtues and better moments, true. Yet he is also remembered for his base passions, adultery, and murder. Truth be told, none of David's successors measure up to the panegyric either—except One. Eyes of faith keep looking, and envisage the Son of David—the Messiah, the One "anointed" above all others. He is the only One who loves, cares, and shares truly, the One who really does "ride victoriously, on behalf of truth, meekness and justice" (5). The first time, He rode in on a humble donkey. The next time, He will ride a spectacular white horse, with His army and bride joining Him on many white horses (Rev. 19:11, 14). Who is this glorious King? Who is His bride (Rev. 19:7–8; 21:2)? Whose Name above all will be "remembered in all generations"? We hope you know. We hope you are praying with anticipation for that glorious wedding day.

Psalm 46

He Makes Wars Cease

¹ For the music director, of the sons of Korah, according to Alamoth, a song.
² God is our refuge and strength,
    an ever-present help in trouble.
³ Therefore we will not fear,
    though the earth change,
    though the mountains topple into the heart of the seas,
⁴ though its waters roar and foam,
    though the mountains quake at their swelling. *Selah*

⁵ There is a river whose streams make glad the city of God—
    the holy dwelling place of *Elyon*.[a]
⁶ God is in the midst of her, she will not be shaken.
    God will help her when morning dawns.
⁷ Nations are in uproar, kingdoms totter,
    He utters His voice, the earth melts!
⁸ *Adonai-Tzva'ot* is with us.
    The God of Jacob is our stronghold. *Selah*

⁹ Come, see the works of *Adonai*,
    who brings devastations on the earth.
¹⁰ He makes wars cease to the end of the earth.
    He breaks the bow and shatters the spear.
    He burns chariots with fire.
¹¹ "Be still, and know that I am God.
    I am exalted among the nations.
    I am exalted in the earth."
¹² *Adonai-Tzva'ot* is with us.
    The God of Jacob is our strong tower. *Selah*

a. 46:5. cf. Ezek. 47:9, 12; Rev. 22:1–2.

Glenn Blank

The sons of Korah have composed an apocalyptic, super-visionary poem. On the earth, "mountains topple" (3) and "waters roar" (4). Yet somehow the visionary is calm, as "God is our refuge and strength" (2). Such repose in the midst of turmoil takes a lot of trust!

Perhaps the explanation is the extraordinary calm of the city that follows. What is this city with its river that makes it glad (5)? Probably not Jerusalem in the hills of Judah—unlike many cities, it has no river flowing through it, unless it's an underwater spring feeding the pool of Siloam. If it is earthly Jerusalem at all, it is either outside time or at least its usual place, looking more like the apocalyptic Jerusalem of Ezekiel 47; Zechariah 14; or Revelation 22, which all feature a supernatural river of healing and gladness. In those visions, as here, the city is serenely perfect in its beauty, simply because "God is in the midst of her" (6).

Such *shalom* within contrasts with the tumult of the nations without. Unlike earthly cities, where towers fall and "kingdoms totter" (7), this city "will not be shaken" (6). On the one hand, the Judge "brings devastations on the earth" (9), while on the other hand, "He makes wars cease to the end of the earth" (10). How are both things possible? It depends on where you are standing. If you "fall into the hands of the living God" (Heb. 10:31), you may quake with fear of the devastations of the world as we know it. But if you dwell in His presence, you can be confident that God is "our strong tower"—for so the refrain sings twice (8, 12).

The next-to-last verse climaxes with a short speech from God Himself. "Be still," for it is futile to fight against God. The city of God cannot be taken by force through human effort but only by exalting God "among the nations" (11). Therefore, exalt ADONAI so that He may be your secure, "strong tower."

PSALM 47

In Celebration of God's Reign

¹ For the music director, a psalm for the sons of Korah.
² Clap your hands, all you peoples!
    Shout to God with the voice of joy!

³ For *Adonai Elyon* is awesome,
    a great King over all the earth.
⁴ He subdues peoples under us,
    and nations under our feet.
⁵ He chooses our inheritance for us,
    the glory of Jacob whom He loved. *Selah*
⁶ God is gone up amidst shouting,
    Adonai amidst the sound of the *shofar*.
⁷ Sing praises to God, sing praises!
    Sing praises to our King, sing praises!
⁸ For God is the King of all the earth.
    Sing praises with a skillful song.
⁹ God reigns over the nations.
    God sits upon His holy throne.
¹⁰ The princes of the peoples are gathered as a people of the God of
    Abraham.
    For the shields of earth belong to God—
    He is greatly exalted!

Glenn Blank

Is *Adonai* the King of Israel or the whole world? The answer is—both. Then again, not so fast! Shouldn't there be a coronation—when the subjects get to recognize their king? Other royal psalms celebrate the coronation of Israel's new king (2, 45, 72). But this one celebrates God Himself as "the King over all the earth," and "over the nations" (3, 8–9). Inasmuch as none of the other nations recognized His rulership in ancient times—and few if any do today—this psalm is expressing a Messianic hope of the kingdom of God. It is a glorious hope! It is an occasion for rambunctious clapping and shouting (1), *shofars* blasting and praises ringing (6–7)—that's how the coronation of Solomon (1 Kings 1:39–40) and other ancient kings went. Those who believe that God truly is our King should be first to exalt Him. Those who do will have the privilege of joining in His conquest, when "He subdues peoples" under His "feet" (4).

Are you uneasy with the idea of God as a conquering King? Then bear in mind the way He must conquer you—not by brute force but by the might of His love. We have a King who first chooses us, then waits for His people to choose Him, freely. Let all the people and their princes exalt Him! For all the "shields of earth" belong to Him (10). For He alone brings lasting *shalom* and fullness of joy.

PSALM 48

Consider Zion's Towers

[1] A song, a psalm of the sons of Korah.
[2] Great is ADONAI, and greatly to be praised
  in the city of our God—His holy mountain.
[3] A beautiful height—the joy of the whole earth—
  is Mount Zion, on the northern side of the city of the great King.[a]
[4] God, in her palaces,
  is known as a stronghold.
[5] For behold, the kings assembled,
  they advanced together.
[6] They saw, then they were astounded,
  they fled in terror.
[7] Trembling seized them there,
  pain like a woman in labor.
[8] With an east wind
  You broke the ships of Tarshish.
[9] As we have heard, so have we seen,
  in the city of ADONAI-*Tzva'ot*,
  in the city of our God.
  God will establish her forever. *Selah*
[10] We have meditated on Your lovingkindness, O God,
  in the midst of Your Temple.
[11] Like Your Name, O God,
  so is Your praise
to the ends of the earth.
  Your right hand is full of righteousness.
[12] Mount Zion is glad,
  the daughters of Judah rejoice,
because of Your judgments.

a. 48:3. cf. Matt. 5:35.

¹³ Walk about Zion, go around her.
     Count her towers.
¹⁴ Consider her ramparts,
     go through her palaces,
     so you may describe it to the next generation.
¹⁵ For this God is our God, forever and ever!
     He will guide us to the end.

Jeffrey Seif and Glenn Blank

Today, many Bible believers are oblivious to the notion of sacred space. When the psalmist speaks of the "city of our God" (2) and "the city of the great King" (3), many people think of heaven—that distant, ethereal abode of God that we hope will be our place of ultimate reward. "Zion" has become a metaphor for the celestial city. The psalmist, one of the "sons of Korah" (1), a priestly singer in the Temple, was thinking about a walled town in the hills of Judea. For him the "holy mountain" (2) was a "beautiful height" located "on the northern side of the city of the great King" (3)—and sure enough, if you check out these places today, the Temple Mount is higher than and due north of the ancient City of David. So this "city of our God" (9) was built with real sticks and bricks. David and Solomon took great pains and pleasure in con-structing "her palaces" and making the God of Israel "known as a stronghold" there (4). Israel's kings wanted neighboring kings to be in such awe of its glory and strength that they would be "astounded" and flee "in terror" (5–6).

God is intent on making His abode on earth, not simply beyond earth. He wants us, here and now, to "have heard" and "seen" that He dwells "in the city of our God" (9). When "we have meditated on Your lovingkindness" therein (10), it should inspire us to take "Your praise to the ends of the earth" (11). No wonder *Yeshua* told His disciples to be His witnesses first in Jerusalem (Acts 1:8). When they did, "the daughters of Judah" (and several thousand sons) did "rejoice" (12).

Verse 13 says, "Walk about Zion, go around her." That's something you might actually want to do. Pilgrims have been journeying to Jerusalem for centuries. They "count her towers" and "her ramparts," they meander about her ways, they recall her history, so that they "may describe it to the next generation" (13–14). They experience the energy and say, "This God is our God, forever and ever!" (15). If you have yet to join the happy throng, why not make plans to go? And if you cannot go this year, or next, you can still open up your heart, here and now, and meditate on His lovingkindness there, now and forever.

PSALM 49

Rich and Poor Alike

[1] For the music director: a psalm of the sons of Korah.
[2] Hear this, all you peoples.
  Give ear, all you inhabitants of the world,
[3] both low and high,
  rich and poor together.
[4] My mouth speaks wisdom,
  My heart's meditation is understanding.
[5] I will turn my ear to a proverb.
  I will utter my riddle on the harp:
[6] Why should I fear in evil days,
  when the iniquity of my deceivers surrounds me?
[7] Or those trusting in their wealth,
  boasting about their great riches?
[8] No man can redeem his brother,
  or give to God a ransom for him.
[9] For the redemption of a soul is costly—
  so, one should stop trying forever.
[10] Will he live forever—
  and never see the Pit?
[11] Surely he must see, even wise men die.
  The fool and the brutish will alike perish,
  leaving their wealth to others.[a]
[12] Their inward thought is:
  Their houses are eternal,
  their dwellings for generation after generation.
  They name their lands after themselves.

a. 49:11. cf. Ps. 39:7(6); Eccles. 2:16–18, 21; Luke 12:20.

¹³ But the pompous man will not endure—
  he is like the beasts that perish.
¹⁴ Such is the way of the self-confident,
  and their followers who approve their sayings. *Selah*

¹⁵ Like sheep they are destined for *Sheol*.
  Death will be their shepherd
  and the upright will rule over them in the morning.
  Their image will decay in *Sheol*—
far from its lofty place.
¹⁶ But God redeems my soul from the power of *Sheol*—
  for He receives me. *Selah*
¹⁷ Do not be afraid when a man gets rich,
  when his house's splendor increases.
¹⁸ For when he dies he takes nothing away.
  His splendor will not follow him down.
¹⁹ Though during his life he congratulates himself,
  and men praise you when you do well for yourself—
²⁰ He will still join his fathers' company,
  who will never see the light.
²¹ A pompous man, without understanding—
  he is like the beasts that perish.

Glenn Blank

Rabbi Benjamin Segal[1] makes several interesting observations about verses 13 and 21. These two verses are a refrain closing each of the two halves of the psalm with a somber warning. But there are subtle differences in the Hebrew for these verses—an additional conjunction here, a different negative particle there, but most significantly, a difference of one Hebrew letter between the main verbs, יָלִין, *yaleen*, in 13 and יָבִין, *yaveen*, in 21. Perceiving that subtle difference (a ל jumping up for our attention) makes a big difference—just as perceiving what is precious can make a big difference in how one looks at this life.

One of the priestly "sons of Korah" (1) imparts important advice. This psalm has more in common with Wisdom literature like Proverbs and Job than with David's songs. The psalmist speaks to "all you inhabitants of the world" (2) and not just the nation of Israel. He speaks to all classes—"both low and high" (3)—and not just the royal court. He speaks "wisdom" (4) rather than a prayer. He turns his ear to "a proverb" and a "riddle" (5). He poses this riddle as a series of rhetorical questions: "Should I fear in evil days?" (6), Will they boast "about their great riches?" (7), Can a man ever "redeem his brother?" (8), "Will he live forever?" (10).

We could answer with a trite proverb—"You can't take it with you." Everyone knows this but tries to forget it. Instead, many in "their inward thought" cherish an illusion that "their houses are eternal" (12)—or, if you can't take it with you, surely future generations will remember your name. Truly? The first refrain (13) vaporizes this fantasy.

Is there any hope? Is there a better destiny than "the Pit" (10) or "decay in *Sheol*" (15)—a dark, shadowy place of negligible existence? That's when the psalmist makes an appeal to God—He "redeems my soul," He "receives me" (16). This verse is the only mention of God in this psalm; it's also the only time the psalmist speaks in the first person. It comes down to a personal relationship, a personal expression of trust in a Redeemer, much like what Job 19:25 declares: "I know that my Redeemer lives!" Without this faith, the rich in this world's wealth "will never see the light" (20). So *Yeshua* warns all in His parable of a rich man "who stores up treasure for himself, and is not rich in God" (Luke 12:21).

So now, do you perceive that temporal pomp perishes (13, 21)? Do you see the light beyond? Truly?

PSALM 50

A Sacrifice of Thanks

 ¹ A psalm of Asaph.
   God, *Elohim ADONAI* has spoken and summoned the earth
      from the rising of the sun to its setting.
² Out of Zion, the perfection of beauty,
      God shines forth.
³ Our God comes, and does not keep silent.
      A fire is devouring before Him,
         and it storms around Him mightily.

⁴ He calls to the heavens above
    and to the earth, to judge His people:
⁵ "Gather My *kedoshim* to Me,
    who cut a covenant with Me with a sacrifice."
⁶ The heavens declare His righteousness,
    for God Himself is Judge. *Selah*

⁷ "Hear, My people, and I will speak,
    O Israel, and I will testify against you:
    I am God, your God.
⁸ I do not rebuke you for your sacrifices,
    for your burnt offerings are continually before Me.
⁹ I have no need of a bull from your house
    nor goats from your pens.
¹⁰ For every beast of the forest is Mine,
    and the cattle on a thousand hills.
¹¹ I know every bird of the mountains.
    Everything moving in the field is Mine.
¹² If I were hungry, I would not tell you—
    for the world is Mine and all it contains!
¹³ Do I eat the flesh of bulls
    or drink the blood of goats?
¹⁴ Offer God a sacrifice of thank offerings,
    then fulfill your vows to *Elyon*.
¹⁵ Call upon Me in the day of trouble.
    When I rescue you, you will honor Me."

¹⁶ But to the wicked, God says:
    "What are you doing, reciting My laws
    and taking My covenant in your mouth?
¹⁷ For you hate discipline,
    and you cast My words behind you.
¹⁸ When you see a thief, you are pleased with him,
    and your portion is with adulterers.
¹⁹ You have unleashed your mouth for evil
    and harnessed your tongue for deceit.
²⁰ You sit, speaking against your brother,
    slandering your own mother's son.
²¹ These things you have done—Should I keep silent?
    You thought I was just like you—but I reprove you,
    and set the case before your eyes.

[22] Now consider this, you who forget God.

Or else I will tear you in pieces with no one to rescue you.

[23] A sacrifice of praise honors Me,

and to the one who orders his way,

I will show the salvation of God."

Jeffrey Seif and Glenn Blank

With supreme majesty, God has "summoned the earth" (1). Those summoned should respond, not just because of His authority but also because of His glorious light and truth, "the perfection of beauty" (2). He is coming, with fire and storms all around Him (3), with a mind to "judge His people" (4). His *kedoshim* ("holy ones") are to gather—those with whom He has made a covenant (5). It is not a casual meeting. It is judgment day—and not everyone can expect to fare very well in the assessment. Will you? How will you respond when the mighty Judge (6) announces, "I will testify against you" (7)?

Because none of us want to be on the minus side of this ledger, we do well to consider how the Judge plans to assess His people. Poor scores are not divvied out because of lack of "sacrifices" or "offerings" (8), because He already owns it all, even "the cattle on a thousand hills" (10). Religious people can serve up offerings with rigor—maybe you don't know anyone offering up live animals, but you may know people who can recite liturgical prayers almost from memory. God is not satisfied with formulaic rituals though. He wants people to do what is right—and many are not doing so. The Judge of souls takes issue with the lack of heartfelt praise (14) and a failure to keep covenantal vows. (Similarly, *Yeshua* expressed dissatisfaction with babbling or boastful prayers; see Matt. 6:7; Luke 18:11–12.) Such indifference or pride catches up with you, as it eventually does in all relationships—be they human or divine. A sluggish or insensitive partner is not going to enjoy much marital bliss or close friendship. Merciful as God is, one can always turn to Him, clean the slate, and start afresh. "Call upon Me," He says, and I will "rescue you" and "you will honor Me" (15). The offer is always on the table. Yet many do not take God up on it.

So He rebukes the unrighteous, especially for their hypocrisy (16–18) and their *lashon ha-ra* (evil tongue, 19–20), with a solemn warning that He does not forget about those who forget about Him (21–22). Then He turns to the righteous with suggestions worth taking to heart: "A sacrifice of praise honors

Me," and "one who orders his way" correctly will eventually see "the salvation of God" (23). Thanks (תּוֹדָה, *todah*, can mean either thanks or praise—it's the same Hebrew word in vv. 14 and 23) is especially valuable to God when it's a "sacrifice." You offer it at a cost to yourself—such as when you might not feel like it. It keeps you humble. It changes your orientation, from yourself to the One who is love. He has sacrificed so much to make us free to love Him, or not. When we didn't love Him, He still loved us, and redeemed us, at a great cost to Himself. How many judges do you know who love you so?

Those anxious to see God's providential hand in their mortal affairs would do well to consider that His hand extends to those who actually reach up to Him with theirs. Turn to Him. Reach up to Him. Reach out to others, too, in love. Doing so will bear fruit. Love never fails. You will see God's hand reaching into your affairs and be the better for it.

PSALM 51

Create in Me a Clean Heart

¹ For the music director: a psalm of David, ² when Nathan the prophet
    came to him, after he went to Bathsheba.
³ Be gracious to me, O God,
      according to Your mercy.
    According to Your great compassion
    blot out my transgressions.
⁴ Wash me thoroughly from my iniquity
    and cleanse me from my sin.
⁵ For I know my transgressions
    and my sin is ever before me.
⁶ Against You, You only, have I sinned,
      and done what is evil in Your sight,
      so that You are just when You speak,
      and blameless when You judge.
⁷ Behold, I was born in iniquity and in sin
    when my mother conceived me.
⁸ Surely You desire truth in the inner being.
    Make me know wisdom inwardly.

⁹ Cleanse me with hyssop and I will be clean.
>Wash me, and I will be whiter than snow.
¹⁰ Let me hear joy and gladness,
>so the bones You crushed may rejoice.
¹¹ Hide Your face from my sins,
>and blot out all my iniquities.

¹² Create in me a clean heart, O God,
>and renew a steadfast spirit within me.
¹³ Do not cast me from Your presence—
>take not Your *Ruach ha-Kodesh* from me.
¹⁴ Restore to me the joy of Your salvation
>and sustain me with a willing spirit.
¹⁵ Then will I teach transgressors Your ways
>and sinners will return to You.
¹⁶ Deliver me from bloodguilt, O God—
>God of my salvation.
>>Then my tongue will sing for joy of Your righteousness.
¹⁷ O Lord, open my lips,
>and my mouth will declare Your praise.
¹⁸ For You would not delight in sacrifice, or I would give it,
>nor be pleased by burnt offerings.
¹⁹ The sacrifices of God are a broken spirit.
>A broken and a contrite heart, O God,
>You will not despise.

²⁰ In Your favor do good to Zion.
>Build up the walls of Jerusalem.
²¹ Then You will delight in righteous sacrifices and whole burnt offerings.
>Then bulls will be offered on Your altar.

Paul Wilbur

Right from the opening two verses you understand that this is one of those songs that is not going to be the happy, clappy kind. Yet there are verses that many will return to time and again to find help in times of need. David was indeed a man after God's own heart, but that obviously didn't make him a perfect man. In fact, there has only been One who walked this earth who can claim the title of altogether "blameless," and that would be *Yeshua* of Nazareth, the Messiah and King of Israel. David fell victim to several common weaknesses of the flesh, one of them being the lust of the eyes and another the pride of life. First, David should have turned away from the view he had of his friend's wife bathing on the rooftop, but he didn't. His eyes became a snare for him just as they do for so many to this day. Many a mighty man has been ensnared by grievous sin that began with only a glance, that became a stare, that became a meditation and then an addiction. Next, the king fell to the sin of pride, which told him that he was above the law; because he was the king, he could have anything he wanted. After stealing what did not belong to him, he hatched a wicked plan to hide the evidence, and when that didn't work, he schemed to remove the injured party by murdering Bathsheba's husband so that he could have what he wanted. The heart of man is deceitful and wicked above all things, and who can even know his own heart (Jer. 17:9)?

Now, after all his plotting and wickedness, David comes to the end of himself, but only after the prophet Nathan comes to him and accuses him of his awful crimes. David cries out to ADONAI for grace, mercy, and compassion to blot out his iniquity and to cleanse him from his terrible sin (3–4). It is interesting that David cries out for the very help that he was not willing to extend to either of his victims—but this is the nature of sin and deceit. The enemy will convince you that this is what you need, want, have to have, and then when you satisfy the lust of the flesh, the lust of the eyes, or the pride of life, he will hammer you with guilt and condemnation for the very acts he persuaded you of in the first place!

I don't really understand verse 6, because the sin was not only against the Lord and His righteousness; David also sinned grievously against Uriah his friend and Bathsheba, Uriah's wife. (Perhaps he recognizes that he can never get right with them if he cannot first get right with God.) He acknowledges that the justice of ADONAI is blameless, but then reminds the Lord that he is human after all. He asks for the cleansing of hyssop (9), which refers to the sprinkling of blood for purification and protection, as in Passover and the ordinance with the red heifer. He calls upon the Lord to blot out all his sins (11). But he gets to the heart of the matter when he prays, "Create in me a clean heart" (12)—the word here is *bara*, referring to the creative power of *Elohim*, the only One who has this power to create. He then asks for a new or renewed (חָדָשׁ, *chadash*) spirit. He implores ADONAI not to remove His face (פָּנֶי, *panei*) from him and not to take His "Holy Spirit" (רוּחַ קָדְשְׁךָ, *Ruach Kod'sh'cha*) from his life (13). For David these were real issues at stake. Above all other punishments he feared that the loss of anointing and presence of ADONAI might be the ultimate price he would pay. Don't forget, David had a front-row seat and saw the very thing he fears happen to Israel's first king, Saul. He watched the favor and strength of the face of ADONAI turn away, saw the torment of Saul's soul, and knew of his death by his own sword. No wonder David cries out; he does not want this to be his legacy as well. Verses 14–18 I might label as David's "foxhole" promises to the Lord—for deliverance and forgiveness he will teach transgressors the ways of ADONAI, and sing and declare His righteousness. Lastly, David affirms that a broken and a contrite or crushed spirit his God will not despise (19)—at least he hopes not.

This psalm is a heavy and weighty one, as there would have been grave consequences should ADONAI not have been moved by David's repentance. Reading the rest of the story, Nathan reports that David was forgiven—though the child of his sin died. His next son with Bathsheba, Solomon, took his place on the throne after David's death.

I recall singing the words beginning with verse 13 many times as I led worship in our Messianic congregation in Rockville, Maryland. We sang with great fervor and passion, "Cast me not away from Thy presence, O Lord, and take not Thy Holy Spirit from me." Surely our hearts were touched by the thought that we could ever displease ADONAI. Sin is something we as human beings have to deal with daily, and yet it is good to have the assurance that if we confess our sins, He is faithful and just to forgive us our sins and cleanse us from all unrighteousness (1 John 1:9). If you should ever be struggling with guilt, remember David and this psalm. Also remember *Yeshua* and the price He paid to forgive *all* of our sins.

PSALM 52

Treacherous Tongue!

¹ For the music director: a contemplative song of David, ² when Doeg the Edomite came and reported to Saul telling him, "David went to Ahimelech's house."

³ Why do you brag about evil, mighty man?
    God's lovingkindness is every day.
⁴ Your tongue plots destruction,
    like a sharp razor, working deceit.
⁵ You love evil instead of good,
    lying rather than speaking right. *Selah*
⁶ You love only devouring words—
    treacherous tongue!
⁷ God will pull you down forever,
    and snatch you, rip you out of your tent,
    and uproot you from the land of the living. *Selah*
⁸ Then the righteous will see and fear,
    and laugh at him:
⁹ "Here is the man who did not make God his stronghold.
    Instead he trusted in his great riches—
and was strong in his evil desire."
¹⁰ But I—I am like an olive tree flourishing in the House of God.
    I trust in God's lovingkindness forever and ever.
¹¹ I will praise You forever for what You have done.
    I will hope in Your Name, for it is good,
    in the presence of Your *kedoshim*.

Jeffrey Seif and Glenn Blank

Betrayal! David agonizes over how Ahimelech and eighty-five other priests of the Lord died, all because Doeg the Edomite told King Saul that David had come to him for help (2; 1 Sam. 22:9–22). How could a man do such an evil thing and then brag about it (3)? How can a tongue plot destruction and treachery (4–6)? In Dante's *Inferno*, the lowest part of hell is reserved for betrayers. Though the psalmist wrote before Dante, he still sees its principle of justice—for "God will pull you down forever" (7). While we wish the number of victims were few, the truth is, we still live in a world where many betray others. Counted among the betrayed are spouses, business associates, and friends—those who thought they knew the other, trusted, and yet were betrayed. The ease with which people can find a place in this story attests to the scope of the problem. You may even know someone who meets this description: "Your tongue" is like "a sharp razor, working deceit" (4). Nevertheless, justice will come. The righteous will laugh at the wicked (8).

A day will come when the righteous will be "like an olive tree"—long-lived and filled with the sap of the Spirit, "flourishing in the House of God . . . forever and ever" (10).

Some commentators think the ancients had little hope for life after death, yet here and elsewhere in the Psalms there are triumphant glimpses of eternal lovingkindness toward the righteous in God's House. So then, what can we say to victims in a world where their efforts are stymied and diminished by the guiles and wiles of the wicked? God is the Judge, both now and forever. In His lovingkindness, He will redeem; in His righteousness, He will judge. He delivers and rewards those who hope in Him. As for the wicked, they also have their deliverance and reward—delivered to destruction, for the reward of ruin.

PSALM 53

A Fool Denies God

¹ For the music director: on Mahalath, a contemplative song of David.
² The fool says in his heart:
   "There is no God."
   They are corrupt, commit vile injustice.
   There is no one who does good.
³ God looks down from the heavens
      on the children of men,
   to see if anyone understands,
   who seeks after God.
⁴ All have turned aside—
   together they have become corrupt.
      There is no one who does good—
   no, not even one!
⁵ Will the evildoers never learn?
      They consume My people as they would eat bread,
      and never call upon God.
⁶ There they are in great dread—
      where there is nothing to fear.

> For God has scattered the bones of those besieging you.
> You have put them to shame,
> for God has rejected them.

> [7] Who will give salvation for Israel out of Zion?
> When God restores His captive people,
> let Jacob rejoice, let Israel be glad!

Jeffrey Seif and Glenn Blank

Closely paralleling Psalm 14, this psalm again raises some eternally important questions. The first is: "Will the evildoers never learn?" (5). So many, in their foolish unbelief, are "corrupt" and "commit vile injustice" (2). From God's perspective, it's a pretty bleak picture—"There is no one who does good—no, not even one!" (3–4) Anyone trusting in the goodness of man or the merit of his own good deeds may want to reconsider. In the end, they will be in "great dread" because "God has rejected them" (6). As Hebrews 10:31 warns, "It is a terrifying thing to fall into the hands of the living God."

The second question is: "Who will give salvation[s] for Israel out of Zion?" (7). The answer is embedded in the word for salvation—יְשׁוּעֹת is the plural form of *yeshuah*. Though all people—even the children of Israel—have "turned aside" from God (4) and become corrupt, God has not turned aside from Israel but remains faithful. Though Israel has suffered the consequences of unbelief and disobedience, "God restores His captive people" (7).

In a world where we are all too easily disappointed in other people's performances, slighted by offenses real or imagined, and outright betrayed, the psalm assures us that God is faithful and will not disappoint. He will show Himself strong on our behalf through a display of His salvation. This deliverance comes in various ways on various days. Even now we see captive Israel restored to the land. In the fullness of time His deliverance came as the Deliverer. David and the prophets looked for this Deliverer, and faithful *kedoshim* are looking for Him to come again, One who truly does good for God, for Israel, and for all—the Messiah. Out of Zion God has revealed His salvation—His *Yeshua*.

 PSALM 54

Surely God Is My Helper

¹ For the music director, on stringed instruments, a contemplative song of
   David, ² when the Ziphites came and said to Saul: "Is not David hiding
   himself among us?"
³ O God, save me by Your Name,
   vindicate me by Your might.
⁴ O God, hear my prayer,
   listen to the words of my mouth.
⁵ For strangers have risen up against me.
   Violent men seek after my soul.
   They do not set God before them. *Selah*

⁶ Surely God is my helper.
   My Lord is the supporter of my soul.
⁷ Let evil return to my foes.
   Silence them with Your truth!
⁸ I will sacrifice a freewill offering to You.
   I will praise Your Name, ADONAI, for it is good.
⁹ For He has delivered me from all trouble,
   and my eye has gazed upon my enemies.

Jeffrey Seif

How can the psalmist conclude, God has "delivered me from all trouble" (9),
on the one hand, and say, "save me" (3), for "violent men seek after my soul" (5),
on the other? Is he in trouble or not? How about both? A unique word comes
to mind—*prolepsis*—it's the "representation of something as existing before
its proper historical time." For example, consider a young woman who feels
burdened by the inability to secure the affections of a potential life mate.
Should she actively seek, and the answer to her dilemma is slow in coming,
she might think it is never coming. Her discouragement could prompt all
sorts of internal dialogue, which in turn could contribute even more toward
her feelings of aloneness and repel potential partners. Similarly Jeremiah 17:6
says, "For he will be like a bush in the desert. He cannot see goodness when
it comes." What would happen if the young woman decided just to believe

that since God loves her, a mate will eventually present himself and love her too? This decision could give her new inner resolutions.

Faith prompts us to believe for things in the future, even to act like they are here in the present before they present in the present. Now, back to our psalmist. Even when he is in trouble, he decides to trust: "Surely God is my helper" (6). His confidence in God helps him to recognize his helper. That's trusting faith, and we need it today as much as David needed it then.

PSALM 55

Betrayal by a Friend

¹ For the music director, on stringed instruments, a contemplative song
of David.
² Give ear, O God, to my prayer
and do not ignore my plea for help.
³ Listen to me and answer me.
I am restless in my complaint and moan—
⁴ because of the voice of the enemy,
because of the pressure of the wicked.
For they thrust trouble on me,
and in anger bear a grudge against me.
⁵ My heart shudders within me
and the terrors of death sweep over me.
⁶ Fear and trembling come upon me
and horror has overwhelmed me.
⁷ So I said, "Oh that I had wings like a dove!
I would fly away and find rest.
⁸ Surely I would flee far away.
I would stay in the wilderness. *Selah*
⁹ I would hurry to my shelter
from the rushing wind of the storm."
¹⁰ Lord, confuse and confound their speech,
for I see violence and strife in the city.
¹¹ Day and night they make the rounds on her walls.
Iniquity and mischief are within her.

¹² Ruins are in her midst.

Oppression and deceit never leave her square.
¹³ For if it were an enemy taunting me,
I could endure it.

If my foe was exalting himself over me,
I could hide from him.
¹⁴ But it is you, a man like me—

my companion and my close friend!
¹⁵ Together we enjoyed great fellowship.

We used to walk with the throng in the House of God.
¹⁶ Let desolation come upon them,

let them go down alive into *Sheol*—
for evil is in their dwelling, among them.

¹⁷ As for me, I will call on God,
and *Adonai* will save me.
¹⁸ Evening, morning and noon, I complain and moan,
then He hears my voice.
¹⁹ He will redeem my soul in *shalom* from the battle against me.
For many are striving with me.
²⁰ God will hear and humble them
—yes, the One enthroned of old. *Selah*
Nothing changes—they do not fear God.
²¹ My companion put forth his hands against those at peace with him,
as he violates his covenant.
²² Smoother than butter was his speech,
yet war was in his heart.

His words were softer than oil,
yet they were drawn swords.

²³ Cast your burden on *Adonai*, and He will sustain you.ᵃ
He will never let the righteous be shaken.
²⁴ But You, O God, will bring them down to the Pit of destruction.
Bloodthirsty, deceitful men will not live out half their days.
But I—I will trust in You.

a. 55:23. cf. 1 Pet. 5:7.

Jeffrey Seif and Glenn Blank

Did you ever just want to run away? Our psalmist did. He sings out: "Oh that I had wings like a dove! I would fly away and find rest. Surely I would flee far away. . . . I would hurry to my shelter" (7–9). We might not say it so poetically, but most of us have felt this way at times. We feel it because pressures from people weigh upon us. The psalmist has felt "the pressure of the wicked," who "thrust trouble on me" (4). The pressures of fear and trembling became so great that it felt overwhelming (5–6). Today we might call it an anxiety attack. So he wants to run, far away to the wilderness, to a "shelter from the rushing wind of the storm" (9). David didn't have a psychologist, so he turned to poetry.

What was really bothering him? He opens up. It was bad enough that enemies were chasing after him with their "iniquity and mischief" (11), their "oppression and deceit" (12). That would be enough to upset most of us. But that was not the worst. He says he could endure an enemy taunting him, since he could hide himself from that (13). Maybe. The worst is that "my companion and my close friend" (14) has betrayed him. Ouch. The worst is when we love, when we open our hearts to someone. We dare. We care. We share. Then we meet a creep and get a wound that goes deep!

This companion "violates his covenant" (21). A covenant is a vow before God. How could anyone appear at God's altar, make a vow—say, wedding or membership vows—and then give himself or herself to another? Worse yet, how could this companion actually "put forth his hands against those at peace with him" (21)? When that happens, you wonder, *How could I be so stupid? Why didn't I see it?* Alas, "smoother than butter was his speech, . . . his words were softer than oil" (22). He was duped, and now he knows it. He's hurting bad. How would he deal with it? How should we? Should we give up on people, since they keep hurting us? Should we give up on God, since He let us get into this mess? The problem with running away to the wilderness or otherwise avoiding people, let alone God, is that we wind up avoiding the one thing that is most worthwhile in life—love. As another poet (Tennyson) said, "'Tis better to have loved and lost, than never to have loved at all."[1]

Consider *Yeshua*, the lover of our souls. In the moment of crisis, His disciples abandoned Him. Worse yet, one of them—one who had walked with Him, slept beside Him, even watched His money for Him for three years— sold Him out. Then the defector comes in the dark of night and identifies

Him with . . . a kiss! Hear what *Yeshua* says: "Friend, would you betray the Son of Man with a kiss?" (Luke 22:48) and "Do what you've come to do" (Matt. 26:50). *Yeshua* never stopped loving. He never gave up on His friends. Though Peter denied Him three times, *Yeshua* reaffirmed His friend's calling three times. He never stopped trusting. And that's what the *Ruach HaKodesh* also taught David—never stop trusting. His poem ends with these words: "But I—I will trust in You" (24). Will you?

PSALM 56

In God I Trust

¹ For the music director: "A Silent Dove Far Away," a Michtam of David,
    when the Philistines had seized him in Gath.
² Be gracious to me, O God!
    For man has crushed me,
    fighting all day he oppresses me.
³ My foes trample me all day.
    For many are fighting me arrogantly.
⁴ In a day when I am afraid,
    I will put my trust in You.
⁵ In God—I keep praising His word—
    in God I trust, I will not fear.
    What can mere flesh do to me?

⁶ All day they twist my words.
    All their thoughts are against me for evil.
⁷ They stir up strife; they lie hidden.
    They mark my steps, eager to take my soul.
⁸ In spite of such sin, will they escape?
    In fierce anger, O God, cast down such people!
⁹ You have recorded my wanderings.
    You put my tears in Your bottle.
    Are they not in Your book?
¹⁰ Then my enemies will turn back in the day I call.
    This I know—that God is for me.

¹¹ In God—I keep praising His word—
    in *Adonai*—I keep praising His word—
¹² in God I trust, I will not be afraid.
    What can man do to me?

¹³ I am under vows to You, O God.
    I will present thank offerings to You.
¹⁴ For You have delivered my soul from death
    and my feet from stumbling,
    that I may walk before God in the light of life.

Glenn Blank

After years on the run from Saul and his troops, David has no place left to hide in his homeland. So he hops over the border to Gath in Philistia (1). That was risky because, as 1 Samuel 10:11–14 records, the Philistines soon recognized David as their old enemy. David had to pretend he had gone insane. *Oy.*

Remarkably, in two musical movements, the singer passes from oppression (2, 6) to praise (5, 11), then climaxes in a reverie for his deliverance. In the first movement, he is oppressed with "fighting all day" (2) and being trampled upon (3). Yet even in his fear, the poet declares his trust in God, for what can "mere flesh do to me?" (4–5). Brave words! But the enemies of our souls do not back away so easily. In the second movement, here they come again—they "twist my words" (6) and "stir up strife . . . eager to take my soul" (7). The psalmist cries out, "O God, cast down such people!" (8).

Then follows a lovely expression of trust that God will never forget him, for He has "recorded my wanderings . . . in Your book" and "put my tears in Your bottle" (9). The intimate poetry calls to mind the promises that *HaShem* makes elsewhere to wipe away all our tears (Isa. 25:8; Rev. 7:17). Renewed, the psalmist can say that his enemies will be turned back, confident "that God is for me" (10). No matter how many are in the army of his enemies, "I keep praising His word" (11). The weapon of praise restores his trust (12) and assures his victory.

Finally, he remembers the vows he made to God—vows to "present thank offerings" (13). David would have looked forward to this celebration in the tabernacle. I don't know about you, but I rejoice to offer thank offerings in the sanctuary of our congregation. For I know that *Yeshua* has "delivered my soul from death" as surely as I know that He has kept "my feet from stumbling" through this life. I know that He alone has made it possible for me to "walk before God"—no matter what battles I have to fight each day—and given me confidence that I will join Him "in the light of life" (14)—of His truth and His resurrection (John 8:12).

PSALM 57

Be Exalted over All the Earth

¹ For the music director, "Do Not Destroy," a Michtam of David, when he
    fled from Saul, in the cave.
² Be gracious to me, O God, be gracious to me,
        for in You my soul takes refuge.
        In the shadow of Your wings I take refuge,
        until destruction passes by.
³ I will cry out to *El Elyon*,
        to God who accomplishes it for me.
⁴ He will send from heaven and save me.
        He rebukes the one trampling on me. *Selah*
        God is sending His mercy and His truth.
⁵ My soul is in the midst of lions.
        I lie among those breathing fire—
    sons of men whose teeth are spears and arrows,
        whose tongue is a sharp sword.
⁶ Be exalted, O God, above the heavens.
        Let Your glory be over all the earth!

⁷ They spread a net for my steps,
        my soul is bowed down.
        They have dug a pit before me—
        they fell into it themselves. *Selah*
⁸ My heart is steadfast, O God,
    my heart is steadfast.
        I will sing, yes, I will make music.
⁹ Awake, my glory! Awake, harp and lyre!
        I will awaken the dawn.
¹⁰ I will praise You, my Lord, among the peoples.
        I will sing praises to You among the nations.

¹¹ For Your lovingkindness is great up to the heavens,
and Your truth to the skies.
¹² Be exalted, O God, above the heavens.
Let Your glory be over all the earth!

Paul Wilbur

This psalm is remanded to the chief musician from David himself as a *Michtam*, a particular kind of song sung to a particular tune, as are Psalms 16, 58, and 59. It is quite easy to understand the opening verses when you realize that David was fleeing from Saul in the caves overlooking Ein Gedi, a natural spring near the Dead Sea and the Judean wilderness. It just so happens that Ein Gedi is where we recorded our project *Desert Rain*. Why record and name a project in such a dry, arid place? Because our worship and prayers were for *HaShem* to end the terrible drought that Israel had experienced for many years ... and it rained in the desert!

Once more David found himself in a difficult situation, to say the least. Saul wanted to spear David through. Why? Because of his disobedience, Saul lost the anointing of kingship, and an evil spirit took its place. So instead of grace and wisdom to lead a nation, there remained only jealousy, rage, and denial, refusing truly to repent. In a cave, David sings his prayer about hiding "in the shadow of Your wings" until the trouble passes (2). This image of an eagle hovering, both gentle and powerful, was dear to David. His cries go up to *El Elyon*, God Most High, who accomplishes (גָּמַר, *gomer*) all things pertaining to him (3). This word *gomer* is an interesting one because it is difficult to interpret as a single word without context. A fuller understanding would be that the Lord will complete, perfect, and finish everything. What confidence David has in God, while he is running for his life, that all God promises will be fulfilled!

The imagery that David uses to describe his plight is as vivid and stark as the desert. He is aware he is surrounded by lions—yet he is less concerned about beasts than rumormongers. Evil words spread like a fire, teeth are like spears and arrows, and a tongue like a sharp sword (5), like the swords the enemy soldiers who are hunting him down carry. Though they set traps of nets and deep pits, they all fall prey to their own schemes (7). The heart of David is steadfast (8), not upon his trials and tribulations but on singing the praise and glory of the One who is his glory (9), even as the sun rises over the Salt Sea. At the end of his song, he echoes this powerful refrain to punctuate his confidence: "Be exalted, O God, above the heavens. [*Rooma al-hashamayim Elohim.*] Let Your glory be over all the earth! [*Al kol ha-aretz kevodecha!*]" (6, 12). Oh, the power of a life lived as a worshiper—it is the secret power of all who overcome. *Selah.*

PSALM 58

God Really Judges

¹ For the music director: "Do Not Destroy," a Michtam of David.
² Do you really speak of justice, O "gods"?
    Do you judge with fairness, sons of man?
³ No, in heart you devise injustice.
    Your hands weigh out violence on earth.
⁴ The wicked are strangers from the womb.
    Speaking lies, they go astray from birth.
⁵ Their venom is like a serpent's venom,
    like a deaf cobra shutting its ear—
⁶ not hearing the voice of charmers,
  or a cunning spell binder.
⁷ O God, break their teeth in their mouths.
    Tear out the fangs of young lions, ADONAI.
⁸ Let them flow away like water that runs off.
    When he bends his bow, let the arrows be cut off.
⁹ Like a slug melting away as it slithers,
    like a woman's miscarriage,
    may they never see the sun.
¹⁰ Even before your pots can feel a thorn
    —whether alive or ablaze—
    He will sweep the wicked away.
¹¹ The righteous one will rejoice
    when he beholds vengeance,
    when he washes his feet in the blood of the wicked.
¹² Then men will say:
    "There really is a reward for the righteous.
    There really is a God who judges on earth!"

Jeffrey Seif

Life is sometimes unfair. People often do not "judge with fairness" (2). Sometimes fairness is in high demand but short supply. One need only go to court to discover that truth can be the first casualty. Too many times it seems to come down to who has the best lawyer. Or consider our electoral process. Or maybe we shouldn't. Wicked people "devise injustice" and "weigh out violence" (3). It gets so bad that the psalmist concludes that they "go astray from birth" (4). He compares their behavior to "a serpent's venom" (5). Would that be like the sly serpent of *Beresheet* (Genesis)?

In such a world, good people are treated unfairly, suffering at the hands of the unjust. How do we deal with this? The psalmist demands that the wicked be called to account. "O God, break their teeth in their mouths" (7). Once toothless, they are like a slug or a woman's miscarriage (9). He certainly holds nothing back! It is a cry to a just God for just deserts. Only then, he says, will men say, "There really is a reward for the righteous" (12).

Until His justice really comes, what do we do? Like the psalmist, we wait and we trust. He teaches us that we can turn our complaints into intercessions before God, without becoming like those who will fall under judgment. Nor can we dig a hole deep enough to avoid errant people. As Rabbi Sha'ul (Paul) pointed out, if you want to avoid dealing with immoral people, "you would have to exit the world" (1 Cor. 5:10). We are in this world, and they are in it too. That's the bad news. The good news is that God gets into the world too—He sent His Word and the Messiah into the world as evidence. Be sure of this: "There really is a God who judges on earth!" (12).

 PSALM 59

God Is My Strong Tower

¹ For the music director: "Do Not Destroy," a Michtam of David, when
    Saul sent men to watch the house to kill him.
² Deliver me from my enemies, my God!
    Set me on high,
away from those who rise up against me.

[3] Deliver me from workers of iniquity.
  Rescue me from bloodthirsty men.
[4] For behold, they lie in wait for me.
  Defiant men stir up strife against me—
  not for my transgression or sin, ADONAI.
[5] For no guilt of mine, they run and set things up.
  Awake! Help me! Look!
[6] For You are ADONAI *Elohei-Tzva'ot*, the God of Israel!
  Rouse Yourself to punish all the nations.
  Show no mercy to any iniquitous traitors. *Selah*
[7] They return at evening, snarling like a dog,
  prowling about the city.
[8] See, they are spewing with their mouth
  —swords in their lips—
  "After all, who is listening?"

[9] But You, ADONAI, are laughing at them.
  You scoff at all the nations.
[10] O my strength, I watch for You—
  for God is my strong tower.
[11] My God in His lovingkindness will go before me.
  God will let me look down on my foes.
[12] Do not slay them, lest my people forget.
  With Your power shake them
  and bring them down, O Lord our shield.
[13] The sin of their mouth is the words of their lips.
  So let them be caught in their pride,
  and for uttering a curse and a lie.
[14] Consume them in wrath,
  consume them till they are no more.
  Let them know that God rules over Jacob to the ends of the earth.
  Selah

[15] They return at evening, snarling like a dog,
  prowling about the city.
[16] They wander around for food.
  If they are not full, they stay up all night.
[17] But I—I sing of Your strength!
  Yes, in the morning I sing aloud of Your lovingkindness.
  For You have been my fortress,
  a refuge in the day of my trouble.

¹⁸ O my strength, to You I sing praises.
For God is my strong tower—
my God of lovingkindness.

Jeffrey Seif and Glenn Blank

People get in trouble. It happens all the time. In many cases, the trials we experience are the monsters of our own making. Though never pleasant, they may be easier to bear than the burden of regret when we know we're getting what we had coming. Sometimes we get what we didn't have coming, or never even saw coming. Alas, that happens too.

David had to deal with Saul sending men to kill him (1). These "bloodthirsty men" (3) were sent to "lie in wait for me," though "not for my transgression or sin" (4). It must have been bewildering. David had sung soothing songs to Saul, had won a great victory for his sovereign, yet now "defiant men stir up strife against me" (4). What had he done? "For no guilt of mine, they run and set things up" (5). Do you know anyone in this predicament?

How about Jeremiah, left to die in a dry water hole, just because he spoke the word of the Lord when it wasn't what people wanted to hear? How about Sha'ul (Paul), stoned and left for dead outside of town, twice, because he shared some good news that was attracting a few Jews and a lot of God-fearing gentiles out of the synagogues? How about *Yeshua*, scorned as He suffered on a Roman stake, because His Messianic claim was a threat to the powers that be?

To this day, those who walk closely with God as David did can also become targets. If that's you, don't be surprised about trouble you don't really deserve. You're up against an ancient enemy who has decided to "rise up against" you (2). You need not be guilty of anything—evil spirits and the people they provoke do not think they have to play fair. Evil spirits and the people they provoke are like snarling dogs with "swords in their lips" (7–8). You can complain to God about it. You can urge Him to "rouse" Himself (6) and rescue you. These are prayers God has actually answered throughout the Bible and beyond. Over and over again, David discovered that "God is my strong tower" (10), who "in His lovingkindness will go before me" (11). The One who is "our shield" (12) will cause those who curse and lie to be caught with their own words and pride (13). It may seem like these snarling dogs (15) keep coming after you—"If they are not full, they stay up all night" (16).

Yet the night will end. David sings, "In the morning I sing aloud of Your lovingkindness." Hang in there. *HaShem* is a "fortress, a refuge" (17), yes, a "strong tower—my God of lovingkindness" (18). If you are tempted to despair, don't. Morning will come. He delivers those who trust in Him.

PSALM 60

Song of Victory over Edom

¹ For the music director, on the "Lily of the Covenant," a Michtam of David, for teaching, ² when he fought with Aram-Naharaim and with Aram-Zobah, and Joab returned and struck down twelve thousand Edomites in the Valley of Salt.

³ O God, You have spurned us.
  You have broken out against us.
  You have been angry. Turn back to us!

⁴ You made earth shake; You split it open.
  Heal its fractures—for it shudders.

⁵ You made Your people see hardship.
  You made us drink wine of staggering.

⁶ To those who fear You,
  You gave a banner, to be unfurled before the archers. *Selah*

⁷ Save with Your right hand and answer us,
  so that Your beloved may be delivered.

⁸ God has spoken in His holiness:
  "I will exult!
  I will parcel out Shechem and measure off the valley of Succoth.

⁹ Gilead is Mine, and Manasseh is Mine,
  Ephraim is a helmet for my head,
  Judah is my scepter.

¹⁰ Moab is my washbasin,
  On Edom I toss my sandal,
  Philistia, cry aloud because of me!"

¹¹ Who will bring me into the fortified city?
  Who will lead me to Edom?

¹² Should it not be You, O God—
    who spurned us and no longer goes out with our armies?
¹³ Give us aid against the adversary,
    for the help of man is worthless.
¹⁴ With God we will do mighty things,
    and He will trample our foes.

Glenn Blank and Jeffrey Seif

To secure his kingdom, David had to deal with enemies rising up against him on every side—Philistines to the west along the Mediterranean Sea and Arameans, Ammonites, Moabites, and Edomites to the east of the Jordan River and the Dead (Salt) Sea. In this context, the warrior-king exulted in his victory over twelve thousand Edomites (2). Later kings would have cause to remember David's battles—surely the God of Israel would give them victory over these same enemies.

While militaristic gloating over enemies may offend the sensibilities of some who prefer to see *Yeshua* as a pacifist, modern readers do well not to impose their standards on ancient writers—especially those who honor soldiers coming back from war. Victory in war doesn't come without a price.

Indeed, much of this psalm deals with the agony of defeat—wondering why God has "spurned us" (3), why He made His people "see hardship" (5), why He "no longer goes out with our armies" (12). A string of setbacks spurred the Israelites to seek their God. "To those who fear You, You gave a banner" (6)—a banner is a signal used to rally and direct the troops. "Save with Your right hand and answer us" (7)—the king and his army recognize that without God's help, they cannot win.

So they listen with eagerness to the oracle of God, speaking "in His holiness" (8). Like a great general, God Himself fortifies His forces with faith. All these territories—the ancient town of Shechem with its famous well in Samaria, the village of Succot to the east of the Jordan, Gilead to the northeast, the tribal areas of Manasseh, Ephraim, and Judah within the Promised Land itself—hadn't they all been conquered before, under the leadership of Moses and Joshua? With rhetorical scorn, the oracle calls Moab a mere washbasin and Edom a place to toss a sandal (10) (presumably dirty and smelly from tramping all over). The Edomites had apparently built up a fortified city (11), and perhaps thought they and their allies were invincible there. So the psalmist beseeches the God of Israel, "Give us aid against the adversary" (13).

If you're wondering, *Does God takes sides in war?*, consider that the battles on earth may reflect spiritual purposes in heaven. Consider the lessons that David and the Israelites learn from their struggles, "for the help of man is worthless" (13), while "with God we will do mighty things" (14).

These principles apply to all who fight the good fight—whether against flesh and blood on earth or "against the spiritual forces of wickedness in the heavenly places" (Eph. 6:12). If you are in such a battle against "the adversary," look up to the One who unfurls a banner of victory.

PSALM 61

Lead Me to the Rock

¹ For the music director, on stringed instrument, of David.
² Hear my cry, O God, listen to my prayer.
³ From the end of the earth I call to You when my heart is faint.
  Lead me to the rock that is higher than I.
⁴ For You have been a refuge for me,
    a tower of strength before the enemy.
⁵ Let me dwell in Your tent forever.
    Let me take refuge in the shelter of Your wings. *Selah*

⁶ For You have heard my vows, O God.
    You have given the inheritance of those who fear Your Name.
⁷ May You add days to the king's days.
    May his years span many generations.
⁸ May he be enthroned before God forever.
    Appoint mercy and truth to protect him.
⁹ So I will sing praise to Your Name forever,
    to fulfill my vows day after day.

Jeffrey Seif and Glenn Blank

The inspirational expression "Lead me to the rock that is higher than I" (3) has special currency when viewed from the eyes of an ancient infantryman. When men fight in the field, those with high ground have a decided tactical advantage. Another military expression speaks of God as a "tower of strength" (4). A strong tower on a fortifying wall was another example of a strategically advantageous position—a stronghold against the enemy.

Does participation in biblical religion translate into similar strengthening of our position today, in the face of opposition we may face? Obviously, pastors and churches benefit from attendees and tithers. Do people in the pews benefit too? The psalmist thinks so. When he pleads, "Let me dwell in Your tent" (5), he's referring to the tent of meeting (אֹהֶל מוֹעֵד, *ohel mo-ayd*), or tabernacle of God, where God promised to meet with His people who seek His presence. Similarly, when we seek His presence as we meet together in an appointed place and time to worship Him, it is like abiding in "the shelter of Your wings" (5).

For this reason David reminds God of "vows" he once made. People in dire trouble often look upward and make vows to the Almighty, but how many actually fulfill those vows when trouble abates? Recalling his vows, this worshiper sticks with God, trusting in "the inheritance of those who fear Your Name" (6). Life with the Lord is a value-added life—especially when we resolve to fight our battles for the Lord rather than for self-preservation. He will "add days to the king's days" (7). When I abide in His tent—a place of security and protection in His lovingkindness—I gain strength within myself as well as in my relationships with others. When I "sing praise" to His Name, I gain strength, both to fight the battles of life and "to fulfill my vows day after day" (9). How about you?

✳✳✳✳✳✳✳✳✳✳✳ # PSALM 62 ✳✳✳✳✳✳✳✳✳✳✳

My Rock and My Salvation

¹ For the music director, on Jeduthun. A psalm of David.
² My soul, wait in stillness, only for God—
   from Him comes my salvation.

144

[3] He alone is my rock and my salvation,
my fortress—I will never be moved.
[4] How long will all of you assault a man,
to crush him, like a leaning wall,
a fence to be torn down?
[5] They only plot to topple him from his rank.
Delighting in falsehood, they bless with their mouth,
but inwardly they curse. *Selah*

[6] My soul, wait in stillness, only for God—
for from Him comes my expectation.
[7] He alone is my rock and my salvation,
my strong tower—I will not be moved.
[8] On God, my salvation and my glory is the rock of my strength.
My refuge is in God.
[9] Trust in Him at all times, you people.
Pour out your heart in His presence.
God is our refuge. *Selah*

[10] Sons of Adam are a vapor,
sons of man are an illusion.
In balanced scales they go up—
altogether they are less than a breath.
[11] Do not trust in extortion,
and do not put vain hope in plunder.
Though these things increase riches,
do not set your heart on them.
[12] Once God has spoken,
twice I have heard this:
might belongs to God.
[13] Also Yours, O Lord, is lovingkindness.
For You reward a man for his work.[a]

Glenn Blank

Many will recognize, from verses 2–3 and 6–7, Marty Goetz's anthem, "He is my defense." From David (1), it is a song of a man who has learned to keep waiting "in stillness, only for God" (2, 6). He has seen enough of the lies and illusions of men. When the heat is on, he knows where to turn—to the rock

a. 62:13. cf. Matt. 16:27; Rom. 2:6.

145

of our salvation, just as he did in Psalms 18:3, 47; 27:5; 61:3, and many others—where he "will never be moved" (3, 7).

When I struggle with anxiety, I sing to the rock of my salvation. It helps to know that God is "my fortress" (3), my "strong tower" (7). When the assault of David's enemies makes him feel like he is just "a leaning wall" or "a fence to be torn down" (4), he accumulates and repeats the imagery of "my rock" (3, 7, 8), my strong tower, "my refuge" (8, 9), my salvation, and "my glory" (8) to describe his almighty Friend. It strengthens his ability to trust in Him and encourages us also to "pour out" our hearts "in His presence" (8). Only the eternal One is trustworthy, for the "sons of Adam" are but "a vapor" and "less than a breath" (10; see also Eccles. 2:17, 26). Using a Hebrew idiom of counting, "once . . . twice," the poet affirms that "might belongs to God" (12)—the strength of His eternal reality. People may pursue the plunder of this world (11), but only the Lord will "reward a man" with mercy and righteousness (13).

For only the Lord—only my Messiah—is my defense and my eternal expectation. Amen?

✳✳✳✳✳✳✳✳✳ PSALM 63 ✳✳✳✳✳✳✳✳✳

You Are My God

¹ A psalm of David, when he was in the wilderness of Judah.
² O God, You are my God,
   earnestly I seek You.
   My soul thirsts for You.
   My flesh longs for You
   in a dry and weary land, where there is no water.
³ So, I looked for You in the Sanctuary,
   to see Your power and Your glory.
⁴ Since Your lovingkindness is better than life,
   my lips will praise You.
⁵ So I will bless You as long as I live.
   In Your Name I lift up my hands.ᵃ

a. 63:5. cf. 1 Tim. 2:8.

⁶ My soul is satisfied as with fat and oil,
  so my mouth praises You with joyful lips.

⁷ When I remember You on my bed,
  I meditate on You through the night watches.
⁸ For You have been my help,
  and in the shadow of Your wings I sing for joy.
⁹ My soul clings to You—
  Your right hand upholds me.
¹⁰ But those who seek my soul to destroy it
  will go down to the depths of the earth.
¹¹ They will be gutted by the sword,
  and become a prey for jackals.
¹² But the king will rejoice in God.
  All who swear by Him will boast,
 when the mouth speaking lies is shut.

Glenn Blank

David was familiar with the wilderness of Judah (1). He was there when running from Saul, and again when fleeing from Absalom—note the reference to "the king" (12). In this same Judean wilderness, the *Yom Kippur* scapegoat *Azazel* was sent to die of thirst, and *Yeshua* fasted and thirsted for forty days. Overlooking the Dead or Salt Sea, it is indeed "a dry and weary land, where there is no water" (2b). Yet, the psalmist says, greater than the thirst of "my flesh" for water is the longing of "my soul" for "my God" (2a). From the Judean desert, it is a hard climb up to Jerusalem and the Sanctuary, where David "looked for You . . . to see Your power and Your glory" (3), as the prophets Isaiah and Ezekiel saw. In the Judean desert, where one is starkly confronted with how difficult life is, it is plain that "Your lovingkindness is better than life"—like a shower for the soul, even as the flesh faints. With the strength of faith, he sings praise with his lips (4, 6) and extends blessing with his hands (5). With the "fat and oil" of rich food "my soul is satisfied" (6)—but not his body, yet.

The scene shifts in verse 7 to David in bed meditating on the Lord. Though night should be a peaceful time, "the night watches" are patrolling. Contemplating the Lord's help, David envisions himself "in the shadow of Your wings" (8)—perhaps the wings of the *cheruvim* over the ark, which he had brought into Jerusalem (2 Sam. 6:2). It is a place of protection for the soul

(9–10)—indeed, those who seek to destroy his soul will become "a prey for jackals" of the desert (11). Therefore the king rejoices in God, and "all who swear by Him will boast" (12).

Would that also include you, dear reader? When you find yourself in a weary wilderness, will you thirst for water only, or for the Spirit of God? Will your life faint, or will you lift up your hands in His Name? Will your soul fear those who seek to destroy it, or will your soul cling to Him, so that His right hand may uphold you?

PSALM 64

Protect Me from Conspiracies

¹ For the music director, a psalm of David.
² Hear my voice, O God, in my complaint.
    Protect my life from terror of the enemy.
³ Hide me from the conspiracy of evildoers,
    from the tumult of workers of iniquity,
⁴ who sharpened their tongue like a sword,
    and aimed their arrow—bitter words,
⁵ to shoot from hiding at the innocent,
    shooting suddenly at him, with no fear.
⁶ They are firming up their evil plan.
    They talk about setting secret traps.
    They asked, "Who would see them?"
⁷ They are plotting injustices:
    "We have completed a perfect plot!"
    A man's inward part and heart are deep.

⁸ But God will shoot them with an arrow—
    suddenly their wounds will appear.
⁹ So their tongue will be their downfall.
    All who see them will flee away.
¹⁰ Then all men will fear.
    So they will declare the work of God,
    and ponder what He has done.

¹¹ The righteous will be glad in ADONAI and take refuge in Him.
Let all the upright in heart give glory!

Jeffrey Seif

Occasionally when you think others are out to get you, they really are! David cried out to God to "protect my life from terror of the enemy" (2). Was "the enemy" a person or *satan*? When David had to "hide . . . from the conspiracy of evildoers" (3), were they Absalom his son and Ahithophel his once-trusted adviser, plotting to overthrow him? He fears "their tongue like a sword" (4). They "shoot from hiding" at him (5), "firming up their evil plan" (6) and "plotting injustices" (7). The extent to which the psalmist was getting ahead of reality here is open for question; he just wants to survive. What's the evil plan against him? We don't know exactly.

We do know he expects that God will lead a counterattack, for "God will shoot them with an arrow" (8). Since God might not actually come with a bow and arrow, does he expect God to work through people with weapons, or did he perceive a spiritual war behind the scenes? God might not actually trip people up, but He may otherwise see to it that "their tongue will be their downfall" (9). The net result is that "all men will fear" (10) and "the righteous will be glad" (11).

Rather than sweat the adversaries, you too can "take refuge in Him" (11). Whether your adversaries are real, spiritual, or imagined, rest assured that God is able to rout them all. When He does—and you acknowledge that He does—everyone will "ponder what He has done" (10).

✻✻✻✻✻✻ PSALM 65 ✻✻✻✻✻✻

Praise Is Awaiting You in Zion

¹ For the music director, a psalm, a song of David.
² Praise is awaiting You in Zion, O God,
and to You the vow will be fulfilled.
³ O You who hear prayer,
to You all flesh will come.

[4] Records of sins overwhelm me—
> You will atone for our transgressions.
[5] Blessed is the one You choose and bring near to dwell in Your courts!
> We will be satisfied with the goodness of Your House—Your holy
> Temple.
[6] You respond to us in righteousness with awe-inspiring works
> —O God of our salvation—
> hope of all ends of the earth and farthest seas,
[7] who establishes mountains by His power,
> being girded with might,
[8] who stills the roaring of the seas,
> the roaring of their waves,
> and the tumult of the peoples.
[9] Those dwelling in the uttermost parts stand in awe of Your signs.
> You make morning and evening shout for joy.
[10] You visit the land and make it abundant,
> greatly enriching it—
> the stream of God is full of water.
> You prepare their grain,
> for so You have prepared the earth.
[11] You drench her furrows,
> leveling the ridges.
> You soften her with showers,
> blessing her growth.
[12] You crown the year with Your goodness.
> Your wagon tracks drip with abundance.
[13] Pastures of the wilderness overflow
> and hills are robed with joy.
[14] Meadows are clothed with flocks
> and valleys are covered with grain—
> they shout for joy, yes, they sing!

Paul Wilbur

I was very pleasantly surprised when I sat to comment on this song to discover that I had set it to modern melody some twenty-five years ago. You can still hear my own version on *Introducing Israel's Hope.*[1] So . . . we're off and running! Let me begin by quoting the chorus, taken almost verbatim from David's words (2–4):

Praise is awaiting You, O God in Zion;
And to You our vows will be performed.
O You who hear prayer, to You all flesh will come,
You have provided atonement for them!

The song carries a nice lilting bounce and a lyrical melody, perhaps too whimsical for the weightiness of the opening verses, but I was younger then and perhaps a little too romantic about how life goes. Truth be told . . . I hope I haven't changed! This setting was written in a church parking lot in McClain, Virginia, waiting for the pastor to arrive and open the building so we (Israel's Hope) could begin setting up our sound equipment and instruments for the Sunday evening service. I opened my Bible to read to pass the time, and it opened right to this psalm—the chorus above nearly leaped off the page at me, and a song was born.

David's dedication to the music director, "a psalm, a song," may seem redundant, but it's not. The term translated as "psalm," *mizmor*, refers to a melody of some kind. The term for "song," *shir*, is a type of lyric, specifically a religious song. So the songs that I write today could be considered both *mizmor* and *shir*, like David's—as could all the songs written for praise and worship.

Verse 5 is particularly interesting and curious. David says *ashrei tivchar*, happy, blessed, or blissful is the "one You choose." He seems to speak about life in heaven in the presence of ADONAI, in His holy Temple. Solomon's Temple was not built for ADONAI until after David's death, so King David must have had a very clear vision and understanding about heavenly dwellings and practices. Perhaps this is one reason he so longed for the courts of the Lord and desired to build something like them on earth. The word for "blessed" at the start of this verse—the Hebrew *ashrei*—is used exclusively of people and never of ADONAI. It illuminates the state of being for all those who are in an intimate relationship with the Lord—blessed, happy, blissful. Another form of this word used as a proper name, Asher, carries the same meaning. Asher was the second son to Leah and Jacob through Zilpah and was also one of the twelve tribes of Israel.

The imagery of David is beautiful in his depiction of how ADONAI cares for His land and His people. He sets the mountains in place, stills the roaring of the seas and His people. He visits the earth and waters it; He enriches it by the river of God (also described by John in Rev. 22). He waters the furrows, feeds the people, blesses the land with showers, makes the morning and evening rejoice, crowns the year with goodness, and causes our endeavors to prosper. Pastures are clothed with flocks and valleys are mantled with grain—all creation shouts for joy and together they sing . . .

Praise is awaiting You in Zion, O God!

PSALM 66

How Awesome Your Deeds

¹ For the music director, a song, a psalm.
  Shout joyfully to God, all the earth!
² Sing the glory of His Name—
  make His praise glorious.
³ Say to God:
  "How awesome are Your deeds!
  Because of Your great power,
  Your enemies cringe before You.
⁴ All the earth bows down to You,
  and sings praises to You.
  All sing praises to Your Name." *Selah*

⁵ Come and see the works of God.
  How awesome His deeds for the children of Adam!
⁶ He turned the sea into dry land.
  They crossed the river on foot.
  There let us rejoice in Him!
⁷ He rules by His might forever.
  His eyes keep watch on the nations.
  Let no rebels exalt themselves. *Selah*

⁸ Bless our God, O peoples!
  Let the sound of His praise be heard.
⁹ Keeping our soul in life,
  He has not let our foot slip.
¹⁰ For You have tested us, O God—
  You have purified us, as silver is refined.

¹¹ You brought us into a net.
　　You laid a burden on our backs.
¹² You caused men to ride over our heads.
　　We went through fire and water.
　　Yet You brought us out to superabundance.
¹³ With burnt offerings I will come to Your House,
　　fulfilling my vows to You
¹⁴ that my lips uttered and mouth spoke,
　　when I was in trouble.
¹⁵ To You I will present burnt offerings of fat animals,
　　with the sweet smoke of rams.
　　I will offer bulls with goats. *Selah*

¹⁶ Come and listen, all you who fear God.
　　I will tell what He has done for my soul.
¹⁷ I cried out to Him with my mouth,
　　and exaltation was on my tongue.
¹⁸ If I had cherished iniquity in my heart,
　　the Lord would not have listened.
¹⁹ But surely God has heard.
　　He has listened to my voice in prayer.
²⁰ Blessed be God, who has not turned away my prayer,
　　nor His lovingkindness from me.

Jeffrey Seif and Glenn Blank

The word *awesome* has made its way into popular vocabulary. Young people will say a new computer product is "awesome," a new friend is "awesome," a sports outing was "awesome." While products may be great, while people may be great, and while athletic competitions may indeed bring out greatness, the psalmist reserves "awesome" for God alone, exclaiming, "How awesome are Your deeds!" (3, 5). Yes. His enemies cringe and "the children of Adam" marvel at His creative genius and His redemptive power (5–7). The scope of His awesomeness is both international—"Bless our God, O peoples" (8)—and intimately personal, "keeping our soul in life" (9).

His awesomeness gives us a different perspective on our trials—instead of complaining as our ancestors did in the wilderness, the psalmist sees testing as further evidence of his awesome relationship with God. "You have purified us, as silver is refined" (10)—one of the first mentions of this theme of comparing life's ordeals to a refiner's fire (see also Isa. 48:10; Zech. 13:9; Mal. 3:3; 1 Pet. 1:7). The image of causing "men to ride over our heads" reflects a cruel practice of ancient kings literally riding the chariots over people they conquered. Yet God brings His people through it all, "to superabundance" (12)—see *Yeshua's* promise of abundant life in John 10:10. That's awesome, isn't it?

The poet has seen the worst of it and has come out on the other side—better than before! So he promises to offer superabundant sacrifices (15) and to share his testimony to all who fear God (16). God is so awesome, he knows your heart—"If I had cherished iniquity in my heart . . ." (18), and He also hears your voice in prayer (19) and will never withhold His mercy from you (20). Does His awesomeness (and His awesome promises) inspire you to put your hope in God? Can you expect that He will lead you through your tests to the absolute best He has for you? Then you will also say, God is "awesome!"

PSALM 67

Let All Peoples Praise You

¹ For the music director, with stringed instruments, a psalm, a song.
² May God be gracious to us and bless us.
　　May He cause His face to shine upon us—*Selah*
³ so that Your way may be known on earth,
　　and Your salvation among all nations.
⁴ Let the peoples praise You, O God.
　　Let all the peoples praise You.
⁵ Let the nations be glad and sing for joy,
　　for You will judge the peoples fairly,
　　and guide the nations on the earth. *Selah*
⁶ Let the peoples praise You, O God.
　　Let all the peoples praise You.
⁷ The earth has yielded its harvest—
　　God, our God will bless us.
⁸ God will bless us,
　　and all the ends of the earth will fear Him.

Jeffrey Seif and Glenn Blank

Some folks disrespect the *Tanakh* (Hebrew Scriptures) these days. "It belongs to yesterday," they say. It's just for Jews—or was for the Jews, before Jesus (*Yeshua*) came. Or, it's just a lot of laws—and now we're no longer "under law but under grace" (Rom. 6:14–15—see our commentary on Ps. 119). This psalmist reminds us that there was plenty of grace in those days too! "May God be gracious to us and bless us. May He cause His face to shine upon us" (2). Actually, he is referencing Numbers 6:24–26, the "Aaronic Benediction." God—back in the *Torah* of Moses—instructed the high priest (*kohen gadol*) to put this gracious blessing on the children of Israel. To this day, rabbis (and Messianic rabbis) close services with this blessing. Many reverends utter it too. Why not? It's in the Bible! With this abiding prayer, Israelites were forever reminded that God wants always to bless His people. He was gracious in His calling of Abraham, gracious in hearing the children of Israel cry out for deliverance, gracious in delivering our ancestors again and again from their oppressors in the land, gracious to Rahab and gracious to Ruth and Naomi, gracious in sending the prophets, gracious in promising the Messiah.

God is gracious—yesterday, today, and forever! This psalm celebrates the way of salvation, which God makes known "among all nations" (3)—would that be looking forward to *Yeshua*? Then there's grace (and rejoicing) because God judges the people fairly (according to the guidance of *Torah*). More blessings come with financial implications: "The earth has yielded its harvest," so much so that we say "our God will bless us" (7).

God hasn't changed. He has always been gracious to people. Thanks to *Yeshua* as well as a better understanding of His Word, people are learning to appreciate Him more and more. Therefore, "Let the peoples praise You, O God" (6).

PSALM 68

Triumphal Procession up to the Temple

¹ For the music director, a psalm of David, a song.
² Let God arise!
    Let His enemies be scattered!
    Let those who hate Him flee before Him.

³ As smoke is blown away,
   may You blow them away.
      As wax melts before the fire,
   may the wicked perish before God.
⁴ But let the righteous be glad.
      Let them exult before God.
      Let them rejoice with gladness.
⁵ Sing to God, sing praises to His Name.
      Prepare the road for Him who rides through the deserts,
   whose Name is ADONAI—
      and rejoice before Him.
⁶ A father of orphans, defender of widows,
      is God in His holy dwelling.
⁷ God settles the lonely in a home.
      He leads prisoners out to prosperity.
      But the rebellious live in a parched land.

⁸ O God, when You went out before Your people,
      when You marched through the desert—*Selah*—
⁹ the earth shook, the heavens rained
      at the presence of God—the One of Sinai—
      at the presence of God, God of Israel.
¹⁰ You poured down abundant rain, O God.
      You sustained Your weary inheritance.
¹¹ Your community settled in it.
      In Your goodness, O God, You provided for the poor.
¹² The Lord gives the word—
      a great company of women proclaims the good news.
¹³ "Kings of armies, flee, flee!"
      She who stays at home divides the spoil.
¹⁴ When you lie among the campfires,
      wings of a dove were covered with silver
      and her feathers with shimmering gold.
¹⁵ When *Shaddai* scattered kings there,
      it was snowing on Zalmon.
¹⁶ Mount Bashan is a mountain of God.
      Mount Bashan is a mountain of peaks.
¹⁷ Why do you gaze with envy, you mountain peaks,
      at the mountain God desired for His dwelling?
      Yes, ADONAI will dwell there forever!

[18] The chariots of God are thousands and thousands
  —my Lord is among them as at Sinai, in holiness.
[19] You went up on high.
    You led captivity captive.
    You received gifts from humanity,[a]
  even from the rebellious—
    so that God might dwell there.

[20] Blessed be my Lord!
    Day by day He bears our burdens—
  the God of our salvation! *Selah*
[21] God is for us—a God of deliverance.
    ADONAI my Lord has escapes from death.
[22] Surely God crushes the head of His foes,
    the hairy scalp of one walking in his guilt.
[23] My Lord said:
    "I will bring them back from Bashan,
    I will bring them back from the depths of the sea.
[24] So your foot may wade in blood,
    and your dogs' tongues may have their share of your enemies' blood."

[25] They have seen Your processions, O God—
    the processions of my God, my King, into the Sanctuary:
[26] The singers go before, the musicians last,
    between maidens beating tambourines.
[27] "Bless God in the congregations—
    ADONAI, from the fountain of Israel."
[28] There Benjamin, the youngest, is leading them,
    there the throng of Judah's princes,
    there the princes of Zebulun,
    there the princes of Naphtali.
[29] Your God commanded your strength.
    Strengthen, O God,
    You who have acted for us.
[30] From Your Temple above Jerusalem,
    kings bring You tribute.
[31] Rebuke the beast of the reeds,
    the herd of bulls with the calves,
    peoples trampling down pieces of silver.
    He has scattered the peoples who delight in war!

a. 68:19. cf. Eph. 4:8.

³² Nobles come from Egypt.

    Cush runs to stretch her hands to God.

³³ Sing to God, kingdoms of the earth,

    sing praises to the Lord—*Selah*—

³⁴ to Him who rides upon the ancient heavens of heavens.

    Look, He utters His voice, a mighty voice!

³⁵ Ascribe strength to God—

    His majesty is over Israel

    and His strength is in the skies.

³⁶ O God, You are awesome from Your holy places.

    The God of Israel gives strength and power to the people.

    Blessed be God!

Glenn Blank

When the *Torah* scroll comes out of the ark in our synagogues, we chant Numbers 10:35, "Whenever the Ark would set out, Moses would say: 'Arise, ADONAI! May Your enemies be scattered! May those who hate You flee from before You!'" After we recite Isaiah 2:3 (a prophecy of the Messianic age), the scroll is carried in a procession through the aisles of the synagogue with honor and singing and great rejoicing. Such a triumphant procession the psalmist envisions, as he paraphrases Numbers 10:35 in verse 2, "Let God arise! Let His enemies be scattered!" God's presence stirs passion—blowing away His enemies like smoke and melting the wicked like wax (3). The presence of God rouses joy and gladness (4), as the people "sing praises to His Name." The procession reminds us of the march of Israel from Sinai, as we "prepare the road for Him who rides through the deserts" (5). (Isa. 40:3 and Matt. 3:3 also speak of preparing a way in the wilderness for *HaShem*.)

    The righteous God of Moses arises as "a father of orphans, defender of widows" (6; Exod. 22:21; Jacob [James] 1:27), the comforter of the lonely and the liberator of captives (7). The procession through the wilderness (8) recalls the scene at Sinai (Exod. 19:18), when "the earth shook" at the presence of the God of Israel (9). A sign of the presence of the God of the heavens is that He "poured down abundant rain" (10) for His community and the poor (11). He sends a company of women to proclaim "the good news" (12)—like Miriam and the women at the Sea of Reeds (Exod. 15:20–21) or the women reporting that *Yeshua* had risen from the tomb (Luke 24:10). God is good!

The excitement spreads. At the coming presence of ADONAI-*Tsva'ot*, other "kings of armies" flee (13), for "*Shaddai* scattered kings" (15). His glorious presence is compared to a dove "covered with silver" and "shimmering gold" among the campfires of Israel (14). Though the peaks of Bashan (16) in Golan and Syria—including snowcapped Mount Hermon—are the tallest in the region, they "gaze with envy" at Zion, "the mountain God desired for His dwelling" (17). Moreover, just as God empowered Israel to conquer Bashan (Num. 21:34), so He has strengthened David and Solomon to subdue and rule over that region (1 Kings 4:7, 13). Like the "mountain . . . full of horses and chariots of fire all around Elisha" (2 Kings 6:17), the psalmist sees the heavenly chariots of God on Mount Zion just as at Sinai (18). Like a sovereign on His throne in heaven, *HaShem* receives gifts from humanity (19).

Yet our God is gracious, daily bearing our burdens (20; see Ps. 55:23; Matt. 11:30). The God of our salvation gives "deliverance" and "escapes from death" to His servants (21). His power assures His people victory over their heathen enemies (24).

Though the nations had idols of metal and stone, the God of Israel is invisible. So the processions of the ark were seen as "processions of my God, my King," to the sanctuary (25). Levitical singers were appointed to lead the procession with maidens (again like Miriam) beating tambourines (26). All the congregations (27) of the tribes sent delegations—including Benjamin, from whom Saul and Jonathan came, and Judah, from whom David and Solomon came, and Zebulun and Naphtali, two prominent tribes of the north (28). The mention of the tribes retains the memory of their role in the Davidic kingdom. The God of Israel has "commanded your strength" (29), so that neighboring kings brought tribute to the Temple in Jerusalem (30). Even Egypt—the beast or hippopotamus in the reeds of the Nile (31) must send nobles, and also Cush to the south of Egypt (32), as well as all the "kingdoms of the earth" (33).

Yet the God of Israel cannot really be contained in the ark or even the Temple. For He "rides upon the ancient heavens of heavens" (34). His "majesty is over Israel" and "His strength is in the skies" (35)—far above all gods (Ps. 97:9) and "far above any ruler, authority, power, leader, and every name that is named" (Eph. 1:21). Truly He is awesome. Truly "the God of Israel gives strength and power to the people" (36). It is no wonder that this psalm has inspired devoted Jews and Christians for generation after generation. O God, let us catch a glimpse of Your glory in our houses of worship! Open the eyes of our hearts to behold Your glory and goodness! Let God arise!

PSALM 69

Scorn and Disgrace, Gall and Vinegar

[1] For the music director, on "Lilies," of David.
[2] Save me, O God,
    for the waters
    have reached my soul.
[3] I have sunk in deep mud,
  and there is no footing,
    I have come into deep waters,
  and a flood sweeps over me.
[4] I am worn out by my crying,
    my throat is parched,
    my eyes fail, waiting for my God.
[5] Those who hate me without a cause [a] outnumber the hairs of my head.
    Powerful are my enemies who would destroy me with lies.
    What I did not steal, must I restore?
[6] O God, You know my folly,
    nor are my trespasses hidden from You.
[7] May those who hope in You
  not be ashamed because of me,
  my Lord, *ADONAI-Tzva'ot.*
    May those who seek You
  not be disgraced because of me,
  O God of Israel.
[8] For I have endured scorn for Your sake.
    Disgrace has covered my face.
[9] I have become a stranger to my brothers,
    a foreigner to my mother's children.
[10] For zeal for Your House consumed me—
    the insults of those who insulted You have fallen on me. [b]

a. 69:5. cf. John 15:25.
b. 69:10. cf. John 2:17; Rom. 15:3.

[11] When I wept and fasted—
　　that became a reproach to me.
[12] When I put on sackcloth,
　　I became a joke to them.
[13] Those who sit at the gate chatter about me,
　　and I am the song of the drunkards.

[14] But as for me, my prayer to You, ADONAI, is for a time of favor.
　　O God, in Your great love, answer me with the truth of Your
　　　salvation.
[15] Deliver me from the mire—
　do not let me sink.
　　Deliver me from those who hate me,
　out of the deep waters.
[16] Do not let floodwaters sweep over me,
　　nor the deep swallow me up,
　　nor the Pit shut its mouth over me.
[17] Answer me, ADONAI, for good is Your mercy.
　　With Your great compassion, turn to me.
[18] Hide not Your face from Your servant.
　　For I am in distress—answer me quickly.
[19] Draw near to my soul and redeem it.
　　Ransom me because of my foes.
[20] You know my reproach, my shame, my disgrace.
　　All my adversaries are before You.
[21] Scorn has broken my heart, so I am sick.
　　I looked for sympathy, but there was none,
　　for comforters, but found none.
[22] They put gall in my food,
　　and for my thirst they gave me vinegar to drink.[c]
[23] Let their table before them be a snare,
　　and what should have been for their well-being,
　　let it be a trap.
[24] Let their eyes be darkened so they cannot see
　　and their backs be bent forever.[d]
[25] Pour out Your indignation on them.
　　Let Your fierce anger overtake them.

c. 69:22. cf. Matt. 27:34, 48; Mark 15:23, 36.
d. 69:23–24. cf. Rom. 11:9–10.

²⁶ Let their encampment be deserted.
    Let none dwell in their tents.
²⁷ For they persecute the one You have smitten,
    so they tell of the pain
    of those You have wounded.
²⁸ Add guilt to their guilt—
    may they not come into Your righteousness.
²⁹ May they be wiped out of the book of life
    and not be recorded with the righteous.[a]

³⁰ But I—I am afflicted and in pain.
    Let Your salvation, O God, set me up on high.
³¹ I will praise God's Name with a song,
    and magnify Him with praise.
³² It will please *ADONAI* better than an ox
    or a bull with horns and hoofs.
³³ The humble will see it and be glad.
    You who seek God, let your hearts revive.
³⁴ For *ADONAI* hears the needy
    and does not despise His captive people.
³⁵ Let heaven and earth praise Him,
    the seas and everything moving in them.
³⁶ For God will save Zion,
    and rebuild the cities of Judah.
    Then they will dwell there and possess it.
³⁷ The children of His servants will inherit it
    and those who love His Name will dwell there.

Jeffrey Seif and Glenn Blank

Those who love the Psalms may not all love this one. It starts off on a down note. Those who come to God to escape their troubles hear that the psalmist was also in desperate straits: "Save me, O God, for the waters have reached my soul" (2). First it's drowning in water, then it's sinking in "deep mud" with no footing (3). Ugh! Hardly an enviable predicament. Yet it's also the stuff of life. Can we learn how to navigate these muddy waters?

It turns out the problem isn't really mud—that was a metaphor—it's problem people. They "hate me without a cause" (5). This problem is more familiar

a. 69:29. cf. Rev. 3:5.

to most of us than mud holes. David begins to wonder if he is responsible—"O God, You know my folly . . . my trespasses" (6). Then he shifts the basis of his appeal away from self-pity to concern for others—"may those who hope in You not be ashamed because of me" (7). Wise move. Nevertheless, he cannot help feeling sorry for himself: "Disgrace has covered my face" (8), for he has became the song of drunkards (12–13). Amid it all, he fixes his gaze toward God (14) and begs deliverance from the metaphorical mire (15–16).

More and more, the protagonist of this poem, as he pours out his soul to God, resembles the Suffering Servant of Psalm 22 and Isaiah 53. Because "zeal for Your House consumed me" (10), more persecution follows (see Matt. 26:67; Mark 14:65). Despite his ordeal, the sufferer retains his faith in *HaShem's* mercy and compassion to answer him, draw near, and ransom him from his foes (17–19). He dramatizes the reproach of all his adversaries, looking for comforters but finding none (20–21). Then comes a verse quoted in all of the Gospels: "They put gall in my food . . . they gave me vinegar to drink" (22).

Some modern readers find the next passage difficult—an imprecatory prayer cursing unjust enemies, urging God to "add guilt to their guilt" (28). Eternal destiny is at stake, as the psalmist asks that "they be wiped out of the book of life" (29). (For more about cursing passages, see our commentary on Ps. 109.)

Having poured out his heart, the psalmist turns to praise. The transition from the curse of verse 29 to the confidence in salvation in verse 30 and the song of praise in verse 31 is striking. Yet from the point of view of passionate and personal faith, it is coherent. Prayer is how you talk directly to God when you really trust Him. He is confident that faith-filled praise "will please ADONAI better than an ox" (32)—a hefty sacrifice! Though the boastful had their moment, the humble with God will prevail, because they "seek God" (33) and God "hears the needy" (34).

Finally, the psalmist goes politically incorrect again—*oy*, he's a Zionist! "God will save Zion, and rebuild the cities of Judah" (36). Throughout the Bible, there is an inextricable relationship between God, Jews, and the land of Israel. As with many other psalms, personal and national concerns mix together. A Jewish reader should understand that his connection with Zion is part and parcel of his identity. What if you are not Jewish? If you have put your trust in *Yeshua*—the Messiah and King of Israel—then your roots and identity are also grounded in the Holy Land.

✳✳✳✳✳✳✳✳✳ PSALM 70 ✳✳✳✳✳✳✳✳✳✳

My Help and My Deliverer

¹ For the music director, of David, for a memorial.
² O God, come quickly to deliver me,
    ADONAI, to help me.
³ May they be put to shame and disgrace
  who seek my life.
    May they be turned back in humiliation
  who delight in my hurt.
⁴ May those who say, "Aha! Aha!"
  be turned away because of their shame.
⁵ But may all who seek You
  rejoice and be glad in You.
    May those who love Your salvation
  always say, "Let God be magnified."
⁶ But I am poor and needy—
  God, come quickly to me.
    You are my help and my deliverer—
  ADONAI, do not delay.

Jeffrey Seif and Glenn Blank

One thing about walking with the Lord is that when we feel we need Him, we tend to need Him *now*—up close and in the moment. We can relate to the immediacy of the petition, "O God, come quickly to deliver me" (2). After troubling about others who are troubling him (3–4), the psalmist lifts up his head: "May all who seek You rejoice and be glad in You" (5). Then back he goes down to the pits: "I am poor and needy—God, come quickly" (6). And that's the psalm. What is the *Ruach HaKodesh*, who inspired and preserved it, telling us? This back and forth, this going from malaise to praise and back, prompts some musing. What does the Spirit of God think when we too weave in and out of our moments of encouragement and discouragement?

Precarious as life is, and difficult as people in our webs of relationships can be, it doesn't take much to get thrown out of kilter. Life happens, and disorientation comes in a moment. So can reorientation—when we decide to fix our gaze on God's "salvation" again (5). Like the psalmist, we are sometimes forced to say, "I need You, and I need You now!" The Comforter hears us. The Counselor reminds us, be determined, seek Him in prayer, and lift up His Name—through good times and bad. He promises: those who seek Him will find Him—and once again "rejoice and be glad."

❋❋❋❋❋❋❋❋❋❋ PSALM 71 ❋❋❋❋❋❋❋❋❋❋

My Hope When I Am Gray

¹ In You, ADONAI, have I taken refuge.
    Let me never be ashamed.
² Deliver me and rescue me in Your justice.
    Turn Your ear to me and save me.
³ Be to me a sheltering rock where I may always go.
    Give the command to save me—
  for You are my rock and my fortress.
⁴ My God, rescue me out of the hand of the wicked,
    out of the grasp of an evil, ruthless man.
⁵ For You are my hope, ADONAI my Lord—
    my trust from my youth.
⁶ From my birth I have leaned on You.
    You took me out of my mother's womb.
    My praise is always about You.
⁷ I am like an ominous sign to many,
    but You are my strong refuge.
⁸ My mouth is filled with Your praise
    and with Your glory all day.

⁹ Do not cast me away in the time of old age.
    When my strength fails, do not forsake me.
¹⁰ For my enemies speak against me.
    Those who watch for my soul conspire together,
¹¹ saying: "God has forsaken him—
    Pursue and take him, for no one will deliver."

¹² O God, be not far from me!
  My God, come quickly to help me.
¹³ Let the accusers of my soul
  be disgraced and destroyed.
    Let those who seek to harm me
  be covered with scorn and confusion.

¹⁴ But I—I will hope continually
  and will praise You more and more.
¹⁵ My mouth will recount Your justice and Your salvation all day,
  though I do not know the sum of them.
¹⁶ I come because of the mighty deeds of ADONAI my Lord.
  I will remember Your righteousness—Yours alone.
¹⁷ God, You taught me from my youth,
  and I still keep declaring Your wonders.
¹⁸ So even until I am old and gray, O God, do not forsake me,
  till I tell of Your strong arm to the next generation,
  Your might to all who are to come.
¹⁹ For Your righteousness, O God,
  reaches to high heaven.
    You have done great things—O God,
  who is like You?
²⁰ You made me see many troubles and evils
  —You will revive me again—
    from the depths of the earth
  You will bring me up again.
²¹ You will increase my greatness,
  and comfort me once again.
²² So I will praise You with the harp for your truth, O my God.
  I will sing praises to You with the lyre, O Holy One of Israel.
²³ My lips will shout for joy
  —when I sing praises to You—
    and my soul, which You have redeemed.
²⁴ Also my tongue will tell of Your righteousness all day.

Glenn Blank and Jeffrey Seif

In this era of ever-increasing life expectancies, assisted living, and nursing homes, this psalm becomes even more relevant. You don't need to be "old and gray" (18) to feel its poignancy. You just have to have a heart of compassion and a willingness to pray. The psalmist appeals to *HaShem* as his "refuge" (1) to rescue and save him (2), to be "a sheltering rock" and a "fortress" (3). What seems to be the problem? An "evil, ruthless man" (4) is bringing him down. For shame! Alas, the elderly are prey. The word "ruthless" reminds us (though it's not the actual etymology) of a woman named Ruth. The covenant loyalty of this Moabite woman for her Jewish mother-in-law so impressed the citizens of Bethlehem (especially the benevolent Boaz) that she became one of the most famous women in the Bible. Those without Ruth's virtues—notably the virtue of loving care for the aged—are truly ruthless.

The elderly poet looks back over his life, going back to his youth (5) and his birth (6). He recalls a life full of praise and glory for God (8). To have this perspective on life lived is invaluable. Yet now "in the time of old age, when my strength fails," he (or she) worries about being "cast . . . away" (9). No wonder grandparents cling to their grandchildren! Yet how many have no one to visit them! It is especially trying when he feels he's become "an ominous sign" (7) or when old foes conspiring against him "watch for" his soul (10) and whisper, "God has forsaken him" (11). These enemies of the soul are not so much flesh and blood as the kind that plagues a lonely heart.

The answer to this dilemma is one that we find—along with much of the language of this poem—throughout the Psalter. It is the answer for dilemmas of all ages. Again and again, the elderly call on God for help and refuge (2, 3, 4, 7, 12). Again and again, they surrender their worries to God and renew their hope in God's justice (4–5, 12–13, 20–21). Again and again, they fill their mouths with praise for God (6, 8, 14, 17, 22, 23). It is ageless wisdom: the praise of *HaShem* renews the soul with hope and *shalom*.

The good news is that no matter how old or young you are, the Eternal One hears your prayers. Though He may allow you to see "troubles and evils" in this life, be sure that the Just One will revive you again and bring you up "from the depths of the earth" (20)—as surely as He has raised *Yeshua* from the dead. Keep calling on the Comforter, for He will comfort you "once again" (21). Keep singing the praises of the "Holy One of Israel" (22), for He will redeem your soul (23), forever.

✳✳✳✳✳✳ PSALM 72 ✳✳✳✳✳✳

A Powerful King for the Poor

¹ Of Solomon.
    Give the king Your judgments, O God,
      and Your righteousness to the king's son.
² May he judge Your people with righteousness,
    and Your poor ones with justice.
³ Let the mountains bring *shalom* to the people,
    and the hills righteousness.
⁴ May he vindicate the poor of the people,
    save the children of the needy,
    and crush the oppressor.
⁵ Let them fear You while the sun endures,
    and while the moon lasts, throughout all generations.
⁶ May he be like rain falling on a mown field,
    like showers watering the ground.
⁷ Let the righteous flourish in his days.
    Let *shalom* abound till the moon is no more.
⁸ May he have dominion from sea to sea,
    and from the River to the ends of the earth.
⁹ Let desert dwellers bow before him,
    and his enemies lick the dust.
¹⁰ May kings of Tarshish and the islands bring tribute,
    kings of Sheba and Seba offer gifts.
¹¹ So let all kings bow down before him,
    and all nations serve him.

¹² For he rescues the needy crying for help,
    also the poor and the one with no helper.
¹³ He will take pity on the poor and needy,
    and the souls of the needy he will save.
¹⁴ From oppression and violence he redeems their soul,
    for precious is their blood in his sight.
¹⁵ Long may he live!
    May gold from Sheba be given to him.
    May he pray for him continually,
and bless him all day.

[16] Let there be abundance of grain in the land.
　　Let it sway on the top of the hills,
　　let its fruit be like Lebanon,
　　and let people of the city flourish like grass of the field.
[17] May his name endure forever.
　　May his name increase before the sun,
　　and may all nations be blessed by him
　　and call him blessed.

[18] Blessed be *Adonai Elohim*, God of Israel,
　　who alone does wonders.
[19] Blessed be His glorious Name forever.
　　May all the earth be filled with His glory!
　　Amen and Amen!
[20] The prayers of David son of Jesse are complete.

Glenn Blank

The poet paints a portrayal of a perfect king. He suggests Solomon (1), who was indeed the most powerful of Israel's kings; the double mention of Sheba's tribute (10, 15) recalls the queen who came from that distant land south of Israel. Yet the king envisioned in this poem is far greater both in dominion—"from sea to sea ... to the ends of the earth" (8) and in righteousness (1, 2). Though Solomon was renowned for the wisdom of his judgment (1 Kings 3:28), neither he nor any of the kings of Israel and Judah demonstrated this ideal king's determination to "judge ... Your poor ones with justice" (2), "vindicate the poor" (4), rescue "the needy crying for help" (12), and "take pity on the poor and needy," let alone "the souls of the needy ... save" (13). Solomon devoted most of his energies to building projects and pleasures. People complained to his successor about the heavy yoke Solomon had put on them (1 Kings 12:4). Neither Kings nor Chronicles mentions a monarch who was so mindful of justice for the needy. Rather, this ideal echoes those of the *Torah* (Deut. 17:16–18), Proverbs (29:18), and the prophets (Isa. 11:4; Jer. 22:16; Amos 8:3–4).

Who is this epitome of emperors, whose justice crushes the oppressor (4), whose grace is "like showers watering the ground" (6), who makes "*shalom* abound till the moon is no more" (7)? Who is it whose "enemies lick the dust" (9) and who "all kings bow down before" (11), who redeems the souls of the needy, "for precious is their blood in his sight" (14)? Who is this king of glory—to whom we must pray continually (15), who causes abundance to flourish (16), whose Name endures as long as the sun and by whom all nations will be blessed (17)? He is certainly no mundane, mortal monarch—He is King Messiah! He is the One anointed to proclaim Good News to the poor (Isa. 61:1; Luke 4:18) and who announced to the poor, "Yours is the kingdom of God" (Luke 6:20). He is the One who will "save the children of the needy" (4). May His Name be blessed and endure forever (17)!

Psalms 41, 72, 89, 106, and 150 each close a collection of psalms with a doxology—from the Greek, *doxa* means "glory" and *logos* means "word," hence verses glorifying *HaShem*. Perhaps each of these five collections was once its own scroll, or perhaps the five books are like the five books of *Torah*. The doxology of this psalm—exalting God "who alone does wonders" (18) and blessing "His glorious Name"—also exalts the ideal King. Only the One in perfect unity with the glorious God of Israel will measure up to these ideals. "May all the earth be filled with His glory! Amen and Amen!" (19).

PSALM 73

God Is the Strength of My Heart

¹ A psalm of Asaph.
    Surely God is good to Israel,
      to the pure in heart.
² But as for me, my feet almost slipped.
      My steps nearly slid out from under me.
³ For I envied the arrogant,
      when I saw the prosperity of the wicked.
⁴ For there are no pains at their death,
      their body is healthy.
⁵ They have none of humanity's trouble,
      nor are they plagued like others.
⁶ Therefore, they put on pride as a necklace,
      and violence wraps around them like a garment.

⁷ Their eyes bulge out from fatness.
    The imaginations of their hearts run wild.
⁸ They scoff and wickedly plan evil.
    From on high they threaten.
⁹ They set their mouth against heaven.
    Their tongue struts through the earth.
¹⁰ Therefore His people return here,
    while they drink their fill.
¹¹ So they say: "How does God know?
    And does *Elyon* have knowledge?"
¹² Behold, such are the wicked—
    always at ease and amassing wealth.
¹³ Surely in vain have I kept my heart pure,
    and washed my hands in innocence.
¹⁴ For all day I have been stricken,
    my chastisement comes every morning.

¹⁵ If I had said: "I will speak thus,"
    surely I would have betrayed a generation of Your children.
¹⁶ But when I tried to make sense of this,
    it was troubling in my eyes—
¹⁷ until I entered the Sanctuary of God,
    and perceived their end.
¹⁸ Surely You put them in slippery places.
    You hurled them down to destruction.
¹⁹ How suddenly they became a ruin—
    terminated, consumed by terrors.
²⁰ Like a dream when one awakes,
    thus when You arise, my Lord,
You will despise their form.
²¹ When my heart was embittered
    and I was pierced in my heart,
²² I was brutish and ignorant.
    I was like a beast before You.
²³ Yet I am continually with You.
    You hold my right hand.
²⁴ You guide me with Your counsel,
    and afterward You will take me into glory.

²⁵ Whom have I in heaven but You?
    On earth there is none I desire besides You.

²⁶ My flesh and my heart may fail,

    but God is the strength of my heart

    and my portion forever.

²⁷ For behold, those far from You will perish.

    You put an end to all who like a harlot are unfaithful to You.

²⁸ But for me, it is good to be near God.

    I have made my Lord *ADONAI* my refuge.

    So I will tell of all Your works.

Jeffrey Seif and Glenn Blank

"Surely God is good to Israel, to the pure in heart" (1). This psalm opens with a promising statement of faith. But it will take awhile to get back to it. With Israel's tough go of it through human history, many Jews have looked at God and said to themselves: "With friends like this, who needs enemies?" So our psalmist admits, he "almost slipped" (2)—not literally but figuratively, in his walk of faith. He couldn't help noticing the "prosperity of the wicked" (3). How come such people appear to be getting the blessings of wealth and health (4) but "none of humanity's trouble" (5)? How come God doesn't seem to notice how "they put on pride as a necklace" (6) and "their eyes bulge out from fatness" (7)? The poet is certainly laying it on thick, isn't he? It climaxes with their big boast, the haughty question (11): "How does God know?"

Then the poet wonders if his pure, godly life has been "in vain" (13). He starts to complain about his chastisement (14), but then catches himself. (Wait a moment. Have you ever caught yourself complaining this way?) Then he remembers his responsibility. If he had vented this way, "I would have betrayed a generation of Your children" (15). In other words, it's one thing to vent to God, but you may want to consider the effect your venting can have on others.

Instead of just trying to "make sense of this" (16) on his own, he "entered the Sanctuary of God." There's wisdom: if something is bothering you, take it to God in prayer. There, he got a perspective from eternity—he "perceived their end" (17). Though the wicked may seem "always at ease" (12), they will suddenly be hurled down to ruin and terrors (19). Though it may seem as if God is sleeping, "when You arise, my Lord," the judgment will come (20). That eternal perspective pierced his heart (21), so that he realized just how "brutish and ignorant" (22) his thoughts had been before God. Now he appreciates that God holds his right hand, guides and counsels him, and afterward will take him "into glory" (23–24).

Scholars debate about whether the poet is actually looking forward to eternal life, but to us it seems so. He might not clearly know what eternal life will be like, but then, how do we? The important thing is the eternal perspective.

The poet recovers his equilibrium, closing with another promising statement of faith: "Whom have I in heaven but You?" (25). In the end, he knows "it is good to be near God" (28). In between, we have the questions of an honest man. Isn't it good to know that we can be honest with God? The psalmist could have slipped into pious self-righteousness but didn't. Isn't it good to know that God will redeem us from ourselves if we let Him? The secret is to take what troubles you to God, enter His sanctuary, and let Him give you His eternal perspective. Then you too will come out saying, "It is good to be near God." Yes, surely God is good.

PSALM 74

Intercession for Restoration of Zion

¹ A contemplative song of Asaph.
   Why have You cast us off forever, O God?
   Why does Your anger smolder against the flock of Your pasture?
² Remember Your congregation, which You purchased of old,
   redeemed as the tribe of Your inheritance,
   and Mount Zion, where You dwelt.
³ Lift Your steps toward the perpetual ruins—
   an enemy has done all evil to the Sanctuary!
⁴ Your adversaries have roared in the midst of Your meeting place.
   They have set up their standards as signs.
⁵ It seemed like bringing up axes
   into a thicket of trees—
⁶ and now all its carved work
   they smash with hatchet and hammers!
⁷ They set Your Sanctuary on fire,
   burning it to the ground.
   They defiled the dwelling place of Your Name.

⁸ They said in their hearts: "Let us crush them totally!"
  They burned down all the meeting places of God in the land.
⁹ We do not see our signs.
  No longer is there any prophet—
  and no one among us knows how long.
¹⁰ How long, O God, will the adversary mock?
  Will the enemy revile Your Name forever?
¹¹ Why do You hold back Your hand, Your right hand?
  Draw it out of Your bosom and consume them!

¹² Yet God is my King of old,
  working salvation in the midst of the land.
¹³ You split the sea with Your power.
  You smashed the monsters' heads in the waters.
¹⁴ You crushed the heads of Leviathan,
  giving him as food to the desert dwellers.
¹⁵ You opened up spring and brook.
  You dried up ever-flowing rivers.
¹⁶ The day is Yours, the night also is Yours.
  You provided moon and sun.
¹⁷ You set all the borders of earth.
  You made summer and winter.
¹⁸ Remember how the enemy mocked, ADONAI,
  and how foolish people despised Your Name.
¹⁹ Do not deliver Your turtledove's soul to the wild beast.
  Do not forget the life of Your afflicted ones forever.
²⁰ Look upon the covenant—for haunts of violence
  fill the dark places of earth.
²¹ Do not let the oppressed turn back in shame.
  But let the poor and needy praise Your Name.
²² Rise up O God, and defend Your cause.
  Remember how the fool mocks You all day.
²³ Do not forget the noise of Your foes,
  the uproar of those rising up against You,
  ascending continually.

Glenn Blank and Jeffrey Seif

Sometimes people ask hard questions. Apparently God can handle it, because the Bible and especially the Psalms are full of them. Here's a doozy: "Why have You cast us off forever, O God?" (1). Job, David, Jeremiah, Habakkuk, *Yeshua*, and plenty of others have thrown such a question at God, when they feel like He has forgotten or forsaken them. Even rabbis and pastors may feel this way when acute problems assail their ministries, just as all people do when troubles seem overwhelming. If God just forgot about us, perhaps a reminder would help—"Hey, we're still down here! How about a little help?" If He has rejected us, a reminder would do little good. But we'd still need His help, more than ever.

The first movement of this song (1–11) is a vivid painting of a tragic scene. Asaph—one of the Levites who ministered in the Temple—feels cast off forever. He begs God to "remember Your congregation"—the one for whom he once had prepared sacrifices—"which You purchased of old" (2). His sense of God's abandonment comes because of the destruction on Mount Zion. It's sometime after 586 BCE and God's Sanctuary—the Temple that Solomon had built four hundred years before—now lies in "perpetual ruins" (3). It is still painful to think that heathen "adversaries have roared in the midst of Your meeting place" and "set up their standards" (4) there (presumably exalting their gods). Ruthlessly they demolished "all its carved work" and smashed "with hatchet and hammers" everything in the holy place (6), then set it "on fire, burning it to the ground" and thus "defiled the dwelling place of Your Name" (7). How it hurts to imagine this same scene replayed when the Romans demolished the Second Temple, or when, century after century, hatemongers burned down precious synagogues.

In the second movement of the psalm (12–17), Asaph calmly sees the calamity as temporary—since "God is my King of old" who is still "working salvation" (12). This faith comes on the basis of God's ancient covenant with Israel. The poet stakes his convictions not on his circumstances, which are bleak, but on the saving power of God through the ages. He is still the One who "split the sea" (13) and "crushed the heads of Leviathan" (14)—a poetic way of describing the chariots of the monstrous Pharaoh. Going back to creation, He "provided moon and sun" and "set all the borders of earth" (16–17). In other words, if God did it then, can we trust Him to do it for us again? Somehow, God can and will turn things around and show His good purposes on the earth, even though at the moment it isn't obvious how or when.

The third movement (18–23) returns to intercessory prayer. Here and now, in real time, Asaph reminds God about "how the enemy mocked" (18) and petitions God piteously, "Do not deliver Your turtledove's soul to the wild beast" (19). Then comes the foundation of his petition: "Look upon the covenant" (20). It is on the basis of *HaShem*'s covenant promises with Israel that the psalmist can make his appeal. He cannot claim that Israel does not deserve some punishment—surely he is aware of the warnings of Moses and the prophets about the consequences of Israel's idolatry and injustice. He claims that God's covenants with Israel are ultimately unconditional. For Leviticus 26:44 says, "Yet for all that, when they are in the land of their enemies, I will not reject them, nor will I hate them into utter destruction, and break My covenant with them, for I am *Adonai* their God." Romans 11:2 again affirms: "God has not rejected His people whom He knew beforehand." Therefore, Asaph can intercede before His Maker with confidence (22): "Rise up O God, and defend Your cause." It's a cry for help from a troubled man. Yet it's a cry for redemption from one who knows that the Eternal One is still faithful.

When you find yourself in a dire situation, when the tide seems to have turned against you, when it feels like God has distanced Himself from you, and you're left trying to look up and hold on—hold on, hold on to the ancient covenant that God made with Israel and the new covenant He made with all humanity through Messiah *Yeshua. Am Israel Chai!* The people of Israel live! That Zion stands today, with the flag of Israel proudly displayed over it, confirms that these prayers do not go unanswered. The "noise of Your foes" (23) will fade. He will redeem His inheritance (2).

Psalm 75

He Lowers One and Lifts Another

¹ For the music director: "Do not Destroy," a psalm of Asaph, a song.

² We praise You, we praise God,
>   for Your Name is near.
>   People declare Your wonders.

³ "When I appoint a set time,
>   I Myself will judge uprightly.

⁴ When the earth wavers with living on it,
  I Myself hold its pillars firm. *Selah*
⁵ I say to the arrogant, 'No more boasting!'
  And to the wicked,
  'Do not be lifting up your horn.'
⁶ Do not lift your horn up high.
  Do not speak with outstretched neck."

⁷ For exaltation comes
  not from the east nor from the west,
  nor even from the desert.
⁸ For God is the Judge:
  He lowers one and lifts up another.
⁹ For in the hand of *Adonai* is a cup of foaming wine mixed with spices,
  and He pours it out.
  Surely all the wicked of the earth will drink,
  draining it down to the dregs.ᵃ
¹⁰ But I—I will declare it forever,
  I will sing praise to the God of Jacob.
¹¹ I will cut off all the horns of the wicked,
  but the horns of the righteous will be lifted up.

Jeffrey Seif and Glenn Blank

Young men try to attract attention from the opposite sex by sticking out their chests and competing with other males. People put their best foot forward to get a mate, secure a job, or maintain presence in the communities where they live, work, and worship. When the psalmist casts aspersions on those who lift their "horn up high" and "speak with outstretched neck" (6), he uses poetic language from the animal kingdom. Given that the psalmist contends that *Adonai* "lowers one and lifts up another" (8), he is not extolling the virtues of self-denial so much as suggesting it's better to let Him do the lifting. This principle is affirmed again in verse 11: "The horns of the righteous will be lifted up."

Private and reclusive sorts may glory in their deprivation, their seeming humility, and think that forever remaining in the background and backwaters of human experience is a sign of superior spirituality. The psalmist, by contrast, differentiates between one's self-glorification and one's glorification

a. 75:9. cf. Rev. 14:10.

by God. "For exaltation comes" not from any direction on earth (7) but from eternal heaven. *Yeshua* makes a similar point in Luke 14:7–11, when he sagely recommends that you take the least important seat, from which the host may invite you to a more honorable place. Serve Him well, "sing praise to the God of Jacob" (10), and see how He proves Himself to be the lifter of your head.

PSALM 76

Who Can Stand in Your Presence?

¹ For the music director, on stringed instruments: a psalm of Asaph, a song.
² In Judah God is known.
    In Israel His Name is great.
³ In Salem is His *sukkah*
    and His dwelling place in Zion.
⁴ There He broke the fiery shafts of the bow,
    the shield, the sword, and the battle. *Selah*
⁵ You are brilliant,
    more majestic than nourishing mountains.
⁶ The valiant have been plundered—
    they slumbered in their sleep.
    The mighty could not lift their hands.
⁷ At Your rebuke, O God of Jacob,
    both horse and rider lay dead asleep.
⁸ You are awesome, yes You are!
    Who can stand in Your presence once You are angry?
⁹ From heaven You pronounced judgment.
    The earth feared and was still—
¹⁰ when God rose up to judgment,
    to save all the humble of the land. *Selah*
¹¹ For wrath upon man will bring You praise,
    a remnant of wrath You put on as a belt.
¹² Make vows to ADONAI your God and fulfill them.
    Let all around Him bring tribute to the One who is to be feared.
¹³ He cuts off the breath of princes.
    The kings of earth are in awe of Him.

Jeffrey Seif

"In Judah God is known" (2). Is this still true? Does He make His will and ways known there? Or has He taken up residency elsewhere? Perhaps in Rome? Or perhaps He's moved to Mecca? This psalmist would never be asking such questions. He would say: "Of course not!" He is absolutely confident that God is, in fact, at work both in and through the commonwealth of Israel. It is there where God is "brilliant," winning battles (4–7) and pronouncing cosmic judgment (8–9), in order to "save all the humble of the land" (10).

What is God up to? Why did He show Himself strong on behalf of Judah then? Why, for that matter, does He show Himself strong on behalf of Israel now? (How else can we explain how Israel has won so many wars against all odds?) Does He think Jewish flesh is worth more than non-Jewish flesh? Pound for pound are we more valuable to Him? No. God does not play favorites (Exod. 23:3; Rom. 2:11). Is it that He prefers Jewish culture over gentile culture? No. The God who is One delights in all humanity. What then? The psalmist says it is so "the kings of earth are in awe of Him" (13). He makes His ways known *there*, so the unique One can be known everywhere! God's work on behalf of the Jews is so He can work through the Jews—and so manifest His grace to all. That "all" extends to you—irrespective of how much or how little Jewish blood flows in your veins, or whether you live in Jerusalem or halfway around the world—He extends His grace to you.

PSALM 77

Remember the Wonders

¹ For the music director, on Jeduthun: a psalm of Asaph.
² My voice to God—and I cried out,
    my voice to God—and He heard me!
³ In the day of my trouble I seek my Lord.
    At night my hand stretches out untiringly.
    My soul refuses to be comforted.
⁴ I remember God and I moan.
    I muse, and my spirit grows faint. *Selah*

⁵ You hold my eyelids open—
 I am so troubled—I cannot speak.
⁶ I ponder the days of old,
 the years long ago.
⁷ In the night I remember my song.
  I meditate with my heart
  and my spirit is searching.
⁸ "Will the Lord reject forever
  and never again show favor?
⁹ Has His mercy vanished forever?
  Has His promise come to an end forever?
¹⁰ Has God forgotten to be gracious?
  Or has He in anger withdrawn his mercies?" *Selah*

¹¹ Then I said: "It wounds me—
  that the right hand of *Elyon* has changed."
¹² I will remember the deeds of ADONAI.
  Yes, I will muse about Your wonders of old.
¹³ I will meditate also on all Your work
  and consider Your deeds.
¹⁴ O God, Your way is holy.
  What god is great like God?
¹⁵ You are the God who works wonders.
  You have made Your power known among the peoples.
¹⁶ With your arm You redeemed Your people,
  the children of Jacob and Joseph. *Selah*

¹⁷ The waters saw You, O God,
  the waters saw You and writhed,
  even the depths shook.
¹⁸ The clouds poured out water,
  the skies resounded,
  Your arrows flashed back and forth.
¹⁹ The sound of Your thunder was in the whirlwind.
  Lightning lit up the world.
  The earth trembled and shook.
²⁰ Your way was in the sea,
  and Your path in the mighty waters,
  but Your footprints were not seen.
²¹ You led Your people like a flock,
  by the hand of Moses and Aaron.

Glenn Blank

What should you do when things get tough? Maybe you've lost your job or you've landed in the hospital or you're going through a stretch of the blues. Asaph—a Levite assigned to Temple worship—knew what to do. He cried out to God with his voice (2). In the day of his trouble, he sought the Lord, refusing to be comforted until he had an answer (3). He remembered God (4).

Not that it was easy. Whatever he was going through—maybe he lived in the aftermath of the destruction of the first Temple?—it wasn't easy for him to find comfort. Sometimes that's how it is. You keep crying out, you moan, your spirit "grows faint" (4); you are so troubled, you can no longer even speak (5). What should you do? Maybe you've experienced intense disappointment, rejection, or loss. What do you do when your "spirit is searching" but cannot find an answer (7), when your heart wonders if the Lord has forgotten you, if He will "never again show favor" (8)? What do you do when you think that maybe God is angry with you, has "withdrawn His mercies" (10)? The ancient poet knew these feelings—the *Ruach Ha-Kodesh* knows too—how "it wounds me" (11).

Asaph—a Levitical servant and a poet of *Elyon*, God Most High—knew what to do. He pondered the "wonders of old"; he remembered "the deeds of *Adonai*" (12). When you meditate on His deeds (13), your focus shifts from your temporary trial to His holiness (14) and everlasting hope. When you wonder at His wonders, you won't miss His arm reaching down to redeem you (15–16). Asaph remembers how "the waters . . . writhed" (17) to make a "path in the mighty waters" (20)—when *HaShem* delivered our people through the Sea of Reeds. He remembers how "the skies resounded" at the "sound of Your thunder" (18–19) at Sinai—when *HaShem* cut a covenant with our people. He remembers how He led His people "like a flock" (21)—when *HaShem* brought our people into the Promised Land. All this, though "Your footprints were not seen" (20)—what an awesome reminder that "we walk by faith, not by sight" (2 Cor. 5:7).

If Asaph could find comfort in the wonders of Exodus, how much more comfort can we find in the wonders of Matthew, Mark, Luke, and John? Or in the wonders God has done in your own life? Keep crying out; keep remembering the wonders He has done. You will again see how great and wonderful our God is.

PSALM 78

Israel from Moses to David

¹ A contemplative song of Asaph.
    Listen, my people, to my teaching.
    Turn your ears to the words of my mouth.
² I will open my mouth with a parable.
    I will utter perplexing sayings from of old,
³ which we have heard and known,
    and our fathers have told us.
⁴ We will not hide them from their children,
        telling to the next generation the praises of ADONAI
    and His strength and the wonders He has done.
⁵ For He established a testimony in Jacob
        and ordained *Torah* in Israel,
        which He commanded our fathers to teach their children,
⁶ so that the next generation might know,
    even the children yet to be born:
    they will arise and tell their children.
⁷ Then they will put their trust in God,
        not forgetting the works of God,
        but keeping His *mitzvot*.
⁸ So they will not be like their fathers—
        a stubborn and rebellious generation,
        a generation that did not prepare its heart,
    whose spirit was not loyal to God.
⁹ The sons of Ephraim were archers armed with bows,
        yet they turned back in the day of battle.
¹⁰ They did not keep God's covenant
        and refused to walk in His *Torah*.
¹¹ They forgot His deeds
        and His wonders that He had shown them.
¹² He did miracles in front of their fathers
        in the land of Egypt, in the plain of Zoan.
¹³ He split the sea and led them through,
        and He made the water stand like a wall.
¹⁴ By day He led them with a cloud
        and all night with a light of fire.

[15] He split apart rocks in the wilderness
    and gave them drink as abundant as the depths.
[16] So He brought streams out of a rock,
    and made waters flow down like rivers.[a]
[17] Yet they added more sinning against Him,
    rebelling against *Elyon* in the desert.
[18] They put God to the test in their heart
    by demanding food for their craving.
[19] Then they spoke against God, saying,
    "Can God set a table in the wilderness?
[20] See, He struck the rock,
    waters gushed out, streams overflowed.
    But can He give bread?
    Will He provide meat for His people?"

[21] When *Adonai* heard, He was angry.
    A fire was kindled against Jacob,
    and fury also rose against Israel.
[22] For they did not believe in God
    or trust in His salvation.
[23] Yet He commanded the skies above
    and opened the doors of heaven,
[24] and rained down manna upon them to eat,
    and gave them grain of heaven.[b]
[25] Man did eat the bread of angels.
    He sent them abundant provision.
[26] He loosed the east wind in the skies,
    and by His power He drove the south wind.
[27] He rained meat upon them like dust,
    and winged fowl like sand of the seas.
[28] And He let it fall amidst their camp,
    all around their tents.
[29] So they ate and were very full—
    for He gave them their desire.
[30] No longer a stranger from their desire,
    while their food was still in their mouths,
[31] the anger of God rose against them
    and slew the stoutest of them,
    and struck down young men of Israel.

a. 78:15–16. cf. 1 Cor. 10:4.
b. 78:24. cf. John 6:31.

³² Despite all this they sinned still more,
  and did not trust in His wonders.
³³ So He ended their days in futility
  and their years in terror.
³⁴ But when He slew them,
  then they sought Him, and turned back,
  and desired God eagerly.
³⁵ Then they remembered that God was their Rock
  and *El Elyon* their Redeemer.
³⁶ But they flattered Him with their mouth
  and kept lying to Him with their tongue.
³⁷ For their heart was not steadfast with Him,
  nor were they faithful to His covenant.
³⁸ But He is compassionate,
 forgives iniquity and does not destroy.
  Yes, many times He restrains His anger,
 and does not stir up all His wrath.
³⁹ For He remembered that they are but flesh,
  a passing breath that never returns.

⁴⁰ How often they rebelled against Him in the wilderness,
  and grieved Him in the desert!
⁴¹ Again and again they tested God,
  and pained the Holy One of Israel.
⁴² They did not remember His hand—
  the day He redeemed them from the foe,
⁴³ when He displayed His signs in Egypt
  and His wonders in the plain of Zoan.
⁴⁴ He turned their rivers into blood,
  so they could not drink from their streams.
⁴⁵ He sent on them flies to devour them,
 and frogs to devastate them,
⁴⁶ and gave their crops to the grasshopper,
 and their labor to the locust.
⁴⁷ He destroyed their vines with hail,
 and their sycamore trees with frost,
⁴⁸ and gave over their cattle to the hail,
 and their flocks to fiery bolts.
⁴⁹ He sent on them the fury of His anger
  —wrath and indignation and trouble—
  a band of evil angels.

⁵⁰ He cleared a path for His anger.
    He spared not their soul from death,
    but gave their life over to the plague.
⁵¹ He struck down all the firstborn in Egypt,
    the firstfruits of their strength in the tents of Ham.
⁵² But He brought His people out like sheep,
    and led them in the wilderness like a flock.
⁵³ He led them to safety, so they did not fear,
    but the sea overwhelmed their enemies.
⁵⁴ Then He brought them to His holy territory,
    to the mountain His right hand had gotten.
⁵⁵ He drove out nations before them,
    and allotted them an inheritance.
    He settled the tribes of Israel in their tents.

⁵⁶ Yet they tested and rebelled against *El Elyon*,
    and did not keep His decrees.
⁵⁷ Like their fathers they turned and were treacherous.
    They turned aside like a faulty bow.
⁵⁸ For they provoked Him
with their high places,
    so they aroused His jealousy
with their graven images.
⁵⁹ God heard and was furious,
    and He greatly detested Israel.
⁶⁰ He abandoned the tabernacle of Shiloh,
    the tent He pitched among men.
⁶¹ He gave up His strength into captivity,
    and His glory into the adversary's hand.
⁶² He gave His people over to the sword,
    when He was angry at His inheritance.
⁶³ Fire consumed their young men,
    and their virgins had no wedding songs.
⁶⁴ Their priests fell by the sword,
    and their widows could not weep.

⁶⁵ Then the Lord awoke as from sleep,
    as a warrior shaking off wine.
⁶⁶ He beat back His foes,
    putting them to lasting scorn.
⁶⁷ Then He detested Joseph's tent
    and chose not the tribe of Ephraim.

⁶⁸ Instead He chose the tribe of Judah,
   Mount Zion, which He loved.
⁶⁹ He built His Sanctuary like the heights,
   like the earth that He established forever.
⁷⁰ He also chose David His servant
   and took him from the sheepfolds,
⁷¹ from following nursing ewes.
   He brought him to shepherd Jacob His people,
   and Israel His inheritance.
⁷² So He shepherded them with the integrity of His heart,
   and led them with His skillful hands.

Jeffrey Seif and Glenn Blank

At seventy-two verses, this is a long psalm. But Israel has a long history, and recounting its development from Moses to David is no small task. The purpose is the "telling to the next generation the praises of ADONAI and His strength and the wonders He has done" (4). Praising God is not relegated to a professional class of clergy. Rather, His testimonies are to be transmitted to all. The "fathers" are "commanded" to "teach their children, so that the next generation might know . . . the works of God" (5–7). Then as now, however, too many "forgot His deeds" (11), prompting a poetic recap of all He did for our fathers on the way from Egypt to Sinai (12–20)—you might want to share these verses at a Passover Seder.

Yet many of our fathers and friends still do "not believe in God or trust in His salvation" (22). Indeed, we get a telling picture of unbelief for most of verses 23–51. Nevertheless, God is "compassionate," for He "forgives iniquity, and . . . many times He restrains His anger" (38). Our ancestors would not have it—"How often they rebelled against Him in the wilderness." Their rebellion "grieved Him . . . tested God" and even "pained the Holy One of Israel" (40–41). Consider how the Holy One views the tests He gives to His people to grow their faith and perseverance, yet how much pain we cause Him when we grieve Him and test His patience! The *Ruach Kodesh* urges us to remember that He redeemed us "from the foe" (42); with many signs and wonders He delivered His people from Egypt (43–51). Yet even when, like a shepherd, He led them "to His holy territory" (54) and "allotted them an inheritance" (55), again "they tested and rebelled" (56) like their fathers, provoking Him with their "high places" and their "graven images" (58). "God heard and was furious, and He greatly detested Israel" (59). So He "gave His people over to the sword" (62).

Through history to the present, there are those who have construed God's anger with His people as permanent rejection—even justifying their own persecution of Jews as God's continuing judgment and wrath. They would do well to read the rest of the story. God again "chose the tribe of Judah" (68), "built His Sanctuary" among them (69), and "chose David" (70). Despite the disappointments and the disciplines, God would not and could not deny His covenant with Israel, "His inheritance" (71). The psalm closes with God again shepherding them and leading Israel with "His skillful hands" (72).

It's a long psalm because it's a long story. Much like our own story, this one is punctuated by examples of God's grace and human beings' less-than-hoped-for responses. Though the heavenly Father gets angry, gets out the paddle, and makes His children feel His wrath—for their ultimate good—He is unwilling to throw them off outright, because the overarching theme of history, from His point of view, is His covenant faithfulness. Though human beings are wayward, there is still a way back to this merciful God. The story of God's perennial and parental faithfulness to Israel, in spite of her chronic and childish unfaithfulness, does not fit so well within the framework of Replacement Theology. The psalmist will have none of it—God is unfailingly faithful, "with the integrity of His heart" (72).

True as He is to Israel, consider the implications for your own life. The psalm is an exhortation to remember the story of God's lovingkindness and to tell the next generation. Believe it, then be proactive in transmitting it. By so doing, you may stave off not only your own tendency to waywardness but also the waywardness that too easily recurs in the next generation. Additionally—of no little importance to the psalmist—reminding ourselves of God's tender and abiding mercy reminds young and old alike that a kindly disposed God stands ready to meet us, not only in "His Sanctuary like the heights" (69) but at the other end of our heartfelt prayers. Draw near to the throne of grace to find mercy. Draw near to the Shepherd to find help in time of need.

PSALM 79

A Lament over Jerusalem

¹ A Psalm of Asaph.
> God, the nations have invaded Your inheritance,
> defiled Your holy Temple,
> and reduced Jerusalem to ruins.
² They gave the carcasses of Your servants as food to the birds of the skies,
> the flesh of Your *kedoshim* to the beasts of the earth.
³ They poured out their blood like water all around Jerusalem,
> and there was no one to bury them.
⁴ We have become a taunt to our neighbors,
> a scorn and derision to those around us.

⁵ How long, ADONAI, will You be angry?
> Forever?
> Will Your jealousy keep blazing like fire?
⁶ Pour out Your wrath
> on the nations that do not acknowledge You,
> on the kingdoms that do not call on Your Name.
⁷ For they have devoured Jacob
> and laid waste his country.
⁸ Do not hold against us the sins of our fathers.
> May Your mercies come quickly to meet us,
> for we are brought very low.
⁹ Help us, God of our salvation—
> for the sake of the glory of Your Name.
> Deliver us, and atone for our sins—
> for Your Name's sake.
¹⁰ Why should the nations say:
> "Where is their God?"
> Before our eyes, let it be known among the nations
> that You avenge the shed blood of Your servants.
¹¹ Let the prisoner's groan come to You.
> By Your great arm preserve those who are doomed to die.
¹² Pay back into the midst of our neighbors sevenfold their reproach—
> the reproach they hurled at You, my Lord.

[13] So we, Your people, the flock of Your pasture,
   will praise You forever.
      From generation to generation
   we will recount Your praise.

Jeffrey Seif

We call it "pay back." Vicious adversaries have "invaded," "defiled," and "reduced Jerusalem" (1) and even disrespected the dead (2–3)—surely an offense to God as well as man. Will God, who is just, give the wicked their due? If so, when? "How long . . . forever?" asks the psalmist (5)—and plenty of others have asked this question ever since.

Some people have the conception that the Lord would have us simply be sheepish in the face of adversity. Some even wonder if a request to "pour out Your wrath" (6) should have a place in biblical literature. Yet it is there, isn't it? Its presence invites readers to consider what to do with it. Victims of abuse cry out for justice. Does God turn a deaf ear to their cry? Does the "prisoner's groan" come before Him, or does His "great arm preserve those who are doomed to die" (11), or not? The psalmist refuses to lie down and accept the prospect of an abysmal future for his people. Instead, he asks that the God of justice "pay back" the wicked (12). When he beseeches God to "avenge the shed blood" of His servants (10), he anticipates the *kedoshim* of Revelation 6:10 who cry out to the Lord, "How long before You judge those who dwell on the earth and avenge our blood?" Trusting in God's justice is a matter of survival. When the vileness of oppressors is visited upon their own heads, then לְדֹר וָדֹר, *l'dor va-dor*, "from generation to generation," this nation of survivors "will praise You forever" (13).

Today as yesterday, victims seek redress. This psalm (and much else in Scripture) proclaims that ultimately God does give justice. Therefore it attests that it offends no biblical virtue to execute justice—though for the sake of the Good News, we are bidden to bear abuse graciously. Therefore, let us pray for and seek justice on the earth—a justice we need very much.

Psalm 80

Restore Us, Revive Us

¹ For the music director, on "Lilies,"ª a testimony: a psalm of Asaph.
² Give ear, Shepherd of Israel,
    You who lead Joseph like a flock.
    You who are enthroned upon the *cheruvim*, shine forth!
³ Before Ephraim, Benjamin and Manasseh,
    stir up Your might, and come to save us.
⁴ O God, restore us, make Your face shine,
    and we will be saved.

⁵ *Adonai-Tzva'ot*, how long will You be angry
    with the prayer of Your people?
⁶ You have fed them the bread of tears
    and made them drink a measure of tears.
⁷ You make us a contention to our neighbors,
    and our enemies mock as they please.
⁸ *Elohei-Tzva'ot*, restore us, and make Your face shine,
    and we will be saved.

⁹ You pulled out a vine from Egypt.
    You drove out nations and planted it.
¹⁰ You cleared a place for it,
    and it took deep root and filled the land.
¹¹ The mountains were covered by its shade,
    the mighty cedars with its branches.
¹² It sent out its branches to the sea,
    and its shoots to the river.
¹³ Why have You broken down its fences,
    so all who pass by the way pick its fruit?
¹⁴ A boar from the forest ravages it,
    whatever moves in the field feeds on it.
¹⁵ *Elohei-Tzva'ot*, please return!
    Look down from heaven and see!
    Now take care of this vine—
¹⁶ the shoot Your right hand planted—
    the son You strengthened for Yourself.

a. 80:1(0). Heb. *Shoshanim.*

[17] It is burned with fire, it is cut down.
> They perish from the rebuke of Your face.

[18] Let Your hand be upon the man of Your right hand—
> the son of man
> You made strong for Yourself.

[19] Then we will not turn away from You.
> Revive us, and we will call on Your Name.

[20] ADONAI *Elohei-Tzva'ot*, restore us.
> Make Your face shine, and we will be saved.

Jeffrey Seif and Glenn Blank

Shepherding has its challenges. If you haven't tried your hand at sheep, imagine trying to herd cats! At least sheep are mindful of the shepherd's staff and eventually recognize the shepherd's voice. People, on the other hand, just figure out how to avoid the rod and ignore the voice. So they drift all over—even people who mean well. Here, God takes on the role of "Shepherd of Israel," trying to "lead Joseph like a flock" (2). Even God Himself finds this flock to be, ahem, unruly. When they wander off and get in trouble, what do they do? Some of them cry out, "come to save us" (3). Never mind how they got into their predicament. Others just wander completely out of sight. The good ones bleat with some trust in the Shepherd, remembering Moses and the promise of the Aaronic blessing, "restore us, make Your face shine" (4). Actually, these words are a refrain, repeated again (8) and again (20). This refrain gives the poem a nice structure; it also tells us something about these sheep.

It seems God's flock has fallen upon some hard times. Alas, it happens—again and again. Can God the Good Shepherd be counted on to help? When it seems like we've tasted enough of "the bread of tears" (6) and our enemies (whether human or spiritual) just "mock as they please" (7), will God restore His sheep to their pasture?

The next section compares Israel to a vine. The same imagery is found in the prophets and the *Besorot* (Gospels) (see, for example, Isa. 5:1, 2, 7; Jer. 2:21; Mark 12:1). God went to a lot of trouble to make room for this vine and it filled the land (10–12), but now it seems that He has removed the "fences" (13) of His protection and a wild "boar"—symbolizing a foreign nation—ravages it (14). Prayer goes up: O God, "take care of this vine" (15), which is also "the son You strengthened for Yourself" (16). Israel is also called

God's son in Exodus 4:22–23—when *HaShem* had compassion on the slaves in Egypt—as well as in Hosea 11:1 and other prophetic passages. On the basis of this intimate relationship, the poet intercedes with God to restore the vine, which has been "burned with fire" and "cut down" (17).

Then the "son of man" appears, whom "You made strong for Yourself." This "man of Your right hand" (18) may be another reference to Israel as God's son or to a king of Israel. Yet we cannot help but glimpse the One who called Himself "the Son of Man," and who now sits "at the right hand of the Powerful One" (Mark 14:62). (See our commentary on Ps. 110.) This Son of Man closely identifies with the flock of Israel, even calling Himself the "good shepherd" who "lays down His life for the sheep" (John 10:11).

Israel keeps crying out, like sheep to their Shepherd: "Make Your face shine, and we will be saved" (20). Our friends in churches often talk about being "saved." Here, though, it is less about the salvation of an individual soul (important as that is) and more about the deliverance and restoration of a devastated nation. God (and the Messiah) seeks and saves both individuals and nations. Does the Shepherd of Israel "give ear" to His people Israel? The incessant, heartfelt appeals, expressed in such poetic language, convince us of the power of prevailing prayer. Because of His compassion, God does hear these prayers, and God does save people—spiritually, materially, socially, and nationally. Praying makes a difference. "In this way all Israel will be saved" (Rom. 11:26). So let's keep calling on His Name—the Name of our Good Shepherd.

PSALM 81

Hear O Israel

¹ For the music director, on the Gittite lyre, of Asaph.
² Sing for joy to God our strength,
    shout to the God of Jacob!
³ Lift up a song and sound a tambourine,
    a sweet lyre with a harp.
⁴ Blow the *shofar* at the New Moon,
    at the full moon for the day of our festival.

[5] For it is a decree for Israel,
  an ordinance of the God of Jacob.
[6] He set it up as a testimony in Joseph,
  when He went throughout the land of Egypt,
  I heard a language I did not understand.

[7] "I relieved his shoulder of the burden,
  his hands were set free from the basket.
[8] You called out in trouble, and I rescued you.
  I answered you from the hiding place of thunder.
  I tested you at the waters of Meribah. *Selah*
[9] Hear, My people, I will admonish you—
  if you would listen to Me, O Israel!
[10] Let there be no foreign god among you,
  and you shall not worship any alien god.
[11] I am ADONAI your God,
  who brought you up out of the land of Egypt.
  Open your mouth wide and I will fill it.

[12] But My people did not listen to My voice.
  Israel was not willing to be Mine.
[13] So I gave them over
  to the stubbornness of their heart,
  to walk in their own counsels.
[14] Oh that My people would listen to Me,
  that Israel would walk in My ways!
[15] I would soon subdue their enemies,
  and turn My hand against their foes.
[16] Those who hate ADONAI would cringe before Him—
  their time of doom would be forever.
[17] But you would be fed with the finest wheat,
  with honey out of a rock would I satisfy you."

Jeffrey Seif and Glenn Blank

Because musical tastes don't necessarily transfer across cultures, perhaps not everyone will appreciate the sound when an ancient or modern Jew decides to "lift up a song and sound a tambourine" (3), much less let loose with a blast of a *shofar* (4). We admit it can be a bit jarring, but that's the point. It's supposed to command your attention, because here comes the Judge!

These sounds were part and parcel of the psalmist's world and a way he and other Levites would liven up a religious celebration, such as a New Moon.

Most likely the New Moon in question is *Yom Teruah*, the Day of Blowing *shofars*—nowadays commonly called *Rosh Hashanah*, which occurs on a New Moon, or the first day of the seventh month. The "full moon for the day of our festival" (4) was most likely during *Sukkot*, the Festival of Tabernacles following *Yom Teruah*. These festivals are always occasions for noisy celebration.

If you don't get why Messianic Jews, like our ancient forebearers, are so exuberant, remember how God acted on behalf of our ancestors when he rescued us from "the burden" and "the basket" (7) of slavery, when He brought us "up out of the land of Egypt" (11). If you're thinking, well, that was a long time ago, and I wasn't there, try looking at it from the Eternal One's point of view—to Him, it is as though it just happened. Furthermore, He is still setting people free—such as you and me.

As He commanded the Israelites, He commands us too—"you shall not worship any alien god" (10)—because He still desires an exclusive relationship with His people. Tragically, Israel "did not listen" to His voice, Israel "was not willing" to be His (12). He who delivered Israel grew weary of "the stubbornness of their heart" (13). Nevertheless, from generation to generation, He holds out the promise that should they opt to "walk" in His ways (14), He would again show Himself strong on their behalf and "subdue their enemies" (15), and once more they would be "fed with the finest wheat" and be satisfied (17).

Though Israel's vacillation may not inspire us to praise and shout, God's enduring faithfulness should. Words like lovingkindness, patience, forbearance, enduring mercies, and more describe a God who disciplines when He must but is forever willing to turn again to His people when they turn to Him. If you have a tambourine, why don't you jingle it? If you have a voice, why don't you lift it up to praise Him?

PSALM 82

A Rebuke for Unjust Judges

¹ A psalm of Asaph.
God takes His stand in the assembly of God.
He judges among the "gods":

² "How long will you judge unjustly
    and show partiality to the wicked? *Selah*
³ Give justice to the poor and fatherless.
    Be just to the afflicted and destitute.
⁴ Rescue the weak and needy.
    Deliver them out of the hand of the wicked.
⁵ They know nothing;
    they understand nothing—
    they walk about in darkness.
    All of earth's foundations are shaken.
⁶ I said: 'You are "gods,"
    and you are all sons of *Elyon*,[a]
⁷ yet you will die like men,
    and will fall like any of the princes.'"

⁸ Arise, O God, judge the earth!
    For You possess all the nations.

Glenn Blank and Jeffrey Seif

Corrupt judges—showing partiality based on any agenda but genuine justice—are ancient news. When those vested with juridical authorization "show partiality to the wicked" (2), it is bad news for the powerless. In a world where underlings can often do little more than grin and bear it, the good news is that God Himself takes the witness stand against the "gods" (actually all too human) of the courtroom (1). He castigates those who "judge unjustly" and are less inclined to "give justice to the poor and fatherless" (2–3). If judges expect to make it "in the assembly of God" (1), they must reflect His justice and compassion, as revealed in *Torah*, the prophets, and the Psalms, and ultimately through Messiah *Yeshua*. They must be willing to "rescue the weak and needy" and "deliver them out of the hand of the wicked" (4). God warns judges that He is ultimately the One who appoints (and removes) them, and He is the One who decides when "you will die . . . and will fall like any of the princes" (7). He is the One who one day will "arise" and "judge the earth" and "possess all the nations" (8). Lest the powerful become overly comfortable in their positions and commit indiscretions, God goes on record warning that even powerful but still mortal "gods" in this world will have to give an accounting to Him.

a. 82:6. cf. Luke 6:35; John 10:34.

You and I may not preside over a courtroom, but we all at times evaluate people around us, such as those who work for or with us. *Yeshua* urged His disciples: "Do not judge, and you will not be judged. Do not condemn, and you will not be condemned. Pardon, and you will be pardoned" (Luke 6:37). In other words, if you're going to judge, remember, you too will be judged—by the Supreme Judge. Those who condemn unjustly will be condemned justly. Those who pardon freely will be pardoned more than they ever deserve. Take a moment to reflect: What kind of justice do *you* want? Now take a moment to pray.

PSALM 83

Nations Conspire against Israel

¹ A song: a psalm of Asaph.
² God, do not keep silent.
     Do not hold Your peace, O God.
     Do not be still.
³ For look, Your enemies make an uproar.
     Those who hate You lift up their head.
⁴ They make a shrewd plot against Your people,
     conspiring against Your treasured ones.
⁵ "Come," they say, "let's wipe them out as a nation!
     Let Israel's name be remembered no more!"
⁶ For with one mind they plot together.
     Against You do they make a covenant.
⁷ The tents of Edom and the Ishmaelites,
     Moab and the Hagrites,
⁸ Gebal, Ammon and Amalek,
     Philistia with the inhabitants of Tyre,
⁹ even Assyria has joined them,
     becoming a strong arm for Lot's sons. *Selah*

¹⁰ Do to them as You did to Midian,
     to Sisera and Jabin at the Kishon River,
¹¹ who perished at En-dor—
     they became as dung for the ground.

[12] Make their nobles like Oreb and Zeeb—
 all their princes like Zebah and Zalmunna,
[13] who said,
 "Let us take possession of the pasturelands of God."
[14] My God, make them like tumbleweed,
 like chaff before the wind.
[15] As a fire burns a forest,
 and as a flame sets mountains ablaze,
[16] so pursue them with Your tempest,
 and terrify them with Your storm.
[17] Cover their faces with shame,
 so they may seek Your Name—*ADONAI*.
[18] Let them be ashamed and dismayed forever.
 Let them be humiliated and perish.
[19] Let them know that You alone
 —whose Name is *ADONAI*—
 are *El Elyon* over all the earth.

Jeffrey Seif

If ever there was a psalm that sounded like today's news clippings, it's this one: "Enemies make an uproar" (3), "shrewd plot" and conspiracy (4). Then there's this line that modern-day Hamans repeat: "Come . . . let's wipe them out as a nation! Let Israel's name be remembered no more!" (5). From time immemorial forces have been hell-bent on destroying God's people and especially the Jewish nation. Because "Isra-el" includes a suffix *El*, which means God, snuffing out Israel's name is tantamount to erasing God, who gave the name. Such an effort is bound to fail, for who will prevail against the Almighty? Nevertheless, history shows that these forces are relentless.

Those desiring to destroy God's people—then as now—are noted. They are represented by Edomites, Ishmaelites, and Moabites (occupiers of modern Jordan), raiders from Philistia (modern Gaza), Tyre (Lebanon), and Assyria (modern Syria and Iraq) (7–9). Pressed by threats of annihilation, the psalmist petitions God to "do to them" as He did to other adversaries (10) and to pursue them with His fire and tempest (15–16).

The modern nation of Israel has found itself beset by the same foes with the same relentless purpose: to destroy the Jewish people. They say, "We will throw the Jews into the sea." It didn't work then; it won't work now. God can be counted on as "*El Elyon* [God Most High] over all the earth" (19).

❊❊❊❊❊❊❊❊ PSALM 84 ❊❊❊❊❊❊❊❊

Pilgrim Road to ADONAI's Courts

[1] For the music director, upon the Gittite lyre, a psalm of the sons of Korah.

[2] How lovely are Your tabernacles,
    ADONAI-*Tzva'ot*!

[3] My soul yearns, even faints, for the courts of ADONAI.
    My heart and my flesh sing for joy to the living God.

[4] Even the sparrow has found a home,
    and the swallow a nest for herself, where she may lay her young
    —near Your altars, ADONAI-*Tzva'ot*—
    my King and my God!

[5] Blessed are they who dwell in Your House
    —they are ever praising You. *Selah*

[6] Blessed is one whose strength is in You,
    in whose heart are the pilgrim roads.

[7] Passing through the valley of Baca,
    they make it a spring.
    The early rain covers it with blessings.

[8] They go from strength to strength—
    every one of them appears before God in Zion.

[9] ADONAI-*Tzva'ot*, hear my prayer,
    give ear, O God of Jacob. *Selah*

[10] O God, look at our shield,
    and look upon the face of Your anointed.

[11] For a day in Your courts is better
    than a thousand anywhere else.
    I would rather stand at the threshold of the House of my God
    than dwell in the tents of wickedness.

[12] For ADONAI *Elohim* is a sun[a] and a shield.
    ADONAI gives grace and glory.
    No good thing will He withhold from those who walk uprightly.

[13] ADONAI-*Tzva'ot*,
    blessed is the one
    who trusts in You.

a. 84:12. cf. Rev. 21:23.

Paul Wilbur

This beautiful song of praise to ADONAI-Tzva'ot is truly one of my favorites. Verses 2–3 simply pull you into the heart of a worshiper and the desire to be in the presence of the living God. The very first words, מַה-יְּדִידוֹת (*mah-yedidot*) are usually translated "How lovely," perhaps for poetic flow, but a better sense is "How beloved" as in "desired" and "longed for" rather than a reference to its beauty. Don't get me wrong, I'm certain that the courts of *HaShem* were the most magnificent of any, but the psalmist is expressing here his deep love and longing *to be* in those courts rather than extolling their unsurpassed majesty.

Many years ago when my first son was nearly one year old, I wrote a musical setting for this psalm that I often share in worship. The chorus of the song was taken from verse 11 almost verbatim and ends with the quote, "No good thing will You withhold from him who walks with You; Almighty One, blessed is the man who trusts in You" (see 12–13). I tagged the end of the song with the words, "Almighty One . . . I trust in You!" Little did I know how important those words of faith would be only a few hours later. In the middle of the night, Nathan woke us up by throwing up all his dinner, but the situation didn't improve with time. He continued to throw up until blood was showing, which prompted a panicked call to the doctor at 3:00 a.m. The pediatrician told us of a severe infection hitting young children and that the local hospital was full of young patients with the same symptoms as our precious son. He prayed for us and then told us to wait for his call from the hospital letting us know there was a bed available. The minutes passed very slowly. As our child's pain grew worse, I heard the Lord say to me, "Worship Me." After a brief hesitation I retrieved my guitar from its case with the new song from Psalm 84 scribbled on notebook paper sitting right where I had left it earlier that night.

Over and over I sang, "No good thing will You withhold from him who walks with You; Almighty One, blessed is the man who trusts in You." Amazingly, with each chorus it seemed that color and strength was returning to my son's tiny frame. By the end of the song, he was standing, walking, and drinking water that stayed down! Psalm 16:11 says, "Abundance of joys are in Your presence, eternal pleasures at Your right hand." This is the presence that David's soul yearned and even fainted to enjoy—and over and over again the psalmist declares the blessing, or *asher*, of the man who enjoys a personal relationship with ADONAI-Tzva'ot. The way to His presence has been opened, He invites us to come and dine, and He leads us in paths of righteousness for His own Name's sake. Enter in . . . and be blessed.

Glenn Blank

Psalm 84 is a song of pilgrimage, sung by people setting their hearts to fulfill a *mitzvah*—that's why they are going up to Jerusalem on "pilgrim roads," passing through the valley of Baca (6–7). As they journey, their focus is not on the dusty road but on their destination, the courts of the Lord where the sparrow dwells (4) and the Levites dwell near His house—including the doorkeepers at the threshold of the great gates. Doorkeeping (or ushering) is a Levitical ministry, even if it may not seem as glamorous as making the sacrifices at the altar, singing on the worship team, or proclaiming the word of the Lord. *HaShem* meets His people at the doorway of His House (Exod. 29:42). So the doorkeeper represents the Lord. If the doorkeeper gets bored with his ministry or starts comparing it to other ministries or expects other people to notice him, then he misses the point and loses the reward of ministry. After all, it is much better to "stand at the threshold of the House of my God than dwell in the tents of wickedness" (11). That's the only comparison I should be making. The praise of the doorkeeper is a reminder of the Lord's call to devotion and humility in ministry. Like anyone else, I can be tempted to puff myself up or compare myself with others or expect others to notice me and give me credit. But like everyone else, I must remind myself that my reward is not outside the House, in the tents of the wicked or even the righteous, but only within the House, in His eternal presence. Abba my Lord, how I long to hear You say, "Well done, good and faithful servant." Help me not to seek a reward on earth for my ministry to You, but to store up my treasure in heaven. Forgive me when I get distracted or am tempted to feel unappreciated, and remind me to be grateful for the good things You will not withhold from me.

 # PSALM 85

Restore Your People from Captivity

¹ For the music director, a psalm of the sons of Korah.
² ADONAI, will You favor Your land?
    Will You restore Jacob from captivity?

3 Will You bear away Your people's iniquity,
    Will You pardon all their sin?[a] *Selah*
4 Will You withdraw all Your wrath?
    Will You turn from Your burning anger?[b]
5 Restore us, O God of our salvation,
    and renounce Your indignation with us.
6 Will You be angry with us forever?
    Will You prolong Your anger from generation to generation?
7 Will You not revive us again,
    so Your people may rejoice in You?
8 Show us Your mercy, ADONAI,
    and grant us Your salvation.

9 Let me hear what God ADONAI will say.
    For He will speak *shalom* to His people, and to His *kedoshim*—
    but let them not turn back to folly.
10 Surely His salvation is near those who fear Him,
    so that glory may dwell in our land.
11 Lovingkindness and truth meet together.
    Righteousness and *shalom* kiss each other.
12 Truth will spring up from the earth,
    and justice will look down from heaven.
13 Yes, ADONAI will give what is good,
    and our land will yield its produce.
14 Righteousness is going before Him
    and prepares a way for His feet.

Glenn Blank

When the sons of Korah appealed to God for salvation (5, 8, 10), what were they looking for? The rabbi at a nearby Reformed synagogue would say, "restoration to the land." Indeed, in painful exile, we Jews have longed for *HaShem* to "favor" His land and "restore Jacob from captivity" (2). The pastor at a nearby Baptist church would say, "forgiveness of sin." And indeed, in shame and brokenness, we sinners need Messiah to "bear away" His people's iniquities and "pardon all their sin" (3). Diaspora and distancing are both consequences of disobedience. Because people who should have known better

a. 85:3. cf. Matt. 9:6; 1 John 1:9.
b. 85:4. cf. Rom. 5:9.

have prolonged their idolatry or their idleness, God will prolong His anger (6). We are all hoping that God will "restore us" (5) and "revive us again" (7). We all want to hear *HaShem* "speak *shalom* to His people" and reveal His glory again (9). Amen? We can all appeal to God on the strength of His glorious nature (10)—His חֶסֶד (*chesed*, mercy, lovingkindness, or loyal love) and אֱמֶת (*emet*, truth or faithfulness), His צֶדֶק (*tzedek*, righteousness or justice) and שָׁלוֹם (*shalom*, peace or wholeness) (11–12). These attributes are all abstract and hence not directly observable. Yet the psalmist beholds them embracing and kissing each other—displaying God's gracious nature.

Six of the first seven verses of this poem, as our translation has rendered them, are questions. These are not complaints, nor are they entirely rhetorical. They are the prayers of intercessors directed to the Merciful One on the basis of His covenant promises. For through Moses and the prophets *HaShem* promised to restore the children of Jacob to the land and to bear away all of Israel's sin. Though from generation to generation it may seem that God is angry with our people, or perhaps giving us the "silent treatment," He cannot and will not be angry with us forever, because His very nature is חֶסֶד, love.

O God, You have been restoring more and more of Your people to the land. Now we appeal to You to revive more and more of Your people with Your *Ruach*. Surely *chesed* and *emet* meet together in Messiah. Surely *tzedek* and *shalom* kiss each other in *Yeshua*. Revive us, ADONAI!

❈❈❈❈❈❈ PSALM 86 ❈❈❈❈❈❈

Slow to Anger, Full of *Chesed*

¹ A prayer of David.
   Turn Your ear, ADONAI, and answer me,
   for I am weak and needy.
² Watch over my soul, for I am godly.
   You are my God—
   save Your servant who trusts in You.
³ Be gracious to me, my Lord,
   for to You I cry all day.

⁴ Gladden the soul of Your servant,
  for to You, my Lord, I lift up my soul.
⁵ For You, my Lord, are good,
  and ready to forgive
 and full of mercy to all who call upon You.
⁶ Give ear, ADONAI, to my prayer,
  listen to the voice of my supplications.
⁷ In the day of my trouble I call upon You,
  for You will answer me.

⁸ There is none like You among the gods,
  my Lord, there are no deeds like Yours.
⁹ All nations You have made will come
  and bow down before You, my Lord,
  and they will glorify Your Name.
¹⁰ For You are great, and do wonders—
  You alone are God.
¹¹ Teach me Your way, ADONAI,
  that I may walk in Your truth.
    Give me an undivided heart to fear Your Name.
¹² I praise You, O Lord my God, with my whole heart,
  and glorify Your Name forever.
¹³ For great is Your lovingkindness toward me.
  You have delivered my soul from the lowest part of *Sheol*.

¹⁴ God, the proud have risen up against me
  and a gang of ruthless people have sought my life,
  and have not set You before them.
¹⁵ But You, my Lord,
  are a compassionate and gracious God,
  slow to anger, full of love and truth.
¹⁶ Turn to me and be gracious to me.
  Give Your strength to Your servant,
  and save the son of Your maidservant.
¹⁷ Make me a sign for good,
  so that those who hate me may see it and be ashamed.
  For You, ADONAI, have helped me and comforted me.

Jeffrey Seif and Glenn Blank

The request "Give me an undivided heart" (11) pierces the heart, in part because our hearts can be so very divided. What the Bible means by the "heart" needs some explanation, because the word is so often used and so little understood. When people talk about "inviting Jesus (or *Yeshua*) into my heart," do they really grasp the implications of this statement? Is there really a literal place in our literal hearts where He now resides? If we get sick and need a heart transplant, must we then invite Him into the new heart? If we get an artificial, nonorganic heart, would there be a place for God in it? These are silly questions, of course, because having God in your heart and having an "undivided heart" are figures of speech. To what do they refer? The heart refers to something—or someone—at the center of one's being, motivating and directing the direction of one's life. The heart is like a steering wheel—you can tell who or what is truly in your heart by looking at the direction your life is taking. *Yeshua* warned, "No one can serve two masters; for either he will hate the one and love the other, or he will stick by one and look down on the other" (Matt. 6:24). If anything or anyone else is sharing that place—whether it be money or job, addictions or your own familiar self—your heart is divided, and you start zigzagging. If you truly have accepted *Yeshua* into your heart and make Him share it with any other god, He is going to be jealous; His Spirit is going to grieve. If we could just remember that all those other things, if they are worth anything at all, are gifts of God, then we could begin to love the Giver more than the gifts with our whole heart. Our hearts would be filled with gratitude to the One who is "full of mercy to all who call" on Him (5). We would praise and glorify God with our "whole heart" (12).

This psalm is a prayer (1, 7), the supplication of one who confesses himself "weak and needy" (1). The psalmist trusts "my Lord" (which is literally what Adonai means) to "be gracious" (3). (Note that grace is a Hebrew word: חֵן, *chen*.) Just as He awesomely revealed Himself to Moses on Sinai (Exod. 34:6), so the Lord will indeed be compassionate, gracious, slow to anger, full of love and truth (15) toward him. Though "a gang of ruthless people" may be hell-bent on his demise (14), the Lord will indeed "be gracious" and "save the son of Your maidservant" (16).

What our gracious God wants above all is that you love ADONAI your God with all your heart and all your soul and all your strength. That total commitment is what it truly means to have *Yeshua* in your heart. Take a moment to affirm that commitment to God and to Messiah *Yeshua* now. Amen.

From now on, may you be undivided in your love for the One who is undivided in His love for you.

✳✳✳✳✳✳✳✳ PSALM 87 ✳✳✳✳✳✳✳✳

This One Was Born in Zion

¹ A psalm of the sons of Korah, a song.
 His foundation is in the holy mountains.
² Adonai loves the gates of Zion
 more than all the dwellings of Jacob.
³ Glorious things are spoken of you,
 city of God. *Selah*
⁴ "I will mention Rahab and Babylon among those who acknowledge Me—
 behold Philistia and Tyre, with Cush:
 'This one was born there.'"
⁵ But of Zion it will be said:
 "This one and that one were born in her."
 And *Elyon* Himself will establish her.
⁶ Adonai will count in the register of the peoples:
 "This one was born there." *Selah*
⁷ Then singing and dancing—
 all my fountains of joy are in You!

Glenn Blank

Why do the sons of Korah exalt Zion "in the holy mountains" (1)? Why are they so sure that "Adonai loves the gates of Zion" (2)? Why is it such a big deal to declare, "This one was born" in Zion, three times (4, 5, 6)? Where does that leave those born in Beersheba or Bethlehem, let alone Boston or Beijing? They say of Zion, "glorious things are spoken of you." They say Zion is the "city of God" (3). They say Zion was chosen as the dwelling place of God's *shekheenah*—His glorious presence. They say Zion in the hills of Judah stands in for Zion in the heights of heaven. Rahab (prideful Egypt, see Isa. 30:7) and Babylon were world powers that often threatened and ultimately destroyed Jerusalem. They will ultimately acknowledge the God of Zion as the one true God (4).

Look up and see! Zion is not only an earthly city, it is a heavenly one—the one the patriarchs and prophets longed to see: "the city that has foundations, whose architect and builder is God" (Heb. 11:10). Those who have been born anew in the Spirit have been born anew in Zion. *HaShem* will count them "in the register of the peoples" (6). They will join the ancient Levites in "singing and dancing," for they have found in Him the "fountains of joy" (7) welling up to eternal life (John 4:14).

Will *HaShem* also say of you, "This one was born there"? If you're not sure, or need to review, I urge you to read John chapters 3 and 4 now, prayerfully. You too can be born anew in the city of God!

✳✳✳✳✳✳✳✳✳ PSALM 88 ✳✳✳✳✳✳✳✳✳

Cry of Desperation

¹ A song, a psalm of the sons of Korah, for the music director, for singing
    Mahalath, a contemplative song[a] of Heman the Ezrahite.
² *ADONAI*, God of my salvation,
    day and night I cried out before You.
³ Let my prayer come before You.
    Turn Your ear to my cry.
⁴ For my soul is full of troubles,
    and my life draws near to *Sheol*.
⁵ I am counted with those who go down into the Pit.
    I have become as one with no strength—
⁶ abandoned among the dead,
    like the slain that lie in the grave,
    whom You remember no more—
    cut off from Your hand.

a. 88:1(0). Heb. *maskil.*

[7] You have laid me in the lowest places,
  in dark places, in the depths.
[8] Your wrath lies heavily on me.
  You afflicted me with all Your waves. *Selah*
[9] You have put my companions far from me.
  You have made me repulsive to them.
  I am shut in and I cannot go out.
[10] My eye fails from affliction.
  I call upon You every day, ADONAI.
  I spread out my hands to You.
[11] Will You work wonders for the dead?
  Or will the departed spirits rise up praising You? *Selah*
[12] Will Your love be declared in the grave?
  Or Your faithfulness in the place of ruin?
[13] Will Your wonders be known in the darkness?
  Your righteousness in the land of oblivion?

[14] But I—I cried out to You, ADONAI,
  and in the morning my prayer meets You.
[15] ADONAI, why do You spurn me?
  Why do You hide Your face from me?
[16] From my youth I have been afflicted and close to death.
  I suffer Your terrors—I am desperate!
[17] Your fury has swept over me.
  Your terrors have cut me off.
[18] Like water they surge around me all day.
  They close in on me together.
[19] Friend and loved one You took far from me.
  Darkness has become my companion.

Jeffrey Seif

Would that all problems resolved themselves immediately, all sickness fled at our command, and the wicked were banished from our sight, after the utterance of our prayers! Alas, the fact that these things don't necessarily happen as immediately as we would like requires us to be flexible and to learn patience. The psalmist keeps crying out to God "day and night" (2). His "soul is full of troubles" and his life "draws near to *Sheol*" (4) and to "the Pit" (5–6). He is in the "lowest" and "dark places" (7), "afflicted" (8), and "cannot go out" because he is "repulsive" to his companions (9). Yuck. He's not only down but also seems to be stuck in a down place. He wonders if it could be any worse if he were dead, but in "the land of oblivion" he couldn't praise God or declare His love and faithfulness (11–13). Talk about determined! Down as he is, he looks up—only to feel rejected by the God he seeks. "In the morning my prayer meets You" (14), only to feel spurned by God (15). The fact that "friend and loved one" also have abandoned him (19) no doubt contributes to his feeling that God has too.

When things are terribly bad, it may seem that God has abandoned us too. *Yeshua* Himself felt this anguish when He cried out, "My God, My God, why have You forsaken Me?" (quoting Ps. 22:2). The Bible is brutally honest in acknowledging the way people feel—so people will know that God knows how we feel. Theologians can help us understand that the Father had to let *Yeshua* bear the penalty of our sins away. Yet at the emotional level, abandonment not only seems real and feels real, it is real—especially in the moment it grips your soul. Rather than deny it, we may be better served to voice it—and voice it to God. "Weeping may stay for the night, but joy comes in the morning" (Ps. 30:6). Despite all his trouble, the psalmist still looks up to God and out to the future. Thus, he positions himself to receive help from the Lord. Don't forget (God doesn't); don't give up (God doesn't); help will come.

✳✳✳✳✳✳ PSALM 89 ✳✳✳✳✳✳

Covenant with David's Seed

¹ A contemplative song of Ethan the Ezrahite.
² I will sing of the love of ADONAI forever.
   To all generations I will make known Your faithfulness with my mouth.
³ For I said, "Let your lovingkindness be built up forever!
   The heavens—let Your faithfulness be made firm there!"

⁴ "I have made a covenant with My chosen one.
   I have sworn to David My servant:
⁵ 'Forever I will establish your seed,
   and will build your throne from generation to generation.'"ᵃ *Selah*

a. 89:5. cf. Luke 1:33.

[6] The heavens praise Your wonders, ADONAI
　　—Your faithfulness, too—
　　in the assembly of the *kedoshim*.
[7] For who in the skies can compare to ADONAI?
　　Who is like ADONAI among the sons of gods?
[8] God is greatly feared in the council of the holy ones,
　　and awesome above all around Him.
[9] ADONAI *Elohei-Tzva'ot*, who is like You, mighty ADONAI,
　　with Your faithfulness all around You?
[10] You rule over the swelling of the sea.
　　When its waves mount up, You still them.
[11] You crushed Rahab like a slain one.
　　You scattered Your enemies with Your mighty arm.
[12] The heavens are Yours, also Yours the earth
　　—the world and its fullness—
　　You have founded them.
[13] You created the north and the south.
　　Tabor and Hermon sing for joy at Your Name.
[14] Your arm is mighty,
　　Your hand is strong,
　　exalted is Your right hand.[b]
[15] Righteousness and justice are the foundation of Your throne.
　　Lovingkindness and truth go before You.
[16] Blessed are the people who know the joyful shout,[c]
　　They walk in the light of Your presence, ADONAI.
[17] They rejoice in Your Name all day,
　　and by Your righteousness they are exalted.
[18] For You are the glory of their strength,
　　and by Your favor our horn is exalted.
[19] For our shield belongs to ADONAI,
　　and our king to the Holy One of Israel.

[20] Then You spoke in vision to Your godly ones, and said:
　　"I have bestowed help on a warrior.
　　I have exalted one chosen from among the people.
[21] I have found David My servant.
　　With My holy oil I have anointed him.

b. 89:14. cf. Heb. 1:3.
c. 89:16. Heb. *teruah*, or *shofar blast*.

²² With him My hand will be established.
    Surely My arm will strengthen him.
²³ No enemy will exact tribute from him,
    no son of wickedness will oppress him.
²⁴ I will crush his adversaries before him,
    and strike down those who hate him.
²⁵ My faithfulness and My lovingkindness will be with him,
    and by My Name his horn will be exalted.
²⁶ I will also set his hand over the sea,
    his right hand over the rivers.
²⁷ He will call to Me: 'You are my Father,ᵃ
    my God and the rock of my salvation.'
²⁸ I also will set him as firstborn—ᵇ
    the highest of the kings of earth.ᶜ ᵈ
²⁹ I will maintain My love for him forever,
    and My covenant with him will be firm.
³⁰ His seed I will establish forever,
    and his throne as the days of heaven.

³¹ If his sons forsake My *Torah*,
    and do not walk in My judgments,
³² if they violate My decrees,
    and do not keep My *mitzvot*,
³³ then I will punish their transgression with the rod,
    and their iniquity with flogging.
³⁴ But I will not withdraw My lovingkindness from him,
    nor will I betray My faithfulness.
³⁵ I will not violate My covenant,
    nor alter what My lips have uttered.
³⁶ Once for all I have sworn by My holiness
    —surely I will not lie to David—
³⁷ his descendants will endure forever,
    and his throne as the sun before Me,
³⁸ and as the moon, established forever,
    and a trustworthy witness in the sky." *Selah*

³⁹ But You have cast off and spurned,
    You have become furious with Your anointed one.

a. 89:27. cf. John 8:54.
b. 89:28. cf. Rev. 1:5.
c. 89:28. cf. Rev. 19:16.
d. 89:27–28. In most English translations, 89:27–28 are verses 26–27.

[40] You have renounced the covenant of Your servant.
     You have defiled his crown even to the ground.
[41] You have broken down all his walls.
     You reduced his strongholds to ruin.
[42] All who pass by have plundered him.
     He has become a taunt to his neighbors.
[43] You exalted the right hand of his foes
     and made all his enemies rejoice.
[44] You turned back the edge of his sword
     and have not supported him in battle.
[45] You brought his splendor to an end,
     and cast his throne down to the ground.
[46] You cut short the days of his youth.
     You covered him with shame. *Selah*
[47] How long, ADONAI, will You hide Yourself?
     Forever?
     Will Your fury keep burning like fire?
[48] Remember how short my life span is!
     For what futility have You created all the children of men?
[49] What man can live and not see death?
     Can he deliver himself from the clutches of *Sheol? Selah*
[50] Where is Your former lovingkindness, my Lord,
     which You swore to David in Your faithfulness?[e]
[51] Remember, my Lord, the mockery against Your servants
     that I bear in my heart from so many peoples.
[52] How Your enemies have mocked, ADONAI,
     how they have mocked
     the footsteps of Your Anointed One![f]

[53] Blessed be ADONAI forever.
     Amen and Amen.

Jeffrey Seif and Glenn Blank

This psalm starts on an up note, with the psalmist immediately commencing to "sing of the love of ADONAI . . . to all generations" (2). His joy stems from the good news of God's covenant with David (4) and his seed—which

e. 89:50. cf. Acts 13:34.
f. 89:52. cf. Matt. 27:29, 41; Luke 23:36.

includes all his descendants "from generation to generation" (5). It's a wonderful family promise, extending down through the royal family line. Ultimately this promise looks forward to *Mashiach Ben-David* (Messiah son of David) of Israel (Matt. 1:1).

Yet blessings through the generations of David weren't just confined to kings. Claiming that God will establish our seed too (5) is not beyond the scope of biblical faith. God desires to be praised among "the assembly of the *kedoshim*" (6)—the saints or holy ones devoted to God. His steadfast love and keeping power for David's progeny give rise to praises, attestations of His faithfulness "all around" (9). ADONAI *Elohei-Tzva'ot* (the Lord God of Armies) is feared in the "council of the holy ones" in heaven (8) as well as by everything on earth, including the sea (10) and mountains in the land (13). With a reference to His "arm" or "right hand" (14), we see the image of Messiah revealing Himself in the world. When He does, the abstract concepts of "righteousness and justice" as well as "lovingkindness and truth" become as real as angelic beings worshiping Him on His celestial throne (15).

The blessings of the covenant affect all the people of Israel, producing a "joyful shout" (16) because God favors "our horn" (18)—the king and ultimately the Messiah. They exalt "our shield" (19) who protects them from warfare. For the king is also a "warrior" (20), who can count on God's help, so long as he is loyal to God. "David My servant" has been "anointed" (21). Since prophets anointed all the kings of Israel and Judah, they foreshadowed the Anointed One, or *Mashiach*, Messiah. This anointing assures that "My arm will strengthen him" (22) and no unfriendly enemy "will exact tribute from him" (23). The descendants of David will say of God, "You are my Father, my God and the rock of my salvation" (27)—looking forward to the special Sonship of the Messiah. God promised to bless all of David's descendants through his promised "seed."

To be sure, these glorious promises have conditions. When waywardness imposes itself in subsequent generations (31–32), there is a warning of discipline with the rod and flogging (33)—a chastening literally fulfilled by invading Chaldeans, and later grievously visited upon Messiah *Yeshua*. Yet even in these circumstances, the Davidic covenant will still somehow stand. For God promises, "I will not withdraw My lovingkindness" (34) or "violate My covenant" (35), since "I have sworn by My holiness" (36). Though many have misunderstood the history of David's people, the Jews, God Himself insists that David's seed will "endure forever" (37). This promise has helped sustain the Jewish people ever since, longing in our liturgy for the Messiah to come and restore us. It may be true that Israel has had its setbacks (39–51), times when it seemed like God had "spurned" (39) David's descendants, when God "cast his throne down to the ground" (45) and "covered him with shame" (46). No wonder the psalmist wonders, "How long . . . will You hide Yourself?" (47).

Even though for millennia Jewish people have been asking this question and praying for restoration, God's Word declares that He has not abandoned His people (Rom. 11:1–2). The time is coming soon for an end to those who have "mocked the footsteps of Your Anointed One" (52). Consider how God has through it all preserved His people. Consider how God has brought His people back to the land. Consider how God has jump-started a Messianic Jewish revival in the hearts of tens of thousands of people all over the world and in the land of Israel. Now can you praise Him for His covenant faithfulness and truth?

PSALM 90

Get a Heart of Wisdom

¹ A prayer of Moses the man of God.
   My Lord, You have been our dwelling
   from generation to generation.
² Before the mountains were born,
      or You gave birth to the earth and the world,
      even from everlasting to everlasting,
   You are God!
³ You turn mankind back to dust, saying,
      "Return, children of Adam!"
⁴ For a thousand years in Your sight
      are like a day just passing by,
      or like a watch in the night.
⁵ You sweep them away in their sleep.
      In the morning they are like sprouting grass—
⁶ in the morning it flourishes and springs up,
      by evening it withers and dries up.

⁷ For we are consumed by Your anger
    and terrified by Your wrath.
⁸ You have set our iniquities before You,
    our secret sins in the light of Your presence.
⁹ For all our days have passed away under Your wrath.
    We spent our years like a sigh.
¹⁰ The span of our years is seventy
    —or with strength, eighty—
    yet at best they are trouble and sorrow.
    For they are soon gone, and we fly away.
¹¹ Who knows the power of Your anger?
    Your fury leads to awe of You.

¹² So teach us to number our days,
    so that we may get a heart of wisdom.
¹³ Relent, ADONAI! How long?
    Have compassion on Your servants.
¹⁴ Satisfy us in the morning with Your love,
    so we may sing for joy
    and be glad all our days.
¹⁵ Gladden us for as many days as You have humbled us,
    as many years as we have seen misery.
¹⁶ Let Your work appear to Your servants,
    and Your splendor on their children.
¹⁷ Let the favor of the Lord our God be upon us.
    Establish the work of our hands for us—
    yes, establish the work of our hands.

Glenn Blank

This poem is unique as "a prayer of Moses"—the great prophet makes no other contributions to the Psalter. He is called "the man of God" (1)—a title he claims just once in the *Torah* in Deuteronomy 33:1, in which "Moses the man of God blessed the *Bnei Yisrael* sons of Israel before his death." The theme of mortality is also the theme of this poem. But there are also interesting differences. The Moses of this poem proposes 80 years as a maximum span of life—and that only "with strength" (10)—though the Moses of *Torah* lived 120 years and was still pretty hale and hearty when God took him on Mount Nebo. The Moses of *Torah* was the humblest man on the face of the earth

(Num. 12:3), but this Moses takes up his theme with *chutzpah*, challenging God—confronting Him throughout this poem as *You*—for an answer to one of humanity's most difficult questions.

Few people like to think about death. Many of us are content to avoid it. We extol the virtues of God's healing power. We hope our faith in God will hold it off awhile. But the truth is, "You turn mankind back to dust" (3)—just as our first father Adam was made of dust, so we return. But the poet, representing all humanity, is determined to dialogue with his Maker about it—"from generation to generation" (1) and "from everlasting to everlasting" (2). Creatures of time dare to exchange words with the Eternal One. Then comes a line famous for the paradoxical way God looks at time: "For a thousand years in Your sight are like a day just passing by" (4). He might as well have said like a moment, snapping His fingers. Then again, at least a day gives the Eternal One the luxury of taking it in. Meanwhile, on earth and in time, human life is compared to grass that sprouts up in the morning and withers in the evening (5–6)—in a land on the edge of the desert, wildflowers perish quickly (see Isa. 40:7–8).

When confronted with death, not everyone is so sanguine and peaceful. The second section erupts with anger and wrath (7)—albeit attributed to God, not humanity. Before humanity can say a word about our fear and frustration with death, God has set "our secret sins in the light of" His presence (8). What can we say? If we ever really had the opportunity to complain to God about our death, He would simply point out "our days have passed away under" His wrath (9), as He reviews with us just how we spent our days. Gulp. Talk about fear of God (11)!

What can we say? The poet backs away from the awesome wrath of God with another famous line: "So teach us to number our days, so that we may get a heart of wisdom" (12). It's lovely even if it's impossible, since none of us knows in advance how many days we're getting. All we can do is ask God, "How long?" (13). Many other psalms ask this question, but it's typically a desperate cry by Israel for relief and redemption from her enemies. Here, it's a personal request—not really a question—for wisdom about how to make the most of our days. We can ask our Maker to "satisfy us in the morning" with His love, for He really *is* love and wants us to "sing for joy" (14). We can ask Him to "gladden us for as many days" as He has "humbled us" with misery (15). We can ask for His favor to be upon us (17). Now that's a line fit for Moses—similar to the Aaronic Benediction—may He "make His face to shine on you and be gracious to you" (Num. 6:25). Other than wisdom, there is little more the man of God—or any of us—can ask of our Maker. With God, apparently, there is no harm in asking.

PSALM 91

Dwell in the Shelter of *Elyon*

¹ He who dwells in the shelter of *Elyon*,
     will abide in the shadow of *Shaddai*.
² I will say of ADONAI,
     "He is my refuge and my fortress,
my God, in whom I trust."
³ For He will rescue you from the hunter's trap
     and from the deadly pestilence.
⁴ He will cover you with His feathers,
     and under His wings you will find refuge.
     His faithfulness is body armor and shield.
⁵ You will not fear the terror by night,
     nor the arrow that flies by day,
⁶ nor the plague that stalks in darkness,
     nor the scourge that lays waste at noon.
⁷ A thousand may fall at your side,
     and ten thousand at your right hand,
     but it will not come near you.
⁸ You will only look on with your eyes
     and see the wicked paid back.
⁹ For you have made *Elyon* your dwelling,
     even ADONAI, who is my refuge,
¹⁰ so no evil will befall you
     nor any plague come near your tent.
¹¹ For He will give His angels charge over you,
     to guard you in all your ways.
¹² Upon their hands they will lift you up,
     lest you strike your foot against a stone.[a]

a. 91:11–12. cf. Matt. 4:6; Luke 4:10–11.

¹³ You will tread upon the lion and cobra,
  trample the young lion and serpent.

¹⁴ "Because he has devoted his love to Me,
  I will deliver him.
    I will set him securely on high,
  because he knows My Name.
¹⁵ When he calls on Me, I will answer him.
    I will be with him in trouble, rescue him, and honor him.
¹⁶ With long life will I satisfy him
    and show him My salvation."

Jeffrey Seif and Glenn Blank

Generals and their soldiers have long extolled the benefits of fighting from high ground—better yet, from the upper levels of a well-fortified stronghold. The advantage of height and secure walls was so much desired that God Himself is pictured as a refuge and fortress (2) here and in many other psalms. What is poetic language for us was and is real-world language for those endeavoring to secure footholds in precarious places. You can still visit such strongholds in Israel, both ancient and modern. God is also one's personal "armor and shield" (4)—in the Hebrew, these refer to a large body shield and a small fending shield—and protection from "the arrow that flies by day" (5). Military language continues as "a thousand may fall at your side, and ten thousand at your right hand, but it will not come near you" (7).

David and his mighty men believed they experienced God's protection in actual battles, yet as the psalm progresses one has the impression the psalmist is not contending with just human adversaries. For one thing, he mixes in other imagery, such as the gentle "shadow of *Shaddai*" (1) and the calming presence of "His feathers . . . under His wings" (4) suggesting a mother eagle. In the midst of the fray, God will "give His angels charge over you, to guard you in all your ways" (11). With such supernatural combatants, it becomes clear that the psalmist is inviting us to look at life's battles from a spiritual perspective. God personally will "set him securely on high" (14). He will rescue us when we are in trouble and call on Him (15). By seeing life's battles from a spiritual perspective—"you will only look on with your eyes and see the wicked paid back" (8)—the poet is unveiling an important secret about how to go through life's struggles victoriously. If you truly trust Him to be your refuge, then "you will not fear" (5). For you will experience His protection in the midst of a battle. If you stay in the place of His presence—if "you have made *Elyon* your dwelling" (9)—you will avoid a lot of spear pricks and pestilence, for they "will not come near you" (7). If you decide, by faith, to make God your refuge, if you ask Him to open the eyes of your heart, then you will experience what David and his mighty men experienced in ancient times and what many Israel Defense Force warriors have experienced in modern times—that the mighty God truly watches over His people.

 # PSALM 92

It Is Good to Praise

¹ A psalm, a song for the *Shabbat*.
² It is good to praise ADONAI
    and to make music to Your Name, *Elyon,*
³ to declare Your love in the morning
    and Your faithfulness at night,
⁴ with a ten-string harp,
    with resounding music on the lyre.
⁵ For You made me glad, ADONAI, by Your deeds.
    I sing for joy at the works of Your hands.
⁶ How great are Your works, ADONAI!
    How profound are Your thoughts!
⁷ A brutish man does not know,
    nor does a fool understand.
⁸ Though the wicked spring up like grass,
    and all evildoers flourish,
    it is only to be ruined forever.

⁹ But You, ADONAI, are exalted forever.
¹⁰ For behold, Your enemies, ADONAI
    —behold Your enemies perish—
    all evildoers are scattered.
¹¹ But You exalted my horn like that of a wild ox.
    I am anointed with fresh oil.

¹² My eye can gaze on those lying in wait for me.

My ears hear about evildoers rising up against me.

¹³ The righteous will flourish like a palm tree.

He will grow like a cedar in Lebanon.

¹⁴ Planted in the House of ADONAI,

they will flourish in the courts of our God.

¹⁵ They will still yield fruit in old age.

They will be full of sap and freshness.

¹⁶ They declare, "ADONAI is upright, my Rock

—there is no injustice in Him."

Paul Wilbur

What a joy-filled celebration! This psalm is a song of praise intended to thank *El Elyon* for His lovingkindness, especially as we rest on *Shabbat*. The psalmist begins, טוֹב, *Tov, l'hodot l'ADONAI ool'zamayr l'shimcha Elyon*. "It is good to praise ADONAI and to make music to Your Name, *Elyon*." You may have heard that there are many words in the Hebrew language that are simply translated as "praise" in the English. Well, right here in the first verse we encounter two of them. First is the word לְהֹדוֹת, *l'hodot*, to throw or give thanks, praise, right before God. Second is לְזַמֵּר, *l'zamayr*, to sing and make music with stringed instruments in praise of God. Back in 1981 when I read this psalm in my quiet time, I picked up my stringed instrument—my guitar—and sang it back to *HaShem*, then shared it with my congregation on *Shabbat*! Israel's Hope recorded it on our first album, and people have used it many times since in approaching the throne.

My verse 2 is basically the psalm's verses 5–6 and goes like this: "You make me glad, by Your deeds, O Lord, so I sing for joy at all Your hands have made. How great are Your works, O Lord, *Elohim, baruch HaShem!*" (God, bless the Name!) Then comes the ever-famous chorus *Lai lai, lai, lai, lai lai*. . . . In the early days, some people thought there must be some hidden spiritual meaning to those words, and occasionally someone would work up the courage to actually ask what *lai, lai, lai* meant! Let me go on record here to say that it is simply a nonsensical lyric to express joy and happiness.

And why not? Look at verse 13. The righteous will flourish like the *tamar*, a water-loving date palm that flourishes in the desert oasis. Its rich foliage and long leaves are still often used in feasts and festivals to wave before the presence of the Lord. These branches were undoubtedly some that were broken off and laid on the road to welcome *Yeshua* into Jerusalem the week before *Pesach*. The psalmist then compares the righteous to the cedars of Lebanon, a stately and fragrant species used in the construction of the House of the Lord. Next comes something to shout about: planted in the House of *HaShem* those of a mature age will continue to bear fruit and stay fresh and green (14–15). Did you know that the best fruit comes from the older trees? It may be contrary to our society today that celebrates youth and tends to ignore the wisdom of those who have lived a long life, but those mature trees really do continue to flourish and produce when they are planted firmly in the courts of the Lord. Stay rooted and grounded in His House, and your future is secure!

⁂⁂⁂⁂⁂ PSALM 93 ⁂⁂⁂⁂⁂

Majestic and Unshakable

¹ ADONAI reigns—He is robed in majesty!
  ADONAI has robed and armed Himself with strength.
  Yes, the world is firmly established—unshakable.
² Your throne is established from of old.
  You are from everlasting.
³ The floods have lifted up, ADONAI,
  the floods have lifted up their voice,
  the floods lift up their crashing waves.
⁴ More than the sounds of many waters—
  more majestic than the breakers of the sea—
  so majestic is ADONAI on high!
⁵ Your testimonies are very sure.
  Holiness befits Your House, ADONAI, for endless days.

Glenn Blank

Genesis 1 tells how God imposed order on the waters, forcing the seas into their place, so that dry ground would appear. "ADONAI reigns"—since He has "firmly established" the world (1), it is equally sure that His throne is firmly established and unshakable "from of old" (2). Though the ancient floods dare to lift up their voice—surging three times with their crashing waves (3), the majesty of ADONAI reigns on high above the roar of the surging waters. We moderns haven't quite outgrown the dread of dark depths: the earth trembles, a tsunami rises and roars over the land, and people run for their lives! We still confront the chaotic unknown. This ancient poet responds: "So majestic is ADONAI on high!" (4). Then he dramatically changes the subject, from the din of the dark depths below to the serene sureness of His House above. There His "testimonies are very sure" (5). The words that His finger wrote on the stone tablets assure us—He reigns!—in absolute holiness for all eternity.

PSALM 94

He Will Not Abandon His People

¹ God of vengeance, ADONAI,
  God of vengeance, shine forth!
² Rise up, O Judge of the earth!
  Pay back to the proud what they deserve.
³ How long will the wicked, ADONAI,
  how long will the wicked gloat?
⁴ They gush out, they speak arrogance—
  all the evildoers keep boasting.
⁵ They crush Your people, ADONAI,
  and afflict Your heritage.
⁶ They slay the widow and the outsider,
  and murder the fatherless.
⁷ So they say: "ADONAI does not see—
  the God of Jacob pays no attention."

⁸ Pay attention, stupid among the people!
  Fools, when will you comprehend?
⁹ He who planted the ear, does He not hear?
  He who formed the eye, does He not see?
¹⁰ He who chastens nations, will He not rebuke—
  One who teaches humanity knowledge?

[11] *Adonai* knows human thoughts—
  they are but a breath.

[12] Blessed is the one You discipline, *Adonai*,
    and teach him from Your *Torah*,
[13] to give him rest from days of trouble
    —until a pit is dug for the wicked.
[14] For *Adonai* will not forsake His people.
    He will never abandon His inheritance.[a]
[15] For rightness will be restored to justice,
    and all the upright in heart will follow it.

[16] Who will rise up for me against the wicked?
    Who will stand up for me against evildoers?
[17] Unless *Adonai* had been my help,
    my soul would soon have dwelt in the abode of silence.
[18] If I say: "My foot has slipped,"
    Your mercy, *Adonai*, will hold me up.
[19] When my troubling thoughts multiply within me,
    Your consolations comfort my soul.
[20] Can a throne of corruption be aligned
    with You—planning distress by decree?
[21] They band together against the life of the righteous,
    and condemn innocent blood.[b]
[22] But *Adonai* has been my fortress
    and my God the rock of my refuge.
[23] He will repay them for their wickedness,
    and will annihilate them in their evil.
    Adonai our God will annihilate them.

Jeffrey Seif and Glenn Blank

Because divorce is so common in our culture, and parents abandoning children and children abandoning parents, and people wandering from relationship to relationship and from congregation to congregation, it is increasingly difficult for people today to live out lifelong commitments or even emotionally wrap their arms around a sense of faithfulness. Because people so chronically break faith, a sense of its lack subtly and forcefully imposes itself on us. Words like trust,

a. 94:14. cf. Rom. 11:2.
b. 94:21. cf. Matt. 27:4.

loyalty, and steadfast love, though perhaps understood in the mind, become incomprehensible in the heart. As a result, many may have trouble truly taking in the implications of this psalm. If that's you, because of broken relationships you have experienced, you might want to pray for healing within as you meditate on this psalm. If you are still struggling with an inner desire for vengeance against those who have hurt you, can you trust God to "shine forth" (1) and let Him be the "Judge" who will "pay back to the proud what they deserve" (2)? Perhaps unresolved tensions within your soul are like the ancient complaints against the "wicked" who still seem to "gloat" (3)—and you wonder how long you have to abide with those who "speak arrogance" (4). Have you ever felt like "they crush . . . and afflict" you (5) and wonder why the Lord allows it? When you reflect on what you have experienced, is there something within you that says, "the God of Jacob pays no attention" (7)? If so, this psalm tells you that God already knows what you are feeling: "ADONAI knows human thoughts" (11), just as *Yeshua* knew the thoughts of those who were muttering against Him.

This psalm has some truth to impart to you. The "One who teaches humanity knowledge" (10) has surely not forgotten you. He will rebuke those who betrayed you. He also wants to teach you something life-giving out of your experience (12). He wants to give you "rest from days of trouble" (13). He wants you to know in your heart that no matter who else has forsaken you, God "will not forsake His people" and "will never abandon His inheritance" (14). He wants you to know that He is the One who restores all things "to justice" for "the upright in heart" (15). When you ask, as many have, Who will rise up for me? . . . Who will stand up for me? (16), He wants you to know that He is your "help," that He will hold you up (17–18). When those "troubling thoughts multiply within," He wants you to know that He is the Comforter whose "consolations comfort my soul" (19). The one who experiences His consolations will know where to turn when an evil "throne of corruption" seems to be "planning distress" (20), or when spiritual adversaries "band together" (21) to attack the soul. Turn to the One who is your "fortress" and "rock of . . . refuge" (22), to the One who surely "will repay them for their wickedness" (23).

So, who are you going to trust? Sometimes in your inner thoughts and feelings, trusting God is easier said than done. Yet it is surely better—indeed a blessing—to pay no attention to the wicked and pay all attention to the Righteous One. For He will redeem the righteous, and those who take refuge in Him will see their reward.

PSALM 95

Today, Hear His Voice

[1] O come, let us sing for joy to ADONAI.
    Let us shout for joy to the rock of our salvation.
[2] Let us come before His presence with thanksgiving.
    Let us shout joyfully to Him with songs.
[3] For ADONAI is a great God
    and a great King above all gods.
[4] In His hand are the depths of the earth,
    the mountain peaks are His also.
[5] The sea is His—He made it,
    and His hands formed the dry land.
[6] Come, let us worship and bow down.
    Let us kneel before ADONAI our Maker.[a]
[7] For He is our God,
    and we are the people of His pasture,
    the flock of His hand.
    Today, if you hear His voice:
[8] "Do not harden your heart as at Meribah,
    as in the day of Massah in the wilderness,
[9] when your fathers tested Me,
    they challenged Me, even though they had seen My work.
[10] For forty years I loathed that generation.
    So I said: 'It is a people whose heart goes astray,
    who do not know My ways.'
[11] Therefore I swore in My anger,
    'They shall never enter into My rest.'"

Paul Wilbur

Yet another one of my King David favorites—I believe it was the second musical setting that I did for a psalm back in 1978. Although it ends on a down note, the first seven verses give us a pattern, if you will, for approaching the presence of the Holy One of Israel. Its thought is similar to one

a. 95:6. cf. Phil. 2:10.

David expresses in Psalm 100:4, but I will leave that for you to discover in a couple of pages.

The psalmist invites us to come and sing for joy to the Lord—*L'choo ne-ra-ne-na l'Adonai*—and to shout aloud to the rock of our salvation—*naria l'tsur yisheinu* (1). These words help to usher in the traditional evening *Shabbat* service. Singing praise is a good way to begin to gather our thoughts, take the focus of our daily lives off ourselves, and place the attention where it belongs—on the rock of our deliverance and salvation. Notice that the name of Messiah appears again in the last word of verse 1—*yisheinu* means "our salvation" or "our *Yeshua*." These first three verses always bring a smile to my face, because I have fond memories of leading people into the courts of the Lord with them. No matter where your life may be at the moment, it will be better by far if we only apply these few words. Why? Because our God inhabits the praises of His people (Ps. 22:4). So come let us sing for joy to the Lord! For in His presence there is fullness of joy (Ps. 16:11)!

We can walk in victory if we simply invite the presence of *Adonai* through praise. Now that we have come through His gates with a joyful song, David tells us to come before His presence with thanks and praise (2). The word תּוֹדָה, *todah*, can be translated as either praise or thanksgiving—it comes with shouts of jubilation and is given with the thank offering and the fellowship or *shalom* offering. In other words, the way to approach *Adonai* is not with religious gobbledygook, long faces, or a grocery list of requests but with songs and shouts of thanks and praise! We can praise Him for who He is (3) and thank Him for the things He has made (4–5).

Once we have come through the gates and entered the courts, what do we do now? David instructs us: "Come, let us worship and bow down." Actually, the Hebrew for "worship" and "bow down" means to prostrate oneself, as before a monarch. He follows that with, "Let us kneel before *Adonai* our Maker" (6). The root word for *kneel* here is *barakh*, which means to bless, salute, or bend the knee in humility and reverence. In our Western culture, these ways of understanding worship and honor are somewhat foreign concepts. How would you feel walking into a worship service late (of course, you wouldn't do that), only to find everyone kneeling on the floor? Though a strange sight to most of us, it is how David emphatically recommends that we approach the throne of our Maker. The words that we translate as worship in our Bibles mean that worshipers are kneeling or lying prostrate on their faces before the presence of the Lord.

One thing we learn about ourselves in this Middle Eastern book is that since we are not God, we need to walk in the ancient paths of wisdom and humility if we desire to draw near to the God of Abraham, Isaac, and Israel. David declares that ADONAI is our God, and we are His sheep, His flock (7). His words remind us of who we are, and who He is, so that we can keep our hearts right and do all things decently and in order as we worship the King. Human hearts can go astray and even provoke the anger of God, so David warns us to keep our hearts soft and not harden them (9) against the voice of ADONAI. *Yeshua* asked His disciples if His words offended them (John 6:61). Solomon warned us that an offended brother was like a walled-up city and quarrels like bars of iron (Prov. 18:19). If we desire to be a true community of faith, we need to be an exuberant people of praise and a humble and faithful flock of worshipers.

PSALM 96

Sing a New Song

¹ Sing to ADONAI a new song!
    Sing to ADONAI, all the earth.
² Sing to ADONAI, bless His Name.
    Proclaim the good news of His salvation from day to day.
³ Declare His glory among the nations,
    His marvelous deeds among all peoples.
⁴ For great is ADONAI, and greatly to be praised.
    He is to be feared above all gods.
⁵ For all the gods of the peoples are idols,
    but ADONAI made the heavens.
⁶ Splendor and majesty are before Him.
    Strength and beauty are in His Sanctuary.
⁷ Ascribe to ADONAI, O families of peoples.
    Ascribe to ADONAI glory and strength.
⁸ Ascribe to ADONAI the glory of His Name.
    Bring an offering and come into His courts.
⁹ Bow down to ADONAI in holy splendor.
    Tremble before Him, all the earth.

[10] Say among the nations: "ADONAI reigns!"
  The world is firmly established—it will not move.
  He will judge the peoples with fairness.
[11] Let the heavens be glad, let the earth rejoice.
  Let the sea roar—and all that fills it.
[12] Let the land exult—and all that is in it.
  Then all the trees of the forest will sing for joy—
[13] before ADONAI, for He is coming!
  For He is coming to judge the earth.
  He will judge the world with righteousness
  and the peoples in His faithfulness.[a]

Jeffrey Seif and Glenn Blank

Music is joy with melody. What prompts people to engage in this sort of activity—singing? Love songs are popular because we want love and security—and need it. We assuage our aggravations by letting music give voice to what we desire or possess, and through music we transcend less-than-hoped-for circumstances. Music can emotionally take us to places we want to inhabit, places that give us peace. How much more so, when music turns our hearts to the Eternal One? Here (and again in Ps. 98) we are bid to "sing . . . a new song." How can we sing a new song about the Ageless One? Surely "all the earth" has heard it all before (1)? Yet there is always something new that the birds are warbling and the bees are humming. Or are they just courting each other? No, the psalmist insists, we know better!

Sing the song to *HaShem*—"proclaim the good news of His salvation from day to day" (2). Have you ever shared the Good News—declaring "His glory" and "marvelous deeds among all peoples" (3)—through song? Our friend Paul Wilbur does it all the time. You and I may not be Paul, but can we share his songs with others who aren't singing yet? Or could those of us who can hold a tune sing of His glory to our neighbors? After all, isn't it true that He "made the heavens" (5) and "strength and beauty are in His Sanctuary" (6)? What can we do to get other people to agree that He really does have "glory and strength" (7)? How can we invite others to "come into His courts" (8)? The psalmist sings about the awesomeness of bowing in the presence of His "holy splendor" (9) within the Temple courts. Have we ever experienced His

a. 96:13. cf. Rev. 19:11.

splendor in a congregational worship service? Then let us "say among the nations: 'ADONAI reigns!'" (10).

Though it is easy and natural to sing love songs when we feel swept off our feet by a sense of "falling in love" (whatever that is), sometimes real love requires an act of the will. Optimism also sometimes comes naturally and sometimes requires an act of the will. Optimists are uplifting sorts in an otherwise downward-moving world. Do you like to be around people of hope and praise, or do you prefer rather depressing "realists"? It doesn't take much imagination, let alone faith, to point out the problems of life. Then there are possibility thinkers, people who see problems as opportunities—such as David when he saw Goliath as an opportunity to win a victory for God. Be that kind of person! Be a person with a "new song," one who approaches life with a new, fresh, faith-filled perspective. When you do, you will discover that darkness will fade into light in your own life. You will hear the heavens and the earth already rejoicing (11) and "all the trees of the forest" singing for joy (12). If you keep walking and singing faithfully, other people will want to walk alongside you and sing of His faithfulness too.

PSALM 97

Exalted above All Gods

¹ ADONAI reigns, let the earth rejoice,
    let the many islands be glad.
² Clouds and darkness are all around Him.
    Righteousness and justice are the foundation of His throne.
³ Fire goes before Him
    and burns up His adversaries on every side.
⁴ His lightning lights up the world—
    the earth sees and trembles.
⁵ The mountains melt like wax
    at the presence of ADONAI,
    at the presence of the Lord of all earth.
⁶ The heavens declare His righteousness,
    and all the peoples have seen His glory.

[7] Let all who serve graven images be ashamed—who boast in idols.
Bow down before Him, all you gods!

[8] Zion hears and is glad,
and the daughters of Judah rejoice,
because of Your judgments, ADONAI.

[9] For You, ADONAI, are *Elyon* above all the earth.
You are exalted far above all gods.

[10] You who love ADONAI, hate evil!
He watches over the souls of His godly ones.
He delivers them out of the hand of the wicked.

[11] Light is sown for the righteous
and gladness for the upright in heart.

[12] Rejoice in ADONAI, you righteous ones,
and praise His holy Name.

Jeffrey Seif and Glenn Blank

If God is a King worthy of exaltation and adoration, then the Levitical poet needs words to describe Him. Describing the invisible, within the parameters of a covenant that prohibits the making of images for Deity, is a challenge. The poet begins with "clouds and darkness" (2)—recalling the scene when God descended onto Mount Sinai. He adds fire—like the fire that never consumed the bush yet does burn up "His adversaries on every side" (3). Then "lightning lights up the world" (4)—a stunning display of His sudden splendor! This display calls for a response of awe, as "mountains melt . . . at the presence of the Lord" (5). Moreover, His glory is not just in physical things, for "the heavens declare His righteousness" (6). Others "serve graven images" (7), presumably because they are visible in their shrines, but they are powerless compared to the God of Israel, who is "above all the earth . . . exalted far above all gods" (9).

In verse 10 the poet shifts direction and tone, turning from exalting God to urging His worshipers: "You who love ADONAI, hate evil!" Praising Him is one way to worship God; righteous living is another. Those who know God personally can be confident that "light is sown for the righteous" (11). There is a kind of knowing God that goes way beyond words. We can experience how He "watches over . . . His godly ones" (10). Amazingly, the God of the universe, exalted above all, also watches over the lives of His godly ones. He is the One who delights to fill our hearts with gladness and to lead us in paths of righteousness for His Name's sake. Open your heart to the God of glory and rejoice when He calls you one of His "righteous ones" who "praise His holy Name" (12).

⁘⁘⁘⁘⁘⁘ PSALM 98 ⁘⁘⁘⁘⁘⁘

Creation Rejoices in His Salvation

¹ A psalm.
　　Sing to ADONAI a new song,
　for He has done marvelous things.
　　His right hand and His holy arm
　have won victory for Him.
² ADONAI has made His salvation known.
　　He has revealed His righteousness before the eyes of the nations.
³ He has remembered His lovingkindness,
　His faithfulness to the house of Israel.
　　All the ends of the earth have seen the salvation of our God.
⁴ Shout joyfully to ADONAI, all the earth.
　　Break forth, sing for joy, and sing praises.
⁵ Sing praises to ADONAI with the harp,
　　with the harp and a voice of melody.
⁶ With trumpets and sound of the *shofar*
　　blast a sound before the King, ADONAI.
⁷ Let the sea roar and all within it,
　　the world and those who dwell in it.
⁸ Let the rivers clap their hands,
　　let the mountains sing for joy together—
⁹ before ADONAI, for He is coming to judge the earth.
　　He will judge the world with righteousness
　　and the peoples with fairness.

Glenn Blank

They say singing to God is like praising God twice. So sing another song! Sing about His marvels. Sing about "His right hand and His holy arm" (1)— traditionally understood as an image of the Messiah reaching into the world

230

to save us. The word הוֹשִׁיעָה, *hosheeah*, comes from the same root as יְשׁוּעָה, *yeshuah*—appearing in verses 1 and 2—and can mean either victory or salvation. So the people shouted and sang when *Yeshua* came into Jerusalem—*Hosheea-na!* Save us, please! Or, Grant us victory, now! Some folks got grumpy about it, but *Yeshua* responded, "I tell you that if these keep silent, the stones will shout out!" (Luke 19:40). Yes, that's what happens! Let "all the earth . . . break forth, sing for joy" (4). Let the Levitical choir sing praises with harps, silver trumpets, and *shofars* (5–6). "Let the sea roar" along with all creatures in the ocean and on land (7). "Let the rivers clap their hands"—if you cannot imagine rivers with hands, think of them rejoicing over rapids. "Let the mountains sing" (8)—haven't you ever watched *The Sound of Music?* All creation sings because *HaShem* "is coming to judge the earth" (9). Some people may not be so giddy when the Judge comes. Yet when He comes, "the creation itself also will be set free from bondage to decay into the glorious freedom of the children of God" (Rom. 8:21). Come, with Your right hand, Your holy arm—*Hosheea-na, Yeshua,* come!

PSALM 99

Worship at His Holy Hill

¹ ADONAI reigns, let the peoples tremble.
  He is enthroned upon the *cheruvim*—let the earth shake!
² ADONAI is great in Zion
  and He is exalted above all the peoples.
³ Let them praise Your great
  and awesome Name: holy is He.
⁴ The might of a king loves justice.
  You have established fairness.
  You executed justice and righteousness in Jacob.
⁵ Exalt ADONAI our God
  and worship at His footstool: holy is He.

⁶ Moses and Aaron were among His *kohanim*—
  also Samuel among those calling on His Name.
  They called on ADONAI and He answered them.

[7] He spoke to them from the pillar of cloud.
> They kept His testimonies, and the decree that He gave them.
[8] ADONAI our God, You answered them.
> A forgiving God You were to them, though You avenged their
> misdeeds.
[9] Exalt ADONAI our God,
> and worship at His holy hill,
> for holy is ADONAI our God.

Jeffrey Seif

A journey leads people up to Mount Zion, where "ADONAI reigns" (1) and is "exalted above all the peoples" (2). People from all over the earth are urged to "exalt ADONAI our God and worship at His footstool" (5). Where is His footstool? For the Levitical psalmist, it was in the Holy of Holies within the Temple. Therefore, people are beckoned to "worship at His holy hill" (9). Given that Israelites were forbidden to worship on any hill, save for Mount Zion, the instruction is clear: those who place value in the God of Israel, who is the One true God, were to go to Jerusalem and worship Him there.

Do these instructions for ancient Israelites have implications for us, who live far from Jerusalem and its long-since-demolished Temple? Long before the Temple even stood, Moses told the people about a "place *Adonai* your God chooses to make His Name dwell," where they were to bring their tithes and offerings (Deut. 12:11). In the wilderness, the place was a wandering tabernacle. In the land, it was Shiloh and Nob until David captured Zion. After the Temple was destroyed, Jews and Messianic believers kept worshiping in houses of God wherever they were dispersed, wherever He chooses to dwell.

In our individualistic American culture, faith tends to be privatized. People emphasize a personal relationship with God, treating congregational participation with less resolve. In the world of the Psalms, worshiping at His footstool was both public—all Israel gathering at the place He chose for them—and private—each one bowing down and making one's own offerings. If God is worthy of worship to you, make the effort to go to the place He chooses for you, and there bow down at His feet.

✷✷✷✷✷✷✷✷✷ PSALM 100 ✷✷✷✷✷✷✷✷✷

Enter His Gates with Thanksgiving

¹ A psalm of thanksgiving.
  Shout joyfully to ADONAI, all the earth!
² Serve ADONAI with gladness.
  Come before His presence with joyful singing.
³ Know that ADONAI, He is God.
  It is He who has made us, and we are His.
  We are His people, the sheep of His pasture.
⁴ Enter His gates with thanksgiving
 and His courts with praise!
  Praise Him, bless His Name.
⁵ For ADONAI is good.
  His lovingkindness endures forever,
  and His faithfulness to all generations.

Paul Wilbur

This psalm is one of the best known of the psalms—and not simply because of its brevity but because it has been set so often in song. It begins *Hari-u l'ADONAI*—"Shout joyfully to ADONAI" (1) or "Make a joyful noise to ADONAI." The root of the joyful noise *hari-u* is רוּעַ, *ru-a*, which occurs thirty-three times in the *Tanakh* (Hebrew Scriptures). A *ru-a* was not just a shout or loud noise for the sake of making a sound. It was the call of a *shofar* or a battle cry before engaging the enemy. And yes, it often was a shout of joy in response to the Lord's deliverance of His people from danger. So the psalmist is saying in essence, "Give the Lord a loud shout of joy and praise, *ru-a*! For He has already delivered you from your enemies! Halleluyah!"

"Serve ADONAI with gladness" (2)—with שִׂמְחָה, *simcha*, with joy, gladness, mirth—let's celebrate! It's the same word used for the joy of a wedding day, and why not? He is the bridegroom and we, the body of Messiah, are His bride! Some Jews even name their children *Simcha* because of the joy and gladness they bring to their family. The psalmist goes on, "Come before His presence with joyful singing." The word used for "presence" is פָּנָיו, *panav*, literally, His face. The only request Moses made of ADONAI in Exodus 33 during his eighty days on top of Mount Sinai was to see His face. Now the psalmist says, come before His face with joy-filled singing! Granted, this word *panav* could be used figuratively and idiomatically to refer to His presence. But I prefer to believe that He invites us to come so close in worship that we can see His face. After all, isn't this the reward of the redeemed in Revelation 22:4? Speaking of the servants of ADONAI, John declares, "They shall see His face, and His Name shall be on their foreheads." Call me a little out there, a hopeless romantic, a dreamer if you will, but the reward of the worshiper in spirit and in truth (John 4:24) couldn't get any better than beholding *panav*, His face!

The psalmist reminds us that ADONAI made us to be His people, "the sheep of His pasture" (3). As in Psalm 95, he gives us a prescription or pattern to observe when approaching the presence or *panei* of ADONAI: enter His *sha-ar*, the entrance to His city, with *todah*, a sacrifice of songs of thanksgiving and praise extolling the mighty wonders of ADONAI, and come into His courtyard with תְּהִלָּה, *tehillah*, songs of praise and adoration (4). *Tehillah* is the name given to the Hebrew book of Psalms. It derives from the root word *halal* from which we get the Hebrew word known all over the world as Halleluyah—Praise YAH!

Be thankful, grateful to ADONAI; *yadah*, confess His greatness and bless Him; *barak*, greet and salute Him with bending of the knee. For ADONAI is good (5)—*tov*! His *chesed*, kindness, love, and mercy, and His *emunah*, faithfulness and truth—endure forever and to all generations. Aren't these the very words that Israel declared with Jehoshaphat to defeat Moab and Ammon in 2 Chronicles 20:21? Yes, they are! My *Tanakh* declares that as Israel sang this *tehillah* to ADONAI, thanking Him for the victory before they saw it, ADONAI set an ambush for their enemies, so that not one of them escaped with his life (see v. 22)! O my, the power of praise offered in spirit and truth has the authority to change the situation, the circumstances, and take captive our enemies. Come, let us sing for joy to the Lord!

PSALM 101

Pledge of Integrity

¹ A psalm of David.
   I will sing of lovingkindness and justice.
   To You, ADONAI, I will sing praises.

² I will behave wisely in the way of integrity
—when will You come to me?
I walk in my house with integrity in my heart.
³ No base thing will I set before my eyes.
Twisted behavior I hate—it will not cling to me.
⁴ A perverse heart will depart from me.
I will know nothing evil.
⁵ Whoever slanders his neighbor in secret
—him I will silence.
Who has haughty eyes and a proud heart
—him I will not tolerate.
⁶ My eyes are on the trustworthy of the land,
to be in my company.
One walking in a blameless way will serve me.
⁷ No one who practices deceit will dwell in my house.
No one who utters lies will endure before my eyes.
⁸ Each morning I silence all the land's wicked ones—
to cut off from ADONAI's city every evildoer.

Paul Wilbur

After declaring that he will sing to ADONAI of His חֶסֶד, *chesed* (mercy, loving-kindness, covenant love) and His מִשְׁפָּט, *mishpat* (judgment, righteous legal decision) (1), the poet-king makes a very bold statement of purpose: I will "walk in my house with integrity in my heart" (2). We see in this line the motivation of this song—David longs for the presence of the Lord in his heart. It's a recurring theme, as in Psalm 84:3, "My soul yearns, even faints for the courts of ADONAI." These words bring me back to the words of *Yeshua* in Matthew 5:6 when He declared, "Blessed are those who hunger and thirst . . . for they shall be satisfied." It is a very good place to find ourselves when we are so hungry for the presence of the Lord that we might faint.

The next several verses instruct us *how* to walk with integrity of heart. First, be careful to challenge everything that you set before your eyes (3). Why? Because the eye is the lamp of the body (Matt. 6:22), and so whatever you allow entrance will have power within you, and whatever you allow continual entrance will have increasing authority over you, for good or evil. Second, hate "twisted behavior" (3). There are people who believe for a little while, but then turn aside, slide back, or return to their former way of living. A man of integrity cannot afford to cling to such double-mindedness. Third, guard yourself against those with a "perverse heart" (4). The spiritual principle here is "bad company corrupts good morals" (1 Cor. 15:33). Joshua also warned the Israelites not to have anything to do with the evil practices of the people the Lord drove out before them to give them the land. Fourth, silence anyone who slanders or brings a damaging report against your neighbor (5). Silencing slander can be polite yet firm: "Would so and so want us to be talking about him/her this way?" If your goal is integrity, righteousness, and the presence of Adonai, avoid *lashon hara* (evil tongue) at all costs. Finally, welcome the trustworthy and those who seek to walk in a blameless or upright way (6). To these the king opened up his house, delighting to be in their company. David understands that we tend to become more and more like the people with whom we spend time. I met a young man in Bloomington, Indiana, back in 1976, who was so in love with God that I simply couldn't resist hanging around with him. He eventually led me to a personal relationship with *Yeshua*—because the flipside of 1 Corinthians 15:33 is also true. Godly morals and integrity of heart provoked me to a love affair with Adonai!

❉❉❉❉❉❉❉❉❉ PSALM 102 ❉❉❉❉❉❉❉❉❉❉

Prayer in Affliction

¹ A prayer of the afflicted one, when he is faint and pours out his lament before Adonai:

² Adonai, hear my prayer,
let my cry come to You.
³ Do not hide Your face from me in the day of my distress.
Turn Your ear to me—in the day I call,
answer me quickly.
⁴ For my days vanished like smoke,
and my bones were burned like coals.
⁵ My heart is stricken and withered like grass,
so that I even forget to eat my bread.
⁶ Because of the sound of my groaning,
my bones cling to my flesh.

⁷ I am like a pelican of the desert,
   like an owl of the waste places.
⁸ I lie awake, like a lonely bird on a roof.
⁹ My enemies taunt me all day.
   My deriders use my name to curse.
¹⁰ For I have eaten ashes like bread,
   and mixed my drink with tears—
¹¹ because of Your indignation and wrath,
   for You have picked me up and tossed me aside.
¹² My days are like a lengthening shadow,
   and I wither away like grass.

¹³ But You, ADONAI, sit enthroned forever.
   Your renown is from generation to generation.
¹⁴ You will arise and have compassion on Zion,
   for it is time to show favor to her,
   for the appointed time has come,
¹⁵ for her stones are dear to Your servants,
   and they cherish her dust.
¹⁶ So the nations will fear ADONAI's Name
   and all the kings of the earth Your glory.
¹⁷ For ADONAI has rebuilt Zion.
   He has appeared in His glory.
¹⁸ He has turned to the prayer of the destitute,
   and has not despised their prayer.
¹⁹ Let it be written for a generation to come,
   that a people to be created may praise ADONAI.
²⁰ For He looks down from His holy height,
   from heaven ADONAI gazes on the earth,
²¹ to hear the groaning of the prisoner,
   to set free those condemned to death,
²² to declare the Name of ADONAI in Zion
   and His praise in Jerusalem,
²³ when the peoples and the kingdoms
   assemble to worship ADONAI.

²⁴ He brought down my strength in midcourse.
   He shortened my days.
²⁵ I say, "My God,
   do not take me up in the middle of my days.
   Your years endure through all generations!

²⁶ Long ago You founded the earth,
　　the heavens are the work of Your hands.
²⁷ They will perish, but You will remain.
　　All of them will wear out like a garment.
　　Like clothing You change them, so they change.
²⁸ But You are the same,
　　and Your years will never end.
²⁹ The children of Your servants will live.
　　Their descendants will be established before You."

Jeffrey Seif and Glenn Blank

Some years ago a fuss was made when a prominent Protestant minister said, "God does not hear the prayers of Jews." Aside from the anti-Semitic connotations, it seems beyond the pay grade of the minister to inform God and the world what He can and cannot hear. This psalm assures us that God does hear the prayers of an "afflicted one" (1)—who happened to be a Jew, pouring out his ancient lament to the God of Israel.

When this Jew says "ADONAI, hear my prayer" (2) and "do not hide Your face from me" (3), he understands that God may not answer his request as quickly as he wants. Surely, many a Jew has cried out in prayer, "How long?"—including Jews praying in Psalms 4, 13, 35, 62, 74, 79, 80, 89, and 90. Alas, many a Jew has experienced the anguish of "my bones . . . burned like coals" (4) and their bones clinging to their flesh (6). The pelican, the owl, and the lonely bird (7–8) are vivid images of a Jewish soul crying out for the promised Deliverer. This Jew knows what it's like to hear others "use my name to curse" (9). This Jew knows what it's like to have "mixed my drink with tears" (10). Yet this Jew still sees that the God of Israel "will arise and have compassion on Zion" (14). He is sure that "her stones are dear to Your servants, and they cherish her dust" (15). Jerusalem stone is unique, employed worldwide in Jewish buildings as a symbol of Jewish identity. The dust reminds us of the bodies of the generations of Jewish people buried on the slopes of the Mount of Olives, awaiting the coming of Messiah.

The reverend who could not fathom that God would hear Jewish prayers probably could not fathom how God might love this particular place and city—Jerusalem. Yet the Bible indicates that a day is coming when "the nations will fear ADONAI's Name" (16). God, who "has turned to the prayer of the destitute" (18) and hears "the groaning of the prisoner" (21), also "looks down from His holy height" (20) and beholds Zion. He responds to those who declare His Name there, "His praise in Jerusalem" (22). Even if the heavens and the earth perish, the God of Israel will remain the same (27–28). One thing that will never change is His faithfulness to His covenant promises.

Though many disparage Jews and write them off as those God has rejected, pointing out all the suffering they have endured, the psalmist has this prophetic word: "The children of Your servants will live. Their descendants will be established before You" (29). Jews worldwide cry, *Am Yisrael chai*—The people of Israel live! Despite the tormentors, doubters, and even nay-saying theologians, the historical fact of Israel remains. This fact affirms that God hears those prayers. Let's get behind what God is doing. Now that we see the rebuilding of Zion (17), let's pray that He will soon appear in His glory, to those who love Zion!

PSALM 103

As a Father Has Compassion

¹ Of David.
    Bless ADONAI, O my soul,
    and all that is within me, bless His holy Name.
² Bless ADONAI, O my soul,
    and forget not all His benefits:
³ He forgives all your iniquity.
    He heals all your diseases.
⁴ He redeems your life from the Pit.
    He crowns you with lovingkindness and compassions.
⁵ He satisfies your years with good things,
    so that your youth is renewed like an eagle.

⁶ ADONAI executes justice—
    judgments for all who are oppressed.
⁷ He made His ways known to Moses,
    His deeds to the children of Israel.
⁸ ADONAI is compassionate and gracious,
    slow to anger, and plentiful in mercy.

⁹ He will not always accuse,
  nor will He keep His anger forever.
¹⁰ He has not treated us according to our sins,
  or repaid us according to our iniquities.
¹¹ For as high as the heavens are above the earth,
  so great is His mercy for those who fear Him.
¹² As far as the east is from the west,
  so far has He removed our transgressions from us.
¹³ As a father has compassion on his children,
  so *Adonai* has compassion on those who fear Him.
¹⁴ For He knows our frame.
  He remembers that we are but dust.
¹⁵ As for man, his days are like grass—
  he flourishes like a flower of the field,
¹⁶ but when the wind blows over it, it is gone,
  and its place is no longer known.
¹⁷ But the mercy of *Adonai* is from everlasting to everlasting
  on those who revere Him,
    His righteousness to children's children,
¹⁸ to those who keep His covenant,
  who remember to observe His instructions.

¹⁹ *Adonai* has set up His throne in the heavens,
  and His kingdom rules over all.
²⁰ Bless *Adonai*, you angels of His:
  mighty in strength, performing His word,
  upon hearing the utterance of His word.
²¹ Bless *Adonai*, all you His armies,
  His servants who do His will.
²² Bless *Adonai*, all His works everywhere in His dominion.
  Bless *Adonai*, O my soul!

Paul Wilbur

I find myself returning to this psalm over and over again, as a strong reminder of eternal truths. David begins by demanding praise to *Adonai* from his soul (נֶפֶשׁ, *nefesh*) (1). This word appears 753 times in the *Tanakh* and carries a variety of meanings, but generally it refers to a man's inner being, thoughts, emotions, and will. But David goes a little further than "my soul" when he adds, "and all that is within me," which carries with it even the physical parts of a man's core, his bowels and organs—this guy is a very serious worshiper! Have you ever prayed or worshiped so deep and hard that you felt doubled over at the waist? I think this is the kind of praise that David is demanding of himself here, the kind that gives birth to something of substance from the depths of an individual.

After repeating this demand of his soul (2), David gives a litany of reasons why *ADONAI* is worthy of such praise. First, he reminds us that our God forgives *all* our iniquity (3)—the word David uses refers to sin that is particularly evil, the conscious twisting or perverting of the truth. Next he declares very boldly that *ADONAI* heals *all* our diseases, reminding us of one of His covenant names, *ADONAI Rofechah*, the Lord who heals you (Exod. 15:26). David reminds us that it is *ADONAI* who has redeemed—or purchased our lives back—from שַׁחַת, *shachat*, the Pit (4). It could refer to a deep pit that was dug in order to catch lions or the kind of hole that Joseph's brothers used to imprison him where he would have died a slow, painful death, with no water or food. Or it could refer to the bowels of hell. Each of us who know the Lord should be very glad that He has come to rescue us from this place of terror and eternal torment! After forgiving us of the worst kind of sin, healing us from life-threatening diseases, and purchasing us back from an inescapable prison, *ADONAI* bestows on us the unbelievable honor of His lovingkindness, compassion, and blessing! David has summarized the entire Good News of Messiah *Yeshua* in a few very exciting verses. Forgiveness, healing, redemption, and sonship—what an awesome God we serve! Are you ready to bless Him yet?

To top all this good news off to overflowing, David now promises that the Lord "satisfies your years with good things" and renews your youth "like an eagle" (5). There are several stages of life for eagles when their plumage changes color for protection and maturity, signaling the stage of life they are in. It is a glorious image for us. The God of Israel protects all who are wronged or oppressed (6). He makes known His ways (7). He is compassionate and gracious and slow to anger (8)—reminding me of the admonition to us in Jacob (James) 1:19, "Be quick to listen, slow to speak, and slow to anger." In so doing we show ourselves more like our gracious Father.

David reminds us that *ADONAI* "has not treated us according to our sins" (10), but rather "as far as the east is from the west, so far has He removed our transgressions from us" (12). These verses always take me back to the priestly prayer *Yeshua* taught us to pray, "Forgive us our debts as we also have forgiven our debtors." We have been forgiven for so much! David reminds us that we were made from the dust (14) and our days on this earth are fleeting (15–16), but the lovingkindness of ADONAI is everlasting (17). He reserves this lovingkindness for all "who keep His covenant" (18). Finally, after entreating the angels and His servants and everything else to bless ADONAI (20–22), David ends as he began: "Bless ADONAI, O my soul!" Is your soul ready to bless Him yet?

PSALM 104

ADONAI Rejoices in His Works!

¹ Bless ADONAI, O my soul.
  ADONAI my God, You are very great!
  You are clothed with splendor and majesty—
² wrapping Yourself in light as a robe,
  stretching out heaven like a curtain,
³ laying beams for His upper rooms in waters,
  making the clouds His chariot,
  walking on the wings of the wind,
⁴ making His angels spirits,
  His servants a flaming fire.
⁵ He set the earth upon its foundations,
  so it should not totter forever and ever.
⁶ You covered it with the deep as with a garment—
  the waters standing above the mountains.
⁷ At Your rebuke the waters fled.
  At the sound of Your thunder they hurried away.
⁸ The waters go up the mountains,
  then down to the valleys—
  to the place that You assigned to them.
⁹ You set a boundary to the waters
  that they may not cross over,
  so they may not return to cover the earth.

[10] You make springs gush into the valleys.
>> They run between the mountains.
[11] They give drink to all the beasts of the field—
>> the wild donkeys quench their thirst.
[12] Beside them the birds of the sky dwell—
>> they sing among the branches.
[13] He waters mountains from His upper rooms.
>> The earth is full of the fruit of Your labors.
[14] He causes grass to spring up for the cattle,
>> and vegetation for man to cultivate,
> to bring forth bread out of the earth,
[15] wine that makes man's heart glad,
> oil to make his face shine,
> and bread that sustains man's heart.
[16] The trees of ADONAI are satisfied,
>> the cedars of Lebanon that He planted,
[17] where birds make their nests,
>> and the stork—her home is the fir trees.
[18] The high mountains are for wild goats,
>> the cliffs a refuge for rock badgers.

[19] He made the moon for appointed times,
>> the sun knows its going down.
[20] You bring darkness, so it becomes night,
>> when all the beasts of the forest prowl.
[21] The young lions roar for prey,
>> seeking their food from God.
[22] But when the sun rises, they gather
>> and lie down in their dens.
[23] Man goes out to his work,
>> and to his labor until the evening.

[24] ADONAI, how countless are Your works!
>> In wisdom You made them all—
>> the earth is full of Your creatures.
[25] There is the sea, vast and wide,
>> teeming with gliding things innumerable,
>> living creatures, both small and large.
[26] There, ships go to and fro.
>> Leviathan—You formed to frolic there.

²⁷ They all look to You to give them
    their food at the right time.
²⁸ When You give it to them, they gather it up.
    When You open Your hand, they are satisfied with good.
²⁹ But when You hide Your face—they are dismayed.
    You take away their breath—they perish,
    and return to their dust.
³⁰ You send forth Your *Ruach*—they are created,
    and You renew the face of the earth.

³¹ May the glory of *ADONAI* endure forever!
    May *ADONAI* rejoice in His works!
³² He looks at the earth, and it trembles.
    He touches the mountains, and they smoke.
³³ I will sing to *ADONAI* as long as I live!
    I will sing praise to my God yet again!
³⁴ Let my meditation be sweet to Him.
    I—I will rejoice in *ADONAI*.
³⁵ Let sinners vanish from the earth
    and let the wicked be no more.
    Bless *ADONAI*, O my soul. *Halleluyah!*

Glenn Blank and Jeffrey Seif

The ancient psalmist is filled with wonder at the splendor of God (1). We live in fine homes; they lived in tents or in rooms inserted into the thick walls of their towns. Speaking of God "stretching out heaven like a curtain" (2) requires that we imagine what a tent dweller would have seen when he pulled back the flap of his tent to look up at the unpolluted sky. The phrase "beams for His upper rooms" (3) requires that we think about the rough wood construction of simple houses. When the poet sees God wrapping Himself "in light as a robe" (2), we need to see Joseph's coat as a glorious yet simple garment. Visualizing clouds as His chariot and angels as flaming fire (3–4), we may imagine the swiftest jets and fiercest tanks of ancient armies.

Then the ancient Hebrew poet, living in a land surrounded by deserts, sees life-giving water flowing everywhere. He sees water in the deep oceans and in the high mountains (6), water hurrying from the thunder (7), water flowing down to the valleys (8), water staying within boundaries (9), yet gushing forth in wadis between mountains (10), water giving drink to the wild donkeys and birds in the branches (11–12), water filling up fruit and bringing forth bread and wine (13–15), and water satisfying the trees (16). Can you see all this water shimmering the splendor of God? Should we with our modern plumbing be as excited? Let's not take life-giving water for granted! Water symbolizes the life of the Spirit of God. As the risen *Yeshua* says in Revelation 21:6, "To the thirsty I will freely give from the spring of the water of life."

Next the poet turns to time—not in terms of days and months named after pagan gods (Thors-day, Saturn-day, Janus-ary), but in terms of "the moon for appointed times" (19) and the cycle of the sun to govern the activities of prowling animals by night (20), young lions (21–22), and working man (23).

The wonder expands even wider, as the poet considers all the creatures on God's earth (24), and then "the sea, vast and wide" (25). To the ancient Hebrew living in the Jerusalem hills, what goes on under the surface must have been mostly a mystery. Creatures washed ashore, but what was Leviathan (26)—a whale, a giant squid, or some other sea monster? With scuba gear and automated submarines, how much more can we wonder! These days, many people worry whether earth can survive as it overheats with greenhouse gases and its resources are being depleted. They would do well to consider the confidence of the Hebrew poet who sees the Creator opening His hand to satisfy all living things with good (28). On the other hand, watch out when He hides His face and takes away the *Ruach* or breath of life (29). Humanity's only hope is to draw near to the One who has the power and goodness to "renew the face of the earth" (30).

After extolling the virtues of God's masterpiece, the poet exclaims, "May ADONAI rejoice in His works!" (31). The poem ends with a song of "praise to my God yet again" (33). Meditating on our God who sustains and renews all things, the poet rejoices. Because God is good (all the time!), those who look to Him can count on Him to renew all things, while "sinners vanish from the earth" and the wicked will "be no more" (35). The implications are striking. God is at work in life, new life and renewed life, whereas the godless fall into disorientation, disarray, and decay. Better to be on God's side, don't you think?

✳✳✳✳✳✳✳ PSALM 105 ✳✳✳✳✳✳✳

Tell His Wonders for Israel

¹ Praise ADONAI, call upon His Name.
　　Make known His deeds among the peoples.
² Sing to Him, sing praises to Him—
　　tell about all His wonders!　.
³ Glory in His holy Name.
　　Let the heart of those who seek ADONAI rejoice.
⁴ Seek ADONAI and His strength,
　　seek His face always.
⁵ Remember His wonders that He has done,
　　His miracles and the judgments of His mouth,
⁶ O seed of Abraham, His servant,
　　O children of Jacob, His chosen ones.

⁷ He is ADONAI our God.
　　His judgments are in all the earth.
⁸ He remembers His covenant forever—
　　the word He commanded for a thousand generations—
⁹ which He made with Abraham,
　　and swore to Isaac,
¹⁰ and confirmed to Jacob as a decree,
　　to Israel as an everlasting covenant,
¹¹ saying, "To you I give the land of Canaan,
　　the portion of your inheritance."
¹² When they were but few in number,
　　few indeed, and foreigners in it,[a]
¹³ wandering from nation to nation,
　　from one kingdom to another people,
¹⁴ He allowed no one to oppress them—
　　for their sake He rebuked kings:
¹⁵ "Touch not My anointed ones,
　　and do My prophets no harm."

¹⁶ He called down a famine on the land.
　　He broke the whole supply of bread.

a. 105:12. cf. Heb. 11:9.

¹⁷ He sent a man before them—
　　Joseph, sold as a slave.
¹⁸ They hurt his feet with shackles,
　　　he was put in irons—
¹⁹ till the time that his word came true—
　　the word of ADONAI proved him true!
²⁰ The king sent and released him.
　　　The ruler of the peoples set him free.
²¹ He made him lord of his house,
　　　ruler over all his possessions,
²² to discipline his princes at his will,
　　　and teach his elders wisdom.
²³ Then Israel came into Egypt,
　　　Jacob sojourned in the land of Ham.
²⁴ He made His people very fruitful,
　　　and made them more numerous than their foes.
²⁵ He turned their hearts to hate His people,
　　　to deal shrewdly with His servants.
²⁶ He sent Moses His servant,
　　　and Aaron, whom He had chosen.
²⁷ They performed His signs among them
　　　—miracles in the land of Ham.
²⁸ He sent darkness, and it was dark,
　　　so they did not rebel against His words.
²⁹ He turned their waters into blood,
　　　causing their fish to die.
³⁰ Their land swarmed with frogs,
　　　even in their royal chambers.
³¹ He spoke, and a swarm of gnats came
　　　within all their borders.
³² He gave them a rain of hail,
　　　flames of fire throughout their land.
³³ He struck their vines and their fig trees
　　　and shattered the trees of their country.
³⁴ He spoke, and the locust came
　　　—young locusts without number—
³⁵ to eat up every green thing in their land
　　　and eat up the fruit of their ground.
³⁶ Then He struck all the firstborn in their land,
　　　the firstfruits of all their vigor.

[37] Then He brought them out with silver and gold,
　　　and no one among His tribes faltered.
[38] Egypt was glad when they left—
　　　for dread of them had fallen on them.
[39] He spread a cloud as a covering
　　　and fire to give light at night.
[40] They asked, and He brought quail,
　　　and satisfied them with the bread of heaven.[a]
[41] He opened a rock, and waters gushed out,
　　　flowed as a river in dry places.
[42] For He remembered His holy word
　　　to Abraham His servant.
[43] So He brought forth His people with joy,
　　　His chosen ones with singing.
[44] He gave them the lands of the nations,
　　　so they inherited the labor of the peoples
[45] so that they might keep His statutes
　　　and observe His laws.
　　　Halleluyah!

Paul Wilbur

Psalm 105 brings back such fond memories for me that I simply cannot help relaying a short story of grace and love. The year was 1981 and my small yet budding family had left the familiarity of Bloomington, Indiana, for the strange shores of Rockville, Maryland, and a small house of worship called Beth Messiah Congregation. My son was merely six months old, and my wife and I had been married for only three and a half years, but the call to minister "to the Jew first" was too great to ignore. The invitation to be worship leader and cantor came from some formidable folks as well—Sid Roth, Dan Juster, and Paul Lieberman were among those eager for us to say yes. So with no promises, jobs, or living quarters, off we went. Packing was easy; it all fit in a four-by-eight-foot rental trailer.

Once on-site I learned about a very gifted musician who had recently given his life to *Yeshua* and had also sworn off music, as it had been a big lifestyle

a. 105:40. cf. John 6:31–40.

trap for him. After some talk and prayer at my apartment, Marc Chopinsky asked me to pray for him about using music for ADONAI and for the ability to write songs that would glorify the Lord. I did, and then stood back and watched what *Yeshua* could do with a surrendered gift. About a week later, Marc came back to me with the very first song he had written—taken from Psalm 105. He sang for me with a hesitating voice:

> O give thanks to the Lord, call upon His name.
> Seek the Lord and His strength, glory to His name.
> Ha-le-lu-yah!

This song and many others of his became foundational worship songs for the Messianic movement for decades, and now his son also writes and sings worship songs from their home in Israel.

Psalm 105 serves us today not only as yet another call to worship but also as a history lesson and a stark reminder of both covenant and faithfulness. David entreats the people of Israel to praise and seek ADONAI, to remember His marvelous works and judgments, and to make them known (1–7). He then reminds them of the covenant made with Abraham, Isaac, and Jacob "for a thousand generations" (8–10). Is it just a rehashing of old material? Oh no, for even today the rightful ownership of that tiny piece of land is still in contention by right of lineage and inheritance! Verse 11 is a very specific deed of ownership, and the language is crystal clear.

Next David launches into a detailed telling of the history of that covenant and people and how it all worked out. We hear about the nation that started as a family; the story of Joseph and enslavement in Egypt; the increase of the people and the hatred of a pharaoh who knew not Joseph; the coming of Moses and the ten plagues, all to let the people of the covenant go free. There is a detailed telling of the great exodus, feeding and watering millions of people in a desert for forty years—all because ADONAI remembered His covenant promise to His friend Abraham, all so that Israel would know Him. Then, as a priestly nation among nations, they would make His ways and Name known among the gentiles. Praise ADONAI!

So do we really need a moral to the story, or is it clear? When ADONAI makes a covenant promise, a *brit*, He keeps it to the full. He is faithful, loving, and kind, and His track record is without a blemish since the beginning of time. Praise ADONAI!

PSALM 106

ADONAI Still Faithful to Israel

¹ *Halleluyah!*
    Praise ADONAI, for He is good,
    for His lovingkindness endures forever.
² Who can speak of ADONAI's mighty acts
    or declare His praise?

³ Blessed are those who maintain justice,
    who do what is right at all times.
⁴ Remember me, ADONAI,
    when You show favor to Your people.
    Visit me with Your salvation,
⁵ so I may behold the prosperity of Your chosen ones,
    exult in the joy of Your nation,
    and give praise with Your inheritance.

⁶ We have sinned with our fathers,
    we have committed iniquity,
    we have acted wickedly.
⁷ Our fathers in Egypt did not ponder Your wonders.
    Nor did they remember Your abundant lovingkindness,
    but rebelled by the sea—at the Sea of Reeds.
⁸ Yet He saved them for His Name's sake,
    to make His mighty power known.
⁹ He rebuked the Sea of Reeds
    and it dried up,
    and He led them through the depths as through a wilderness.
¹⁰ So He saved them from the hand of those who hated them,
    redeemed them from the enemy's hand.
¹¹ The waters covered their adversaries—
    not one of them was left.
¹² Then they believed His words.
    They were singing His praise.

¹³ How quickly they forgot His works,
    and would not wait for His counsel!
¹⁴ In the wilderness they craved ravenously,
    in the desert they tested God.

[15] So He gave them what they asked for,
  but sent a wasting disease among them.
[16] Then they envied Moses in the camp,
  and also Aaron, the holy one of ADONAI.
[17] The earth opened up, swallowed Dathan,
  and covered the company of Abiram.
[18] Also a fire blazed in their company,
  a flame consumed the wicked.

[19] They made a calf in Horeb
  and worshipped a molten image.
[20] Thus they exchanged their glory
  for an image of a grass-eating ox.
[21] They forgot God their Savior,
  who had done great things in Egypt—
[22] miracles in the land of Ham,
  awesome things by the Sea of Reeds.
[23] So He commanded their extermination,
  had not Moses, His chosen one,
  stood in the breach before Him,
  to turn His wrath from destroying them.

[24] Then they scorned the pleasing land—
  they did not trust in His word.
[25] Instead, they grumbled in their tents.
  They would not listen to ADONAI's voice.
[26] Therefore He swore to them
  that He would make them fall in the desert,
[27] and disperse their offspring among the nations,
  and scatter them through the lands.

[28] Then they yoked themselves to Baal of Peor,
  and ate the sacrifices of dead things.
[29] So they provoked Him with their deeds,
  and a plague broke out among them.
[30] But Phinehas stood up and intervened,
  so the plague was stopped.
[31] It was credited to him as righteousness,
  from generation to generation forever.

[32] By the waters of Meribah they angered Him,
  and trouble came on Moses because of them.

[33] For they embittered his spirit
    and he spoke rashly with his lips.

[34] They did not destroy the peoples,
    as ADONAI had commanded them.
[35] Instead they mingled with the nations
    and learned their practices.
[36] They worshipped their idols,
    which became a snare to them.
[37] They even sacrificed their sons
    and their daughters to demons.
[38] They shed innocent blood—
    the blood of their sons and their daughters,
    sacrificed to the idols of Canaan.
    So the land was desecrated with blood.
[39] So they defiled themselves by their deeds,
    and prostituted themselves by their practices.
[40] Therefore the anger of ADONAI was kindled against His people,
    and He abhorred His inheritance.
[41] He handed them to the nations—
    those who hated them ruled over them.
[42] Their enemies oppressed them,
    so they were subdued under their hand.
[43] Many times He delivered them,
    but they kept rebelling deliberately,
    and so sank low into their iniquity.
[44] Yet He saw their distress,
    when He heard their cry,
[45] remembered His covenant to them,[a]
    and relented in the greatness of His mercy.
[46] He caused them to be pitied
    in the presence of all their captors.

[47] Save us, ADONAI our God,
    and gather us from the nations,
    so we may praise Your holy Name
    and triumph in Your praise.
[48] Blessed be ADONAI, the God of Israel,
    from everlasting even to everlasting!

a. 106:45. cf. Luke 1:67–79.

Let all the people say, "*Amen!*"
Halleluyah!

Glenn Blank

There are many reasons to praise ADONAI. This psalm begins with several noble ones elaborated upon elsewhere: His goodness and lovingkindness (1), His mighty acts (2), His justice and righteousness (3), His grace and salvation (4), the blessings of prosperity and joy He has given His chosen people (5)—when they have been faithful to Him.

But the rest of this psalm offers an unusual rationale for praise—our sin! Well, if our iniquity and wickedness (6) could actually be any good to God at all, we certainly have plenty to offer! We go back to Egypt, when our unbelieving ancestors were ignorant of His wonders, and after the miracle at the Sea of Reeds, actually had the *chutzpah* to grumble and rebel (7). But His mercy, saving them "for His Name's sake" (8), magnifies praise for His power. Though they didn't deserve it, He "saved them from the hand of those who hated them" (10). And sure enough, they shook off their stupor and believed and sang His praise (12). But it didn't last (13). Soon they were craving and testing the patience of the Almighty (14). So He disciplined them. He gave them what they craved, but along with it came "a wasting disease" (15). That's something for us to ponder—should we ever act like our ancestors with our appetites, or scorn the leaders God has appointed over us (16), or make idols of ordinary things (19–20), or simply forget God our Savior and His awesome deeds (21–22).

The consequences for such brazen disobedience were disastrous—and indeed would have destroyed them had not Moses "stood in the breach" on their behalf (23). When we have grieved God, who has stood in the breach for *us*? *HaShem* doesn't ask much from us. In response to His wonderful love, He would appreciate us thanking and trusting Him. Things go well for us when we do, but our ancestors showed what happens when we grumble in unbelief instead (25). Eventually, it brought on a curse, not only making them collapse in the desert (26) but ultimately dispersing their descendants among the nations (27).

And on it went. Because they attached themselves to a false god with horrible sacrifices, He sent a plague among them (28–29). Only the zeal of Phinehas put a stop to it (30–31). They provoked Moses, who had for so long interceded for them, to rash anger (32–33). Though the next generation was better, entering the Promised Land, they did not destroy the nations with their idols but joined them in worshiping their idols (34–36), even destroying their children as sacrifices to demons (37–38). Because our ancestors "defiled themselves" (39), *HaShem* "abhorred His inheritance" (40) and gave them over to the nations who hated them (41). Now it's getting uncomfortable for us. Our more recent forebearers—our parents and grandparents—have experienced this oppression of the nations. When will our people stop "rebelling deliberately" that we might not sink so low into iniquity (43)?

Amazingly, even the long, sad history of our people gives praise and honor to *HaShem*. "But where sin increased, grace overflowed even more" (Rom. 5:20). When a corrupt, powerful king of France asked Blaise Pascal for evidence of God's power, the great philosopher replied, "Why, the Jews, your Majesty—the Jews!" Though our people have been unfaithful and suffered the terrible consequences of exile, nevertheless God has "remembered His covenant to them" (45) and "caused them to be pitied" (46). The Puritans, contemporaries of Pascal (four centuries ago), foresaw that God would keep His promise and "gather us from the nations." Why? So that "we may praise" His holy Name (47). Truly, the record of Israel, risen from the ashes, a nation reborn in a day (Isa. 66:8), is a "triumph in Your praise" (47). Therefore, let all people bless ADONAI, the God of Israel, forever! Amen!

PSALM 107

His *Chesed* and His Wonders

¹ Praise ADONAI, for He is good,
    for His lovingkindness endures forever.
² Let the redeemed of ADONAI say so—
    whom He redeemed from the hand of the foe,
³ whom He gathered out of the lands,
  from the east and from the west,
  from the north and from the sea.
⁴ Some wandered in a desert, a wasteland.
    They found no way to an inhabited city.

⁵ Hungry and thirsty,
    their souls ebbed away.
⁶ So they cried out to ADONAI in their distress,
    and He delivered them out of their troubles.
⁷ Then He led them by a straight way
    to go to a city where they could live.
⁸ Let them praise ADONAI for His mercy
    and His wonders for the children of men,
⁹ for He satisfies the thirsty soul
    and fills the hungry soul with goodness.

¹⁰ Some sat in darkness and deep gloom,
    prisoners in misery and iron chains,
¹¹ for they had defied God's words,
    and spurned the counsel of *Elyon*.
¹² So He humbled their heart with trouble.
    They stumbled, and no one was helping.
¹³ So they cried out to ADONAI in their distress,
    and He delivered them out of their troubles.
¹⁴ He brought them out of darkness
    and deep gloom, breaking their chains.
¹⁵ Let them praise ADONAI for His mercy,
    and His wonders for the children of men,
¹⁶ for He shattered bronze gates,
    and broke into pieces iron bars.

¹⁷ Some became fools because of their rebellious ways,
    and were afflicted due to their iniquities.
¹⁸ Their soul abhorred all food,
    and they drew near the gates of death.
¹⁹ So they cried out to ADONAI in their distress,
    and He delivered them out of their troubles.
²⁰ He sent His word and healed them,
    and rescued them from their pits.
²¹ Let them praise ADONAI for His mercy,
    and His wonders for the children of men.
²² Let them sacrifice thank offerings
    and tell of His works with joyful singing.

²³ Some go out to the sea in ships,
    doing business on the mighty waters.

²⁴ They saw the works of ADONAI,
 and His wonders in the deep.
²⁵ For He spoke and raised a stormy wind,
 lifting up towering waves.
²⁶ They mounted up to the sky
 and plunged down to the depths.
 In their peril their souls melted away.
²⁷ They reeled and staggered like a drunk,
 and all their skill was bewildered.
²⁸ So they cried out to ADONAI in their distress,
 and He brought them out of their troubles.
²⁹ He stilled the storm to a whisper—
 the waves were hushed.^a
³⁰ They were glad when it became calm,
 and He led them to their desired haven.
³¹ Let them praise ADONAI for His mercy,
 and His wonders to the children of men.
³² Let them exalt Him in the congregation of the people,
 and praise Him at the assembly of elders.

³³ He turns rivers into a wilderness
 and springs of water into thirsty ground,
³⁴ and a fruitful land into a salt waste,
 because of the evil of its inhabitants.
³⁵ He turns a desert into a pool of water,
 a dry land into springs of water.
³⁶ There He brings the hungry to live,
 and they establish a city for a dwelling.
³⁷ So they sow fields and plant vineyards
 that yield a fruitful harvest.
³⁸ He blesses them, they multiply greatly,
 and He does not let their herds diminish,
³⁹ after they were few and crushed
 by oppression, calamity and sorrow.

⁴⁰ He pours contempt on princes,
 making them wander in trackless waste.
⁴¹ But He lifts the needy high above affliction,
 and makes their families like a flock.

a. 107:29. cf. Luke 8:24–25.

[42] The upright see it and are glad,
    and all iniquity shuts its mouth.
[43] Who is wise?
    Let him observe these things,
    and consider ADONAI's lovingkindness.

Paul Wilbur

Opening with the familiar refrain, "Praise ADONAI, for He is good, for His lovingkindness endures forever" (1), this psalm is set more like a modern chorus than most others. The entire forty-three verses underscore this refrain, "Let them praise ADONAI for His mercy, and His wonders for the children of men" (8, 15, 21, 31). This line appears almost as a pre-chorus would in today's style of musical writing, and the recurring cry carries more revelation than may be evident at first reading. What is this hidden wisdom? The psalmist knows—not simply by revelation but also by experience—that ADONAI inhabits the praises of His people (Ps. 22:4). He knows almost instinctively that if Israel would turn from their ways and open wide their mouths (Ps. 81:11) that the Lord would open their prison doors and set the captives free. David had an incredible revelation about praise and the presence of God, which he passed on to other Levitical poets and sings and declares over and over again in his songs.

Then there are the four statements of deliverance (6, 13, 19, 28). After each section about hardship and destruction he interjects verses of hope and deliverance. These stories reflect patterns that Jews have experienced over and over again, and especially in recent times. Verses 2–8 give a short telling of the gathering of Israel—could it also be a prophetic reestablishment of modern Israel, "whom He gathered out of the lands" (3)? Verse 10 sounds to me like a foreshadowing of the Holocaust—there is much in this song about our struggles with "darkness and deep gloom" and the deliverance of ADONAI. Verse 11 explains that the cause of our exile is rebellion against God's words. This may seem harsh, but Moses foretold the same thing, at length, at the end of Deuteronomy. God responds to rebellion not by rejecting His people but by humbling "their heart with trouble" (12). When our people "cried out to ADONAI in their distress" (13), He delivered them—though not all acknowledge what He has done. Yet many Holocaust survivors have found their way back to the Lord.

Many "became fools because of their rebellious ways" (17). Some practiced empty self-denial (18), but only God's word healed them (20). Some set out to do commerce on the seas (23), but found that in the storm "all their skill was bewildered" (27), for only God can still "the storm to a whisper" (29)—looking forward to the One who is the Master of the waves.

In verses 33–36 ADONAI reveals His mastery over the land, either to make it a barren, thirsty ground, or to restore the dry land with springs of water. God is so gracious! How often our friends in Israel have asked us to pray for rain during the winter, and we rejoice when our prayers are answered! Yet how much He wants His people to know He is the One who "brings the hungry to live" (36), He is the One who gives them a fruitful harvest (37), He is the One who blesses them (38) after they were "few and crushed" (39). When will all Israel "see it" and be glad (42)? When will our people be wise and "observe these things, and consider ADONAI's lovingkindness" (43)? O Lord, open the eyes of our hearts!

✳✳✳✳✳✳✳ PSALM 108 ✳✳✳✳✳✳✳✳

With God We Do Valiantly

¹ A song, a psalm of David.
² My heart is steadfast, O God.
> I will sing, sing praises with all my soul.
³ Awake, harp and lyre—
> I will awaken the dawn!
⁴ I will give thanks to You, ADONAI, among the peoples,
> I will sing praises to You among the nations.
⁵ For Your love is higher than the heavens,
> Your faithfulness reaches to the clouds.
⁶ Be exalted, O God, above the heavens,
> let Your glory be above all the earth.
⁷ Let Your beloved ones be delivered.
> Save with Your right hand, answer me!

⁸ God has spoken in His Sanctuary:
> "I will triumph! I will parcel out Shechem,
and measure out the valley of Succot.

⁹ Gilead is Mine, Manasseh is Mine.
 Also Ephraim is a helmet for My head,
 Judah is my scepter.
¹⁰ Moab is My washbowl.
 I throw my shoe on Edom.
 I shout in triumph over Philistia."

¹¹ Who will bring me into the fortified city?
 Who will lead me to Edom?
¹² O God, have You not spurned us?
 Will You go out no more with our armies?
¹³ Give us help against the adversary—
 for useless is deliverance through man.
¹⁴ With God we will do valiantly—
 and He will trample our foes.

Jeffrey Seif and Glenn Blank

Many do not know what to do with God commanding wars or the songs of warriors. Are they out of place with a modern religion? Since *Yeshua* teaches His disciples to turn the other cheek (Matt. 5:39), does that mean He wants believers to be sheepish, letting the wicked walk over them? What about soldiers and sailors, as well as police and security officers, who put their lives on the line to defend their country? Petitions for help are profound when one's own life is on the line. When the lives of comrades, friends, and loved ones hang in the balance, everything is on the line—there at the front line.

Actually, this psalm begins as a song of praise (2), with harp and lyre awakening the dawn (3). It calls for praise "among the peoples" (4), perhaps reminding us of the victory of Jehoshaphat through the Levites singing God's praises before the armies (2 Chron. 20:20–24). Far above the earth and the heavens, God is exalted in His glory (5–6). Far away from battlefields, tucked away in our respective houses of worship, we can also sing these songs. But if you are closer to the front line—as everyone in the land of Israel was then and is today—it's not hard to remember that when we ask God to "save with Your right hand" (7), it's a reference to the sword or weapon hand.

The rest of the poem is a war cry, repeating a passage from Psalm 60. From His sanctuary, the Almighty is the Commander in Chief, declaring, "I will triumph!" The Lord of Israel's armies will secure the home territories of

Shechem, Gilead, Manasseh, Ephraim, and Judah (8–9). Then He will take possession of the ever-threatening neighbors—Moab, Edom, and Philistia (10–11). Yet the armies of Israel cannot prevail without God's help, leading them to wonder if God has "spurned" them (12), "for useless is deliverance through man" (13). But "with God we will do valiantly" (14).

It is a source of comfort and strength to know that God is there to help us with our real-world struggles. The battle belongs to the Lord (1 Sam. 14:47). Whatever your battles, take courage, knowing that the Lord of armies will show Himself strong on behalf of those who put their trust in Him.

❋❋❋❋❋❋❋ PSALM 109 ❋❋❋❋❋❋❋

Prayer against an Accuser

¹ For the music director, a psalm of David.
    O God of my praise, be not silent.
² For the wicked and the deceitful
    have opened their mouth against me.
    They spoke to me with a lying tongue,
³ with hateful words surrounded me,
    and fought against me without cause.
⁴ In return for my love they are my accusers,
    but I am in prayer.
⁵ They repay me evil for good,
    and hatred for my love.

⁶ Set a wicked man over him,
    let an accuser[a] stand at his right hand.
⁷ When he is judged,
    let him be found guilty,
    and may his prayer be as sin.
⁸ Let his days be few,
    let another take his position.
⁹ May his children be fatherless,
    and his wife a widow.

a. 109:6. Heb. *satan*.

¹⁰ Let his children wander and beg
    and may they search in their ruins.
¹¹ Let a creditor seize all he has,
    and may strangers plunder his labor.
¹² Let no one show him mercy,
    or take pity on his fatherless children.
¹³ Let his posterity be cut off,
    and his name be blotted out in the next generation.
¹⁴ May the guilt of his fathers be remembered before ADONAI,
    the sin of his mother never blotted out.
¹⁵ Let their sins be before ADONAI continually,
    that He may cut off the memory of them from the earth.
¹⁶ For he never remembered to show mercy.
    But he persecuted a poor and needy man,
    crushed in spirit, to put him to death.
¹⁷ How he loved cursing—
    may it fall on him!
    He had no pleasure in blessing—
    may it be far from him!
¹⁸ He wore cursing like his robe,
    until it filled his belly like water, and his bones like oil.
¹⁹ May it be like a cloak wrapped around him,
    like a belt tied around him always.
²⁰ Let this be ADONAI's reward to my accusers,
    and to those who speak evil against me.

²¹ But You, ADONAI my Lord,
    deal with me for Your Name's sake.
    Because Your lovingkindness is good, deliver me.
²² For I am afflicted and needy,
    and my heart is wounded within me.
²³ I fade away like an evening shadow,
    shaken off like a locust.
²⁴ My knees totter from fasting,
    and my flesh is lean, with no fat.
²⁵ And I have become a taunt to them.
    When they see me, they wag their head.
²⁶ Help me, ADONAI my God,
    Save me through Your lovingkindness.
²⁷ Let them know that it is Your hand—
    that You, ADONAI, have done it.

[28] They may curse, but You bless.
   When they arise, they will be ashamed,
      but Your servant will rejoice.
[29] My accusers will be clothed in disgrace,
      and wrapped in shame as in a cloak.
[30] I will greatly thank ADONAI with my mouth,
      and in the midst of a throng will I praise Him.
[31] For He stands at the right hand of the needy,
      to save him from those who condemn his soul.

Glenn Blank

Many modern readers puzzle over the imprecatory or cursing psalms, notably 35:4–10; 59:10–13; 69:22–28; 83:9–18; 109:6–20 (the longest vitriol); 137:7–9 (perhaps most shockingly, dashing Babylonian infants on rocks); and 139:19–22. Cursing enemies, however bad their behavior, seems to be politically incorrect. Before the advent of PC concerns, C. S. Lewis wrote ambivalently about these psalms, calling them "terrible," "contemptible," "devilish," "profoundly wrong," and "sinful" prayers.[1] We may wonder how to reconcile vindictive and violent wishes with what *Yeshua* says about loving our enemies or what Paul says about leaving vengeance to God. Does that include vengeful wishes? Some have argued that the imprecatory passages in the Psalms represent "pre-Christian" thought, which presumably "Christian" thought should clean up nicely.

Our Messianic Jewish thought notes some problems with such thinking. First, "progressive revelation" ought not to imply a progress from error to truth—2 Timothy 3:16 confirms that "all Scripture is God-breathed" (that should cover all of the Psalms)—though it might imply a progress of clarity about truth for subsequent writers looking back at earlier ones. If we believe that the Scriptures are coherent because the same Holy Spirit inspired them all, we cannot conclude that there is something fundamentally incorrect about these cursing passages. Second, as Jews, we want to encourage our Christian brethren to avoid a bias against the Hebrew Scriptures. Third, there are many imprecatory passages in the new covenant, notably Paul's venom for those advocating another gospel (Gal. 1:8; 5:12) or *Yeshua's* curse of Bethsaida and Capernaum (Matt. 11:21, 23) or the provocative "woes" of Matthew

23. Fourth, who can say it is morally wrong for believers to intercede for the destruction of Nazis or terrorists?

One noble thought is to hate the sin while loving the sinner. What would the psalmist say? I suspect he would agree that praying for the sinner to repent is fine and good—certainly David prayed for Saul and for Absalom. But so long as the wicked are unrepentant, actively resisting God's will to the point of seeking the destruction of godly or innocent people, they are enemies of God and His kingdom, so justice militates against them. Justice may not be as popular or gentle as mercy; nevertheless, justice is also an attribute of God and necessary for His will to be done, on earth as it is in heaven.

Having said all that, here are a few comments about this particular psalm. This adversary is deceitful (2), hateful without a cause (3), and returns accusation and evil for love (4–5). So he has it coming, doesn't he? It is proposed that an accuser or advocate be set over him (6)—reminiscent of *satan* making his case against Joshua the high priest (Zech. 3:1). Once the accused is found guilty (7), the recommended sentence is severe (that's the imprecatory part, piling on for another twelve verses). But bear in mind that it's a recommendation; the actual sentence is left to the Judge. The psalmist adds to his argument an appeal to *HaShem*'s lovingkindness (which does seem a bit ironic) (21), reminds him of his own sorry state (22–24) because he has "become a taunt to them" (25), and finally puts his trust in the saving power of *HaShem*'s hand (27). For *HaShem* has a way of turning cursing into blessing (28).

Intercessors take note—though you may not want to pile on penalties, Scripture indicates that there is merit in appealing to the true Judge against wicked adversaries.

 # PSALM 110

My Lord Is a *Kohen* Forever

¹ A psalm of David.
    ADONAI declares to my Lord:
    "Sit at My right hand
    until I make your enemies a footstool for Your feet."ᵃ

a. 110:1. cf. Matt. 22:44; Acts 2:34–35; 1 Cor. 15:25; Heb. 1:13.

² *ADONAI* will extend your mighty rod from Zion:

"Rule in the midst of your enemies."ª

³ Your people will be a freewill offering in a day of your power.

In holy splendors, from dawn's womb,

yours is the dew of your youth.

⁴ *ADONAI* has sworn, and will not change His mind:

"You are a *Kohen* forever according to the order of Melchizedek."ᵇ

⁵ My Lord is at your right hand.

He will shatter kings in the day of His wrath.

⁶ He will judge among the nations, heaping up corpses.

He will crush heads over the entire land.

⁷ He will drink from a stream along the way

—so His head will be exalted.

Glenn Blank and Jeffrey Seif

This short psalm is by far the most quoted one in the new covenant, because it has the most mysteries to reveal about the nature of Messiah. *Yeshua* challenged His opponents, in Matthew 22:44, to explain the meaning of "*ADONAI* declares to my Lord:'Sit at My right hand'" (1). In Hebrew, "*ADONAI*" spells out the Tetragrammaton (which only the high priest pronounced, with great solemnity, on *Yom Kippur*), while "my Lord" is literally *ADONAI* (which Jews say rather than utter the Name in vain). So here's the conundrum: If "*ADO-NAI*" is God, then who is "my Lord"? Not David, as Peter explains in Acts 2:34, since no mortal ever ascended into heaven to "sit at My right hand." In Mark 14:61–62, the *kohen gadol* (high priest) demanded of *Yeshua*, "Are you *Mashiach*, Son of the Blessed One?" *Yeshua* answered, "I am . . . and you shall see 'the Son of Man sitting at the right hand of the Powerful One,' and 'coming with the clouds of heaven'!" First, note that *Yeshua*, like other Jews, avoided pronouncing the Holy Name by using a euphemism, "the Powerful One." Second, *Yeshua* connected "sitting at the right hand of the Powerful One" of Psalm 110:1 with the "Son of Man coming in the clouds of heaven" of Daniel 7:13–14. In his vision, Daniel saw "one like a son of man" coming before "the Ancient of Days." So here's the conundrum again: if the "Ancient

a. 110:2. cf. Heb. 1:8; Rev. 12:5; 19:15.

b. 110:4. cf. Heb. 5:6, 10; 6:20; 7:17, 21.

of Days" is the all-powerful God, then who is this Son of Man coming to Him on the clouds of heaven, and why do "all peoples, nations, and languages" serve Him—the Son of Man? Do you get it? The *kohen gadol* understood what *Yeshua* was getting at—either *Yeshua* is making a blasphemous claim about Himself or He really is the Son of the Blessed One! Which do you believe? How you answer has eternal significance. To Him, *HaShem* promises to "make your enemies a footstool for Your feet" (1) and "extend your mighty rod" (2) to reign as the Messianic King. Just as Daniel saw the peoples worshiping the Son of Man, so David saw "your people" offering themselves (not animals, but their own lives, see Rom. 12:1) as "a freewill offering in a day of your power" (3).

Then comes another mystery: "You are a *Kohen* forever according to the order of Melchizedek" (4). Hebrews 7 explains how this mysterious figure reveals something further about the nature of Messiah. Melchizedek, whose name means "king of righteousness," was both the ruler of Salem and a priest, receiving a tithe from Abraham (Gen. 14:18–20). Therefore, "my Lord" is also both a king and "a *Kohen* forever." No other king of Israel—not even David—could make this claim. When King Uzziah dared to offer incense in the Temple (2 Chron. 26:16–21), the high priest confronted him, and then leprosy broke out on his forehead. Only the Messiah can be both king and *kohen* forever!

The God of Israel resolves to "shatter kings in the day of His wrath" (5). This mighty warrior is the same One who comes "in holy splendors, from dawn's womb" (3). Nevertheless, He comes to "judge among the nations, heaping up corpses," and crushing "heads" (6). He is also the One who calmly takes "drink from a stream along the way" (7)—reminding us of Psalm 23. What a paradox! Is He a gentle shepherd or a formidable war chief? It is another mystery of Messiah: He is both—both mortal Son of Man and Son of the Blessed One, both King and Priest, both Good Shepherd and Mighty Conqueror. The One who bears our burdens and forgives our sins is also the One who will return in power to defeat those who still defy God. Both operations will work together to establish His kingdom on earth—as it already is in heaven, where He already sits. In that day, Messiah will return to show Himself strong, fulfilling the victory speech the Father has prepared for His Son: "ADONAI has sworn, and will not change His mind" (4)—until all is understood and all is accomplished.

❊❊❊❊❊❊❊ Psalm 111 ❊❊❊❊❊❊❊

The Beginning of Wisdom

¹ *Halleluyah!* I praise ADONAI with all my heart
    in the company and congregation of the upright.
² Great are the works of ADONAI—
    searched out by all who delight in them.
³ Glorious and majestic is His work,
    and His righteousness endures forever.
⁴ He made His wonders memorable.
    ADONAI is gracious and full of compassion.
⁵ He gives food to those who fear Him.
    He remembers His covenant forever.
⁶ He shows His people His powerful deeds,
    giving them the heritage of the nations.
⁷ The works of His hands are truth and justice.
    All His precepts are trustworthy—
⁸ they are upheld forever and ever,
    made in truth and uprightness.
⁹ He has sent redemption to His people.
    He has ordained His covenant forever.
    Holy and awesome is His Name.
¹⁰ The fear of ADONAI is the beginning of wisdom.
    All who follow His precepts have good understanding.
    His praise endures forever!

Jeffrey Seif

Knowledge is one thing; wisdom is another. A confident young son or daughter can come home from college with more knowledge than his or her parents, but wisdom takes more than four years of study, term papers, and exams. The tests of life and observing the consequences of living in the real world develop, over time, another kind of knowing—what our elders call wisdom. Yet even elderly wisdom is not necessarily the same as what the Bible means by wisdom. This psalm closes with sayings worthy of Proverbs: "The fear of ADONAI is the beginning of wisdom," and "All who follow His precepts have good understanding" (10). You don't necessarily get this kind of wisdom just by observing life. You need this awe of God that motivates you to see how good it is to follow His precepts.

Many secular individuals, young and old, are disposed to give no credence to this point whatsoever. Armed with microscopes and telescopes, enthralled by discoveries in science and industry, they throw themselves into the game of life only to come up empty because they never come to terms with the essence of life. There is wisdom "in the company and congregation of the upright" (1). There is life in the great, "glorious and majestic" work of God (2–3), through which He reveals His grace and compassion (4). There is life in His covenant that He remembers forever (5) and wisdom in the heritage He has given (6). There is wisdom in His "truth and justice" (7–8), and there is life in the redemption He has sent to His people—yes, "holy and awesome is His Name" (9). The true starting point for a successful life is revering Him and understanding His ways.

PSALM 112

Blessed Is the Righteous Man

¹ *Halleluyah!* Happy is the man who fears ADONAI,
   who delights greatly in His *mitzvot.*
² His offspring will be mighty in the land.
   The generation of the upright will be blessed.
³ Wealth and riches are in his house,
   and his righteousness endures forever.
⁴ Light shines in the darkness for the upright.
   Gracious, compassionate and just is he.
⁵ Good comes to a man who is gracious and lends.
   He will order his affairs with fairness.
⁶ Surely he will never be shaken.
   The righteous are remembered forever.
⁷ He is not afraid of bad news—
   his heart is steadfast, trusting in ADONAI.
⁸ His heart is secure, he will not fear—
   until he gazes on his foes.

⁹ He gives freely to the poor.
　His righteousness endures forever.
　His horn is lifted high in honor.
¹⁰ The wicked will see it and be indignant.
　He will gnash with his teeth and waste away.
　The desire of the wicked will perish.

Glenn Blank

On *Erev Shabbat* (the eve of Sabbath), it is customary for a Jewish husband to honor his "wife of valor" by reading some verses of Proverbs 31. I especially enjoy pausing to let our children "arise and bless" their mother. Occasionally, my beloved will reciprocate with a reading of Psalm 112. What a treat, to be considered one "who delights greatly in His *mitzvot*" (1)—and motivating! "His offspring will be mighty" (2)—may it be so, Lord! "Wealth and riches" are his (3)—presumably they will come with wisdom and seeking God's kingdom (see Prov. 3:16; 8:18; Matt. 6:33). "Light shines in the darkness" (4)—may it be the light of truth, the light of Messiah! Verse 5 encourages me to be gracious about lending and to order my affairs with fairness. Then may I "never be shaken" (6) and not be "afraid of bad news"—as I keep trusting in *HaShem* (7). How secure my heart will be in *HaShem* (8), as I give freely with righteousness—צְדָקָה, *tzedaka* (9). Let the wicked get indignant (10)—but blessed and happy (אַשְׁרֵי, *ashrei*) will be the God-fearing man!

✳✳✳✳✳✳✳✳ PSALM 113 ✳✳✳✳✳✳✳✳

From the Rising of the Sun

¹ *Halleluyah!* Praise, O servants of ADONAI,
　praise the Name of ADONAI.
² Blessed be the Name of ADONAI
　from now and forever.
³ From the rising of the sun to its going down
　the Name of ADONAI is to be praised.

268

⁴ *Adonai* is high above all nations,
   His glory is above the heavens.
⁵ Who is like *Adonai* our God,
   enthroned on high,
⁶ who brings Himself down to look
   upon heaven and upon earth?
⁷ He raises the poor from the dust,
   lifts up the needy out of the dunghill,
⁸ to seat him with princes,
   with the princes of His people.
⁹ He settles the barren woman in her home
   as a joyful mother of children.
      Halleluyah!

Paul Wilbur

Many modern choruses have been lifted out of these verses. In the 1980s I set many of them as choruses that I never recorded, but maybe now is the time to unveil the work. Paul Baloche penned the song "Praise *Adonai*," based on verse 3, that was introduced to the world on my recording *Jerusalem Arise!* in 1998 from Israel. He originally wrote the song as "Praise Yahweh," but I told him I couldn't sing the holy Name because of Jewish sensitivity and suggested the title it now carries. It has been recorded in English, Spanish, Portuguese, German, and Hebrew, and it is sung in many other languages as well. Verse 5, for which I've also made a modern setting, is close to a well-known prayer in the *Siddur*, the Jewish Book of Prayer.

The psalmist declares to us the humility of *Adonai*: though "enthroned on high," He "brings Himself down to look upon heaven and upon earth" (5–6). Could this be another riddle about the Messiah? (See Phil. 2:6–9.) He goes on to say that this One "raises the poor" and "lifts up the needy" (7). He even "settles the barren woman in her home" with children (9). Who else—certainly no other ancient god—can do such marvelous things? Who is like the Lord our God? Truly there is none else! Halleluyah!

✳✳✳✳✳✳✳✳ PSALM 114 ✳✳✳✳✳✳✳✳

Passover Song

¹ When Israel came out of Egypt,
  Jacob's house from a people foreign-speaking,
² Judah became His Sanctuary,
  Israel His dominion.
³ The sea saw and fled,
  the Jordan turned back.
⁴ The mountains skipped like rams,
  the hills like lambs.
⁵ Why was it, O sea, that you fled?
  O Jordan, that you turned back?
⁶ O mountains, that you skipped like rams?
  O hills, like lambs?
⁷ Tremble, O earth, at the presence of the Lord,
  at the presence of the God of Jacob,
⁸ who turned the rock into a pool of water,
  the flint into a spring of water.

Jeffrey Seif and Glenn Blank

Jews love Passover—and not just because we get to eat matzah ball soup and gefilte fish! We get to tell our children the ancient story about how God delivered us from slavery in Egypt. This story, along with a host of other tales that have been added to it over the ages, has become for us a genre of litera-ture called *Haggadah*, which means "telling." We read our *Haggadah* booklet dutifully, as it recounts the Passover experience with picture, ritual, and food. Toward the end, after the meal, we read the *Hallel*—Psalms 113–118—as our forefathers have done for ages, even before *Yeshua* came to Jerusalem. So it is apropos that this psalm begins, "When Israel came out of Egypt" (1). By the blood of the Passover lamb, "Judah became His Sanctuary, Israel His dominion" (2). When our ancestors came to the Sea of Reeds with nowhere to turn, "the sea saw and fled" (3, 5). When God shook Sinai and some sur-rounding peaks, "the mountains skipped like rams" (4, 6)—indeed the whole earth trembled (7). When our gracious Provider "turned the rock into a pool of water" (8), it renewed life in the wilderness. It is good to remember God's works on our behalf, isn't it? Remembering how He helped our ancient ancestors renews our confidence that He helps us too.

✻✺✻✺✻✺✻✺✻ PSALM 115 ✻✺✻✺✻✺✻✺✻

Bless the Maker of Heaven and Earth

¹ Not to us, ADONAI, not to us,
    but to Your Name be the glory—
    because of Your love and Your faithfulness.
² Why should the nations say:
    "Where is their God now?"
³ Our God is in the heavens—
    He does whatever pleases Him!
⁴ Their idols are silver and gold,
    the work of human hands.
⁵ They have mouths, but cannot speak;
    eyes, but cannot see.
⁶ They have ears, but cannot hear;
    noses, but cannot smell.
⁷ They have hands, but cannot feel;
    feet, but cannot walk,
    nor utter a sound with their throat.
⁸ Those making them will become like them
    —everyone trusting in them.

⁹ O Israel, trust in ADONAI—
    He is their help and their shield!
¹⁰ O house of Aaron, trust in ADONAI—
    He is their help and their shield!
¹¹ O you who fear ADONAI, trust in ADONAI—
    He is their help and their shield!
¹² ADONAI has been mindful of us,
    He will bless:
    He will bless the house of Israel;
    He will bless the house of Aaron;

[13] He will bless those who fear ADONAI,
   the small together with the great.
[14] May ADONAI increase you more and more
   —you and your children.
[15] May you be blessed by ADONAI,
   Maker of heaven and earth.
[16] The heavens are the heavens of ADONAI,
   but the earth He gave to the children of men.
[17] The dead do not praise ADONAI,
   nor do any who go down into silence.
[18] But we—we will bless ADONAI
   both now and forever. *Halleluyah!*

Jeffrey Seif and Glenn Blank

Confidence is a good thing, and pity the man without it. It is good to be confident about life because of our relationship with *HaShem* (see Ps. 27:3). It is even good to be proud of others we care about, such as when our children do something special. But watch out when it develops into a haughty or self-focused attitude. As Jacob (James) 4:6 says, "God opposes the proud, but gives grace to the humble." So it is good to confess: "Not to us, ADONAI, not to us, but to Your Name be the glory" (1). God gets the glory because He is the ultimate doer (3), actively involved in His creation through works of redemption, unlike the idols of the heathen nations, which are merely the "work of human hands" (4), powerless to smell, hear, walk, or "utter a sound with their throat" (5–7). Those who trust in them will also be powerless.

Those who trust in God, however, will experience His active aid and protection (10–13). They will also see "increase" (14)—the multiplying of sowing and reaping by faith. Only the "Maker" can give this blessing (15), because the heavens are His, and "the earth He gave to the children of men" (16). He is the God of the living, not the dead (Matt. 22:32)—who are powerless to praise Him (17). Are we serving worthless, lifeless idols of our own making or the powerful, living Maker of all things? If the latter, then let us express it with confidence by gratefully blessing Him, "both now and forever" (18).

✳✳✳✳✳✳✳ PSALM 116 ✳✳✳✳✳✳✳

Lift Up the Cup of Salvation

¹ I love ADONAI,
  for He hears my voice, my cries.
² Because He has turned His ear to me,
  I will call on Him all my days.
³ The ropes of death entangled me,
  and the torments of *Sheol* found me.
  I found trouble and sorrow.
⁴ Then I called upon the Name of ADONAI:
  "ADONAI, save my soul!"
⁵ ADONAI is gracious and righteous—
  yes, our God is compassionate.
⁶ ADONAI protects the simple-hearted.
  When I was brought low, He saved me.
⁷ Return to your rest, my soul,
  for ADONAI has been good to you.
⁸ For You delivered my soul from death,
  my eyes from tears,
  my feet from stumbling.
⁹ I will walk before ADONAI
  in the lands of the living.
¹⁰ I trusted even when I said,
  "I am very afflicted"—
¹¹ even when I said in my haste,
  "All men are liars."
¹² How can I repay ADONAI
  for all His bounties to me?
¹³ I will lift up the cup of salvation,
  and call on the Name of ADONAI.
¹⁴ I will fulfill my vows to ADONAI
  in the presence of all His people.
¹⁵ Precious in the sight of ADONAI
  is the death of His *kedoshim*.
¹⁶ O ADONAI! Surely I am Your servant.
  I am Your servant,

the son of Your maidservant.
You have freed me from my bonds.
¹⁷ To You I will offer a sacrifice of praise,
and will call on the Name of ADONAI.
¹⁸ I will fulfill my vows to ADONAI
in the presence of all His people,
¹⁹ in the courts of the House of ADONAI,
in your midst, O Jerusalem. *Halleluyah!*

Glenn Blank and Jeffrey Seif

This psalm, the fourth in the *Hallel* (praise) series, which Jews and Messianic believers read during Passover and *Sukkot* (Tabernacles), fits well as it gives thanks to God for deliverance. It would be so easy to take the story of God delivering our ancestors from slavery for granted—all that happened so long ago! But we need to bear in mind that He still delivers—"I love ADONAI, for He hears *my* voice" too (1, emphasis added). We pray with faith when we really believe that "He has turned His ear to me" (2). *HaShem* commanded us to eat the dry *matzah* and bitter *maror* so that we, too, would taste and experience affliction ourselves. For haven't we all tasted some affliction, and don't we all need God to deliver us from the bondage of sin?

Lest you think you have not literally experienced the entanglement of "the ropes of death" and "the torments of *Sheol*" (3), pause and consider those who have died without hope and gone to that terrible place. If somebody you know is in danger of going there, you could encourage that person that it's not too late to call "upon the Name of ADONAI: 'ADONAI, save my soul!'" (4). Yes, call upon Him now, because "our God is compassionate" (5). God has not made the Good News too complicated, for He "protects the simple-hearted" (6). His salvation gives rest to the soul (7), deliverance from death, and keeps "my feet from stumbling" (8). Instead, those who put their trust in Him "will walk before ADONAI in the lands of the living" (9). You can walk there too. All that He asks is that you believe, that you trust Him. Even when you are afflicted and it seems like "all men are liars" (10–11), God is still true. When you call on His Name, you will "lift up the cup of salvation" (13). There's that word again—יְשׁוּעָה, *yeshuah*.

Once you put your trust in Him, you are in a covenant with Him and are determined to "fulfill" vows to Him (14, 18). Your heart says, "Surely I am

Your servant," and your soul declares, "You have freed me from my bonds" (16). Indebted as you feel, you desire to offer Him "a sacrifice of praise" (17). Whether it's Passover or any other appointed time, never forget what God has done for us. Let's remember His goodness, recall where He found us, recall what He did for us. Let's also pray for those who are still afflicted or who have not yet experienced His gracious salvation, that they also will "call on the Name of ADONAI"—the Name of *Yeshua* (17). Together we will fulfill our vows and worship Him "in the presence of all His people" (18), "in the courts of the House of ADONAI" (19).

 # PSALM 117

Praise Him, All You Nations

¹ Praise ADONAI, all you nations!
  Glorify Him, all you peoples.
² For great is His lovingkindness toward us,
  and ADONAI's truth endures forever.
  Halleluyah!

Glenn Blank

The shortest psalm sounds the chief note. Praise Him, everyone! Let Israel say, "Praise ADONAI, all you nations!" The ultimate destiny of Israel—connected with the coming of the Messiah—is to enjoin "all you peoples" to "glorify Him" (1). Israel sings this song as a pickup to the final, climactic psalm of the *Hallel* (Praise) during *Pesach* (Passover) and *Sukkot* (Tabernacles). Sing with us, for His lovingkindness is awesome. Nothing is more trustworthy than His covenant faithfulness. Halleluyah!

✳✳✳✳✳✳✳✳✳ PSALM 118 ✳✳✳✳✳✳✳✳✳

His *Chesed* Endures Forever

¹ Praiseᵃ ADONAI, for He is good.
    For His lovingkindness endures forever.
² O let Israel say:
    For His lovingkindness endures forever.
³ O let the house of Aaron say:
    For His lovingkindness endures forever.
⁴ O let those who fear ADONAI say:
    For His lovingkindness endures forever.

⁵ Out of a tight place I called on ADONAI—
    ADONAI answered me with a spacious place.
⁶ ADONAI is for me—I will not fear!
    What can man do to me?
⁷ ADONAI is for me, as my helper.
    I will see the downfall of those who hate me.
⁸ It is better to take refuge in ADONAI
    than to trust in man.
⁹ It is better to take refuge in ADONAI
    than to trust in princes.
¹⁰ All nations surrounded me—
    in the Name of ADONAI I cut them off.
¹¹ They surrounded me, yes, all around me—
    in the Name of ADONAI I cut them off.
¹² They swarmed around me like bees—
    they were extinguished like burning thorns—
    in the Name of ADONAI I cut them off.
¹³ You pushed me hard to make me fall,
    but ADONAI helped me.
¹⁴ ADONAI is my strength and song,
    and He has become my salvation.ᵇ
¹⁵ Shouts of joy and victory
    are in the tents of the righteous:
    "ADONAI's right hand is mighty!"ᶜ

a. 118:1. Heb. *hodu*, or *Give thanks to*.
b. 118:14. cf. Luke 1:68–69.
c. 118:15. cf. Luke 1:51a.

[16] *Adonai's* right hand is lifted high!
    Adonai's right hand is mighty!"

[17] I will not die, but live,
    and proclaim what *Adonai* has done!
[18] *Adonai* has chastened me hard,
    but has not given me over to death.

[19] Open to me the gates of righteousness,
    that I may enter through them and praise *Adonai.*
[20] This is the gate of *Adonai*—
    the righteous will enter through it.[d]
[21] I give You thanks, because You have answered me
    and have become my salvation.
[22] The stone the builders rejected
    has become the capstone.[e]
[23] It is from *Adonai:*
    it is marvelous in our eyes!
[24] This is the day that *Adonai* has made!
    Let us rejoice and be glad in it!
[25] *Hoshia-na!* Please, *Adonai,* save now!
    We beseech You, *Adonai,* prosper us!
[26] *Baruch haba b'Shem Adonai*—
    Blessed is He who comes in the Name of *Adonai.*[f]
    We bless you from the House of *Adonai.*
[27] *Adonai* is God, and He has given us light.
    Join the festival with branches, up to the horns of the altar.[g]
[28] You are my God, and I praise You.
    You are my God—I exalt You!
[29] Praise *Adonai,* for He is good,
    for His lovingkindness endures forever.

Paul Wilbur

This one psalm, source of songs and verses quoted more often than one can imagine, carries a rhythm and rhyme, even in English, so that you might hear yourself singing along. From the opening verse, which also closes out the

d. 118:19–20. cf. Rev. 22:14.
e. 118:22. cf. Matt. 21:42; Mark 12:10; Luke 20:17; Acts 4:11; Eph. 2:20; 1 Pet. 2:7.
f. 118:25–26. cf. Matt. 21:9; 23:39; Mark 11:9; Luke 13:35; 19:38; John 12:13.
g. 118:27. Or *bind the festival offering to the horns of the altar.*

psalm, we are treated to the most repeated line in the Bible: *Hodu l'ADONAI ki tov, ki l'olam chasdo.* "Praise [give thanks to] ADONAI, for He is good, for His lovingkindness [*chesed*] endures forever." This line takes me back for several reasons. It's quoted in modern worship choruses in churches around the world. It's also a very popular verse set to music in traditional Jewish worship; my friend René Bloch did a setting that was a hit for Israel's Hope. And . . . it's the faith song sung by Jehoshaphat and Judah after they were surrounded by armies of three nations! I do love that story of Jehoshaphat in 2 Chronicles 20. It's such a striking example of pure faith and trust. There is a dispensationalist notion that the *Tanakh* or "Old Testament" is just law and works, while the "New Testament" is grace and faith. Man, does that ever get my blood boiling! Jehoshaphat and his people were surrounded by a vast army when a prophet of the Lord told them not to fear, just send some Levites out to sing a worship chorus. Those prophets had *chutzpah*, which is Yiddish for bold faith! This prophet was so convincing that they did it—and a great victory was won without even swinging a sword! Psalm 118 is also full of this kind of faith in God's grace.

Let's take a look at the word חֶסֶד, *chesed*—as it recurs in the first four verses. It is a masculine noun indicating lovingkindness, loyalty, kindness, or acts of mercy. If you think the psalmist is beating a drum here, look at Psalm 136, where this word is used no fewer than twenty-six times! All that is accomplished for Israel and all humanity—all that happened, is happening, and is promised—is according to the covenant *chesed* of God. Worth singing about!

Let me highlight a few of these verses that have been so rich in worship over the years. First, verse 6 asks the question, "What can man do to me?" If I've quoted that verse once, I've quoted it a thousand times! It's been a motto for my ministry over the years, as I travel all around the world, including Muslim nations where we minister right out in the open. I say, "I am not ashamed" (Rom. 1:16) and "I will not fear!" (6). Like David, my faith comes from a confidence that my times are in the hands of ADONAI, and no one else. The line is thin, I agree, between arrogance and confidence, and the former should be avoided at all costs. Holy confidence comes from knowing the One who sent you and believing that He will cover and protect you from harm.

Verses 14 and 21 are similar to Isaiah 12:2, and together were the inspiration for a popular song in the '70s: "Behold, God is my salvation, I will trust and will not be afraid. For the Lord my God is my strength and my song, He also has become my salvation. Lai, lai, lai. . . ." We sang that song often and with conviction, and it was a great source of joy and faith.

Verse 15 reminds me of something a seer said in Numbers 23:21 after a very anxious king hired him. Balak of Moab was afraid of Israel and hired Balaam to curse Israel so he could defeat them. But whenever Balaam opened his mouth to curse, only blessing came out, such as "The Lord their God is with them, and the shout of the King is in the tents!" Our psalm says, "Shouts of joy and victory [or salvation, *yeshuah*] are in the tents of the righteous" (15). This shout is the sound of victory! Here in Psalm 118 the righteous are shouting, and back in Numbers 23 ADONAI Himself is shouting—what a glorious sound that must be!

Verse 17 is one I hear or pray often over someone who is very ill but believing God for deliverance and healing. "I will not die, but live, and proclaim what ADONAI has done!" What did I say about faith and grace everywhere in *Tanakh*?

There are many amazing Messianic prophecies in this psalm. The psalmist declares that ADONAI has become my salvation (*yeshuah*) (21)—you might want to point this out to anyone (especially any Jewish friends) who ask where the Name *Yeshua* appears in the Hebrew Scriptures. Then the psalmist warns that this "stone [or rock of salvation] the builders [elders or leaders] rejected has become the capstone" (22)—one on which a whole new Temple would be built! Peter and John quote this exact verse (Acts 4:11) when they stand before the Sanhedrin to give an account of how a lame man got healed in the Temple gates.

How many times have you heard, "This is the day that ADONAI has made! Let us rejoice and be glad in it!" (24)? How about at every Passover Seder, after the meal? Wow, this psalm just overflows with famous, life-giving lines!

And finally: "*Baruch haba b'Shem* ADONAI" (26). I don't need to translate that for you, I'm sure. It's been set to music many times, including by yours truly. *Yeshua* Himself quoted it when He declared to the leaders of Israel in Jerusalem, "You will never see Me again until you say . . ." (Matt. 23:39). Isn't it amazing that the Rock of Israel, the Stone the builders rejected, was standing before the elders when He declared this powerful verse—which they recited every Passover and every *Sukkot*—and yet their blindness kept them from recognizing the salvation of Israel? But let's not forget the hope put forth by Rav Shaul, the apostle Paul, in Romans 11:15, "For if their rejection leads to the reconciliation of the world, what will their acceptance be but life from the dead?" Halleluyah! A day is surely coming when the leaders of Israel will join all who welcome our Messiah back into the holy city!

✳✳✳✳✳✳✳✳✳ PSALM 119 ✳✳✳✳✳✳✳✳✳✳

Learn *Torah* Letter by Letter

ALEPH א

¹ Blessed are those whose way is blameless,
  who walk in the *Torah* of ADONAI.
² Happy are those who keep His testimonies,
  who seek Him with a whole heart,
³ who also do no injustice, but walk in His ways.
⁴ You have commanded that Your precepts
  be kept diligently.
⁵ Oh that my ways were steadfast
  to observe Your decrees!
⁶ Then I would not be ashamed,
  when I consider all Your *mitzvot*.
⁷ I will praise You with an upright heart
  as I learn Your righteous judgments.
⁸ I will observe Your statutes.
  Never abandon me utterly!

BET ב

⁹ How can a young man keep his way pure?
  By guarding it according to Your word.
¹⁰ With my whole heart have I sought You
  —let me not stray from Your *mitzvot*.
¹¹ I have treasured Your word in my heart,
  so I might not sin against You.
¹² Blessed are You, ADONAI.
  Teach me Your statutes.
¹³ With my lips I rehearse
  all the rulings of Your mouth.
¹⁴ I rejoice in the way of Your testimonies
  above all wealth.
¹⁵ I will meditate on Your precepts,
  and regard Your ways.
¹⁶ I will delight in Your decrees.
  I will never forget Your word.

GIMEL ג

¹⁷ Do good to Your servant
    that I may live and keep Your word.
¹⁸ Open my eyes, so I may behold
    wonders from Your *Torah*.
¹⁹ I am a temporary dweller on earth—
    do not hide Your *mitzvot* from me.
²⁰ My soul is crushed with longing
    for Your judgments at all times.
²¹ You rebuke the proud, who are cursed,
    who wander from Your *mitzvot*.
²² Take scorn and contempt away from me,
    for I have kept Your testimonies.
²³ Though princes sit and talk against me,
    Your servant meditates on Your decrees.
²⁴ For Your testimonies are my delight—
    they are also my counselors.

DALET ד

²⁵ My soul clings to the dust.
    Revive me according to Your word!
²⁶ I told of my ways and You answered me.
    Teach me Your statutes.
²⁷ Help me discern the way of Your precepts,
    so I may meditate on Your wonders.
²⁸ My soul weeps with grief.
    Make me stand firm with Your word.
²⁹ Turn me away from the deceitful way,
    and be gracious to me with Your *Torah*.
³⁰ I have chosen the way of faithfulness.
    I have set my heart on Your judgments.
³¹ I cling to Your testimonies.
    ADONAI, do not put me to shame!
³² I run the course of Your *mitzvot*,
    for You open wide my heart.

HEY ה

³³ Teach me the way of Your decrees, ADONAI,
    and I will follow them to the end.

³⁴ Give me understanding,
>> that I may keep Your *Torah*
>> and observe it with all my heart.
³⁵ Help me walk in the path of Your *mitzvot*—
>> for I delight in it.
³⁶ Turn my heart to Your testimonies
>> and not to dishonest gain.
³⁷ Turn my eyes away from gazing at vanity
>> but revive me in Your ways.
³⁸ Fulfill Your word to Your servant,
>> which leads to reverence for You.
³⁹ Make the disgrace I dread pass away,
>> for Your judgments are good.
⁴⁰ Behold, I long for Your precepts.
>> Revive me by Your righteousness.

VAV ו

⁴¹ May Your lovingkindnesses come to me, ADONAI—
>> Your salvation according to Your word—
⁴² so I may answer the one taunting me,
>> for I trust in Your word.
⁴³ Never snatch out of my mouth a word of truth,
>> for I hope in Your judgments.
⁴⁴ So I may always keep Your *Torah*,
>> forever and ever,
⁴⁵ and walk about in freedom.
>> For I have sought Your precepts.
⁴⁶ I will speak of Your testimonies
>> before kings, and never be ashamed.
⁴⁷ I delight in Your *mitzvot*,
>> which I love.
⁴⁸ I reach out my hands for Your *mitzvot*,
>> which I love,
>> and meditate on Your decrees.

ZAYIN ז

⁴⁹ Remember the word to Your servant,
>> on which You have made me hope.

⁵⁰ My comfort in my affliction is this:
    Your word has kept me alive.
⁵¹ The arrogant have viciously ridiculed me,
    yet I did not turn away from Your *Torah*.
⁵² I remember Your judgments from of old,
    A*DONAI*, and comfort myself.
⁵³ Burning indignation grips me,
    because of the wicked who forsake Your *Torah*.
⁵⁴ Your decrees have become my songs
    in the house where I dwell.
⁵⁵ In the night I remember Your Name, A*DONAI*,
    and keep watching over Your *Torah*.
⁵⁶ This is my own:
    that I keep Your precepts.

CHET ח

⁵⁷ A*DONAI* is my portion.
    I promised to guard Your words.
⁵⁸ I have entreated Your favor with all my heart.
    Be gracious to me according to Your word.
⁵⁹ I have considered my ways
    and turned my feet back to Your testimonies.
⁶⁰ I hasten and do not delay
    to obey Your *mitzvot*.
⁶¹ The ropes of the wicked are coiled around me,
    but I did not forget Your *Torah*.
⁶² At midnight I rise to praise You,
    because of Your righteous rulings.
⁶³ I am a companion of all who fear You,
    of those who observe Your precepts.
⁶⁴ The earth is full of Your lovingkindness.
    A*DONAI*—teach me Your decrees.

TET ט

⁶⁵ You do good to Your servant,
    A*DONAI*, according to Your word.
⁶⁶ Teach me good sense and knowledge,
    for I trusted in Your *mitzvot*.

⁶⁷ Before I was afflicted I went astray,
        but now I keep Your word.
⁶⁸ You are good and keep doing good—
        teach me Your decrees.
⁶⁹ Though the proud smeared a lie on me,
        with all my heart I keep Your precepts.
⁷⁰ Their minds are insensible,
        but Your *Torah* is my delight.
⁷¹ It is good for me that I was afflicted,
        so that I may learn Your decrees.
⁷² The *Torah* from Your mouth is better to me
        than thousands of gold and silver pieces.

YOD '

⁷³ Your hands have made me and formed me.
        Give me understanding that I may learn Your *mitzvot*.
⁷⁴ Those in awe of You see me and rejoice,
        because I put my hope in Your word.
⁷⁵ I know, ADONAI, Your judgments are just.
        In faithfulness You have afflicted me.
⁷⁶ May Your lovingkindness comfort me,
        according to Your promise to Your servant.
⁷⁷ Let Your tender mercies reach me,
        Let me live, for Your *Torah* is my delight.
⁷⁸ May the proud be put to shame
        for wronging me with a lie,
        but I will meditate on Your precepts.
⁷⁹ Let those in awe of You return to me—
        those who know Your testimonies.
⁸⁰ My heart will have integrity in following Your decrees,
        so that I would not be ashamed.

KAF ‏כ

⁸¹ My soul faints with longing for Your salvation,
        but I still hope in Your word.
⁸² My eyes are worn out longing for Your promise,
        saying, "When will You comfort me?"
⁸³ Though I became like a wineskin dried in smoke,
        I do not forget Your decrees.

⁸⁴ How many are the days of Your servant?
    When will You execute judgment on my persecutors?
⁸⁵ The proud have dug pits for me—
    that is not in accord with Your *Torah*!
⁸⁶ All Your *mitzvot* are faithful.
    They persecute me with a lie—help me!
⁸⁷ They almost finished me off on earth.
    But I—I will not forsake Your precepts.
⁸⁸ Revive me with Your lovingkindness,
    so I may keep Your mouth's testimony.

LAMED ל

⁸⁹ Forever, A<small>DONAI</small>,
    Your word stands firm in the heavens.
⁹⁰ Your faithfulness endures from generation to generation.
    You established the earth, and it stands.
⁹¹ Your judgments stand today,
    for all things are Your servants.
⁹² If Your *Torah* had not been my delight,
    I would have perished in my affliction.
⁹³ I will never forget Your precepts.
    For with them You have kept me alive.
⁹⁴ I am Yours, save me!
    For I have sought out Your precepts.
⁹⁵ The wicked wait for me to destroy me.
    But I will study Your testimonies.
⁹⁶ I have seen a limit to all perfection,
    yet Your commandment is boundless.

MEM מ

⁹⁷ O how I love Your *Torah*!
    It is my meditation all day.
⁹⁸ Your *mitzvot* make me wiser than my enemies
    —for they are mine forever.
⁹⁹ I have more insight than all my teachers,
    for Your testimonies are my meditation.
¹⁰⁰ I have gained more understanding than all my elders,
    for I have kept Your precepts.

[101] I kept my feet from every evil way,
  in order to follow Your word.
[102] I do not turn away from Your rulings,
  for You Yourself have taught me.
[103] How sweet is Your word to my taste—
  yes, sweeter than honey to my mouth!
[104] From Your precepts I get discernment,
  therefore I hate every false way.

NUN נ

[105] Your word is a lamp to my feet
  and a light to my path.[a]
[106] I have sworn and confirmed
  to observe Your righteous rulings.
[107] I am severely afflicted.
  Keep me alive, ADONAI, according to Your word.
[108] Please accept the freewill offerings of my mouth, ADONAI,
  and teach me Your rulings.
[109] My soul is continually in danger,
  yet I have not forgotten Your *Torah*.
[110] The wicked have set a snare for me,
  yet I did not stray from Your precepts.
[111] Your testimonies I have as a heritage
  forever, for they are my heart's joy.
[112] I turned my heart to do Your decrees,
  forever, to the very end.

SAMECH ס

[113] I hate double-minded ones,
  but Your *Torah* I love.
[114] You are my hiding place and my shield
  —in Your word I hope.
[115] Away from me, evildoers,
  so I may keep the *mitzvot* of my God!
[116] Sustain me according to Your word, so I may live,
  and let me not be ashamed of my hope.

a. 119:105. cf. John 8:12; 12:35.

[117] Support me and I will be saved,
    and study Your decrees continually.
[118] You despise all who wander from Your decrees,
    for their deceitfulness is in vain.
[119] All the wicked of the earth You remove like dross.
    Therefore I love Your testimonies.
[120] My flesh shudders for fear of You,
    and I am in awe of Your judgments.

AYIN ‫ע‬

[121] I did what is just and right.
    Do not leave me to my oppressors.
[122] Guarantee Your servant's well-being.
    Do not let arrogant ones oppress me.
[123] My eyes fail, longing for Your salvation
    and for Your righteous word.
[124] Deal with Your servant as befits Your lovingkindness,
    and teach me Your statutes.
[125] I am Your servant, give me discernment,
    so I may understand Your testimonies.
[126] It is time for ADONAI to act—
    they have violated Your *Torah*!
[127] Therefore I love Your *mitzvot*
    more than gold, more than pure gold.
[128] Therefore I esteem all Your precepts as right in every way
    —every false way I hate.

PE ‫פ‬

[129] Your testimonies are wonderful.
    Therefore my soul obeys them.
[130] The unfolding of Your words gives light,
    giving understanding to the simple.
[131] I opened my mouth wide and panted,
    for I longed for Your *mitzvot*.
[132] Turn to me and be gracious to me,
    as is fitting to those who love Your Name.
[133] Direct my footsteps in Your word,
    and let no iniquity get mastery over me.

¹³⁴ Redeem me from human oppression,
  and I will keep Your precepts.
¹³⁵ Make Your face shine on Your servant,
  and teach me Your decrees.
¹³⁶ Streams of water run down from my eyes,
  because they do not observe Your *Torah*.

TZADHE צ

¹³⁷ Righteous are You, ADONAI,
  and Your judgments are upright.
¹³⁸ You have commanded righteousness,
  Your testimonies, and great faithfulness.
¹³⁹ My zeal has consumed me,
  because my foes forgot Your words.
¹⁴⁰ Your word is thoroughly refined,
  and Your servant loves it.
¹⁴¹ I am insignificant and despised,
  yet I have not forgotten Your precepts.
¹⁴² Your justice is righteousness forever,
  and Your *Torah* is truth.
¹⁴³ Trouble and anguish have overtaken me,
  yet Your *mitzvot* are my delight.
¹⁴⁴ Your testimonies are righteous forever
  —make me understand, so I may live.

KOF ק

¹⁴⁵ I cried out with all my heart,
  "Answer me, ADONAI!
  I will keep Your decrees."
¹⁴⁶ I cried out to You, "Save me,
  and I will keep Your testimonies."
¹⁴⁷ I am up before dawn, crying for help—
  I put my hope in Your word.
¹⁴⁸ My eyes are up before every night watch,
  as I meditate on Your word.
¹⁴⁹ Hear my voice with Your lovingkindness.
  Revive me, ADONAI, with Your judgments.
¹⁵⁰ Pursuers of wicked schemes draw near—
  they are far from Your *Torah*.

[151] You are near, ADONAI,
  and all Your *mitzvot* are truth.
[152] Long ago I learned from Your testimonies
  that You founded them firmly forever.

RESH ר

[153] See my affliction and rescue me,
  for I do not forget Your *Torah*.
[154] Defend my cause and redeem me.
  Restore my life through Your word.
[155] Salvation is far from the wicked,
  for they do not seek after Your decrees.
[156] Great are Your mercies, ADONAI.
  Restore my life with Your judgments.
[157] Many are my persecutors and my foes.
  Yet I do not turn from Your testimonies.
[158] I see the treacherous and loathe them,
  because they do not keep Your word.
[159] See how I loved Your precepts.
  Restore my life, ADONAI, with Your lovingkindness.
[160] Truth is the essence of Your word,
  and all Your righteous rulings are eternal.

SHIN ש

[161] Princes persecute me for no reason,
  but my heart is in awe of Your words.
[162] I rejoice in Your word,
  as one who finds great spoil.
[163] I hate and abhor falsehood,
  but Your *Torah* I love.
[164] Seven times a day I praise You,
  because of Your righteous judgments.
[165] Great peace have they who love Your *Torah*,
  and nothing causes them to stumble.
[166] I hope for Your salvation, ADONAI,
  and do Your *mitzvot*.
[167] My soul has observed Your testimonies
  and I love them exceedingly.

¹⁶⁸ I observe Your precepts and Your laws,
    for all my ways are before You.

TAV ת

¹⁶⁹ Let my cry come to You, ADONAI.
    Grant me understanding by Your word.
¹⁷⁰ Let my supplication come before You.
    Deliver me, according to Your promise.
¹⁷¹ My lips utter praise,
    for You teach me Your statutes.
¹⁷² My tongue sings of Your word,
    for all Your *mitzvot* are righteous.
¹⁷³ Let Your hand be ready to help me,
    for I have chosen Your precepts.
¹⁷⁴ I long for Your deliverance, ADONAI,
    and Your *Torah* is my delight.
¹⁷⁵ Let my soul live and praise You,
    and may Your rulings help me.
¹⁷⁶ I have strayed like a lost sheep—seek Your servant.
    For I did not forget Your *mitzvot*.

Glenn Blank and Jeffrey Seif

Inclined as we are to see blessings as descending from heaven, a wisdom-oriented poet keeps reminding us that the way we direct our steps on earth has much to do with the blessings we receive on earth. "Blessed are those . . . who walk in the *Torah* of ADONAI" (1), "who keep His testimonies" and "who seek Him with a whole heart" (2). Walking in His ways implies that one "do no injustice" (3). God commands justice and teaches it in his "precepts" (4), because it is His nature. Though we cannot earn our salvation in the ultimate sense, the benefits—or blessings—of godly living should not be underestimated. The one so blessed can praise God "with an upright heart" (7). The two of us—cop and professor—heartily agree!

The psalmist uses legal terms from the *Torah*. Since he does not cite any actual laws, it is not clear how precise he wants to be about these terms; he may simply be reciting terms that he heard and studied from the *Torah* scroll. *Torah* (תּוֹרָה) means direction or instruction and can refer to a specific law or the whole body of laws that God gave to Moses. A *mitzvah* (מִצְוָה) is the most general term for a commandment. A *khok* (חֹק) is a statute or decree, sometimes given without explanation (for example, the decree of the red heifer in Num. 19:2). A *mishpat* (מִשְׁפָּט) is a judgment, ruling, or ordinance often spelling out requirements in more detail (see, for example, Num. 9:14). The *edot* (עֵדֹת) or testimonies refer to the code of laws on the two tablets placed in the ark of the covenant (Exod. 21:16). A *pikud* (פְּקֻד) is a precept or principle; applying *Torah*, even when we cannot apply *Torah* literally (such as laws related to sacrifices), we can learn principles that produce wisdom and holiness. The psalmist's overarching theme is his love of *Torah* as a source of spiritual and practical instruction, guidance, and protection.

The way we walk can make the difference between purity and straying into sin (10). By "guarding it according to Your word" (9)—living life according to biblical values and virtues—one secures a good place in this life, not to mention the life to come. Wise is one who has "treasured Your word" in his heart (11)—studying and memorizing the Bible. In ancient times, scrolls were copied by hand and hard to come by, so boys memorized the content of whole scrolls. That's why *Yeshua* was able to quote Deuteronomy three times in response to the tempter—even at the end of forty days of fasting in the Judean desert. When it goes deep within you, you also can "meditate" on His precepts (15), for you "never forget" His word (16).

"Do good to Your servant" (17), he pleads. Note that the petitioner is a "servant" and not simply a "believer." A servant goes a step beyond going to a service. Showing up is good, but serving makes you an actor in the biblical drama. Instead of expecting a community's spiritual leader to be your guide (no disrespect to such leaders intended), you can ask God Himself to "open" your eyes, so you "may behold wonders" (18). God wants a personal relationship with *you*. Once you recognize that you are a "temporary dweller on earth" (19), why would you want to settle for anything less? When you are living for Him, you long for His "judgments" (20)—wise decisions giving direction for your life. The psalmist is humble, knowing that God rebukes "the proud" (21), and he does not want to be counted among those who "wander" from His *mitzvot*. God's "testimonies"—which bear witness to the *mitzvot* within the ark of the covenant—are his "delight" (24). Have you ever thought of the "Ten Commandments" as the "Ten Blessings"? A blessing is spelled out for us in one of them (Exod. 20:12; Eph. 6:1). Now meditate on how keeping each one will lead to long-term honor and blessing, prosperity and love—for your God and your neighbor.

To be faithful in a doubting world can be challenging: "My soul clings to the dust" (25). The psalmist dialogues with God: "I told of my ways and You answered me" (26). Because of this relationship, He can ask God to "help me discern the way" (27). Yes, a godly lifestyle is not always an easy task—so he "weeps with grief," begging for help to "stand firm with" His word (28) amid trying times.

Sometimes, he just needs God to "turn me away from the deceitful way" (29) of temptation rather than staying in "the way of faithfulness" (30). He knows that if he can "cling" to God (31) and "run the course" of His *mitzvot* (32), he can expect to grow in understanding and blessing.

Knowing God's will, ways, and person is experiential—bringing about transformation, not just information. The psalmist asks God to "teach me the way of Your decrees" (33) and to "help me walk in the path of Your *mitzvot*" (35). Walking in the way of the Master is life transforming. Yet like sheep we so easily stray from the good way. With all interior conversions a miracle, he says: "turn my heart" (36) and "turn my eyes away from gazing at vanity" (37). These are the daily choices we need to make in the walk. Jostled about by people, circumstances, and our own imperfect natures, sometimes we also need to pray, "Revive me by Your righteousness" (40). Personal revival is a request the psalmist often repeats, so it must be OK for us to ask too.

Notice the Hebrew letters at the beginning of each stanza. The poem is an acrostic—each stanza begins with the next letter in the Hebrew *aleph, bet*—each one a step in the way of the Word. We're up to ‎ו *vav*, which is also a conjunction (and, but, so) in Hebrew. So, are you ready for the next step?

"Your lovingkindnesses"—plural to emphasize that there is no end to them—include salvation and many promises (41). With God's word, the psalmist has an answer for "the one taunting me" (42). He is confident that he can speak of God's "testimonies before kings, and never be ashamed" (46). For the *Torah* gives true "freedom" (45) and "delight" (47).

It's not that the psalmist has a carefree life. Even those lives that look perfect (from a distance) aren't (up close). So if you're suffering from affliction, take comfort in God's Word, which keeps you alive (50). Have you ever been "viciously ridiculed" (51) for walking with God? Good for you! Take comfort in God's judgments (52). Does "burning indignation" grip you (53)? Make the decrees of God your songs (54). At night, keep remembering His wonderful Name, *Yeshua* (55).

When the pressure is on, you need to make an executive decision to make ADONAI your "portion" and guard His words (57). (As a cop who has to deal with some hotheads, Jeffrey Seif heartily confirms this wisdom!) Instead of forever fretting about others, the psalmist is all about getting his feet on the path and staying there (59). Can you also say that you "hasten and do not delay to obey" His *mitzvot* (60)? When you do, you'll know what to do, even when the "ropes of the wicked are coiled around" you (61). Keep trusting His Word, praise God whether it be morning or midnight (62), and make yourself "a companion of all who fear" the Lord (63). The psalmist puts a premium on the communal aspects of a spiritual life. One should look with suspicion at those who extol the virtues of their personal, private relationship with God yet lead lives characterized by disassociation and aloofness. The *Torah* and the new covenant command us to walk in the Way with a community.

The *Torah* is God's gift, designed to "teach me good sense and knowledge" (66). The poet admits that he "went astray," but affliction has apparently taught him to keep God's Word (67). He even affirms that "it is good for me that I was afflicted" (71). Oh that we would always be so teachable! No matter what is happening, God is "good" (all the time!) and He keeps "doing good" (68). In his case, the afflictions have come from people smearing him with lies (69). When you walk with the Lord, the liar will try to knock you down. Just keep making His *Torah* your delight (70), keep learning His decrees concerning you (71), keep listening to the precious Word from His mouth (72).

The One who is our Maker will continue to form us (73) as we learn how to live according to His *Torah*. Though we may not win a popularity contest, we can be sure that "those in awe of You" will "rejoice" (74). We can be confident in God's faithfulness, lovingkindness, and tender mercies (75–77), when we make *Torah* our delight. Even if others wrong him with a lie (78), the psalmist responds with trust in verse 79: "Let those in awe of You return to me." Walking in the way of God's Word is how "my heart will have integrity" (80). Integrity—a heart that is whole before God and man—is precious to attain!

It's a rough world and there are rough people in it. The psalmist's "soul faints with longing" (81), yet he still hopes. His eyes are "worn out longing for" God's promise (82), and he feels like "a wineskin dried in smoke"—it must be a wretched, desperate feeling!—yet he does not "forget" His decrees

(83). Frankly, he cannot get those bent on making his life miserable out of his mind. His "persecutors" (84) have "dug pits" for him (85) and "persecute" him with lies (86). So bothersome are they that he says, "They almost finished me off" (87). The key word is "almost," however—he is still standing, because God revives him with His lovingkindness (88). We've all been in scrapes. *Yeshua* asks in Luke 18:8, "When the Son of Man comes, will He find faith on the earth?"

No matter what is happening on earth, God's Word "stands firm in the heavens" (89). The authors of this commentary affirm that God's "faithfulness endures from generation to generation" (90), both in their own families and also in the lives of people they have taught and who have taught them the truth of His Word. His "judgments stand today, for all things" are His servants (91). To this day, a statue of Moses stands with the Ten Commandments above the entrance to the Supreme Court of the United States. Rock solid is the Word on which the psalmist stands, as he emphasizes: "If Your *Torah* had not been my delight, I would have perished in my affliction" (92). Though "the wicked wait for me to destroy me" (95), he keeps studying the *mitzvot*, which are "boundless" in "perfection" (96).

How many of us would sing out, "O how I love Your *Torah*!" (97)? Some theologians have made much ado about opposing grace and law, on the grounds that we are now "not under law but grace" (Rom. 6:14–15). But in the same epistle, Paul insists that "we uphold the *Torah*" (Rom. 3:31) and that *Torah* is holy, and the commandment is "holy and righteous and good" (Rom. 7:12). Paul's point is that, through faith in Messiah's death and resurrection, we are no longer under the curse or condemnation (Rom. 8:1) spelled out in *Torah* as the just consequence of our disobedience. Now the righteous requirement of the *Torah* can be fulfilled in us, who walk in the Spirit of Messiah (Rom. 8:2). You don't need to justify yourself before God, since Messiah has taken care of that for you. Nor do you need to feel ambivalent about the psalmist's devotion to *Torah*. You also can enjoy the benefit of the commandments and say that they "make me wiser than my enemies" (98), studying God's Word diligently will give "more insight than all my teachers" (99), and applying it to life will keep "my feet from every evil way" (101). Echoing Psalm 19:11 (another wisdom poem), the psalmist delights in the honey sweetness of God's Word in his mouth (103). Have you developed your spiritual taste buds?

How lovely is verse 105: "Your word is a lamp to my feet and a light to my path." Throughout this psalm and Scripture, there is a special connection between the Word of God and the Way to life in the Spirit. *Yeshua* said in John 8:12, "I am the light of the world. The one who follows Me will no longer walk in darkness, but will have the light of life." Later His disciples called themselves followers of "the Way." For Messianic believers, the light of Messiah multiplies the incandescence of the lamp of God's Word. In the darkness around us, it keeps us alive (107). When "my soul is continually in danger" (109), I remember the goodness of *Torah*. When the wicked one has "set a snare for me" (110), I remember that "Your testimonies" are "a heritage forever" and "my heart's joy" (111).

Let us not be double-minded (113), unstable in all our ways (Jacob [James] 1:8), but wholeheartedly in love with God and His Word. With such single-heartedness, we can be confident that God is our "hiding place and . . . shield" (114). We can trust God to "sustain" us according to His Word (116) and "support" and save us (117), that is, from peril. On the basis of His decrees, God will judge: "All the wicked of the earth You remove like dross" (119). One who "shudders for fear of You" can nevertheless be "in awe of Your judgments" (120).

It's not that the psalmist is so spiritual that he is unearthly. His confidence that he has done "what is just and right" gives him such a practical assurance that he can beckon God to "not leave me to my oppressors" (121). Invested as he is in his personal relationship with God, the guarantee of his personal "well-being" and "salvation" (122–123) is safely in God's hands. Trusting in God to justify his faith, he frankly declares, "Deal with Your servant as befits Your lovingkindness" (124). Then he announces: "It is time for ADONAI to act" (126). Bold? Not at all. He is simply confident that God is who the *Torah* says He is: the Savior of Israel, whose *mitzvot* from heaven are more valuable than "pure gold" (127).

"Your testimonies are wonderful" (129), and "the unfolding of Your words gives light" (130). Let me (Glenn Blank) share a brief story. As a graduate student studying literature at the University of Michigan, and later at the University of Wisconsin, I came to appreciate that the Bible is the greatest book of all. As "I opened my mouth wide" (131), the Spirit of God created in me a longing to know Him. Though I was running from *Yeshua* (even though I learned that the prophets had foretold Him), my heart kept turning to Him and saying, "Turn to me and be gracious to me" (132). Finally, I acknowledged that (a) there is no way for a human to know God unless God makes Himself known; (b) there would be no better way for God to make Himself known to humans than to come and relate to us as a human; (c) He promised He would do just that when He gave the prophets of Israel the hope of the Messiah; and (d) I had to admit that Jesus (I didn't know His Hebrew Name then) had fulfilled this promise when He came as a wonderful human being willing to suffer and lay down His life for the rest of us. So, after many years of seeking, God did "direct my footsteps" in His Word (133). One day I wrote in one of my graduate student notebooks (which I still have), "I am going to Janesville, Wisconsin, to accept Jesus as the Messiah." So I did. No longer will "iniquity get mastery over me" (133; see Rom. 6:9, 14). Ever since, I know that He has made His "face shine on" me (135) as He continues to guide my steps. Many times since have "streams of water run down from my eyes" (136). Though before I could not observe *Torah* in a way that would ever please Him, now I can—not in the flesh but by walking in His Spirit.

One who keeps walking with the Lord and His Word may find that "zeal has consumed me" (139), because "Your servant loves" every word (140). Though one may at times feel "insignificant and despised" (141), one can still exalt the justice and truth of *Torah*. Though "trouble and anguish" may overtake one (143), God's love and His testimonies still "are my delight" (143).

Our readers may wonder, what exactly is this *Torah*, so exalted? For the psalmist (and most Jews), it's the five books of Moses (Genesis–Deuteronomy). Orthodox Jews broaden the concept of *Torah* to include the "Oral Law"—it used to be oral but was written down toward the end of the second century CE as the *Mishna*, a rabbinic commentary on the commandments, statutes, and ordinances of *Torah*. The *Gemara*—a commentary on the *Mishna*— was added later to form the complete *Talmud*. For the Messianic believer, as 2 Timothy 3:16 says, "All Scripture is inspired by God and useful for teaching, for reproof, for restoration, and for training in righteousness." Since the word *Torah* means instruction, *all* Scripture is *Torah*—the first five books are the foundation on which the rest is built.

With this understanding, one can "put my hope in Your word" and continually "meditate on Your word," like a watchman up at night waiting for God to come like the dawn with His help and healing (147–48). Though "pursuers of wicked schemes" are "far from Your *Torah*" (150), we affirm, "Your *mitzvot* are truth" (151), demonstrating that God is "near."

Salvation (*yeshuah*) is a recurrent theme of this psalm, indeed throughout the Psalter. The psalmist looks to God to see his affliction and rescue him (153), defend his cause and redeem him, and restore his life (154). "Salvation is far from the wicked" (155), yet "great are Your mercies" (156). Though many *Yeshua*-believers think of salvation primarily as a ticket to heaven, the psalmist sees it first as deliverance from perils in this life. These two perspectives are not mutually exclusive. The psalmist looks to God to deliver him now, and then proclaims, "Your righteous rulings are eternal" (160).

Therefore, this poet can declare, "Your *Torah* I love" (163), "seven times a day I praise You" (164). Can his zeal inspire us in our own devotions? If so, he has a promise for us: "Great peace have they who love Your *Torah*" (165). Though "princes persecute me for no reason" (161) and falsehood abounds (163), this great peace remains. With this peace—and the blessed assurance that comes from trusting in Messiah *Yeshua*—one can "hope for Your salvation" (166).

Our readers may object that the psalmist did not know about *Yeshua*. True enough. But he did know about *yeshuah*. He also knew that his own knowledge would not be sufficient to save him. To the end, he cries out to God, "Deliver me, according to Your promise" (170). While it is true that His "*mitzvot* are righteous" (172), simply knowing or even doing them is not enough. The psalmist prays, "Let Your hand be ready to help me" (173). Studying the precepts of God always points him back to God Himself. Longing for deliverance (174), he beseeches, "Let my soul live and praise You" (175). He closes by admitting, "I have strayed like a lost sheep" (176). The psalmist understood that he needed a Good Shepherd to "seek" him and bring him back into the fold and good pasture. May we all have his humility, as well as his zeal.

PSALM 120

I Am for *Shalom*

¹ A Song of Ascents.
    In my trouble I cried out to ADONAI,
    and He answered me.

² *ADONAI*, deliver my soul from lying lips,
    from a deceitful tongue.
³ What can be given to you,
    and what more can be done to you, O deceitful tongue?—
⁴ sharp arrows of the mighty,
  with burning coals of a broom tree!
⁵ Woe to me, for I sojourn in Meshech,
    for I dwell among the tents of Kedar!
⁶ My soul has too long dwelt
    with those who hate *shalom.*
⁷ I am for *shalom* and thus I speak,
    but they are for war!

Glenn Blank

This Song of Ascents is the first of fifteen. Ancient Jews could chant or meditate on them as they made their way up into the hill country of Judea to Mount Zion for one of three pilgrimage festivals (*Pesach* or Passover, *Shavuot* or Pentecost, and *Sukkot* or Tabernacles). Another tradition holds that they would recite one of these short psalms on each of the fifteen steps into the Court of Israel in the Temple. The musical Levites may have sung these songs as the sons of Israel ascended these steps. As we meditate on them, we can try to imagine what they must have meant and felt like to our ancient forebearers.

This song starts the series off on a somber note: "In my trouble I cried out to *ADONAI*" (1). Part of the trouble seems to be "lying lips" and "a deceitful tongue" (2–3). Alas, such *tsouris* (a Yiddish word derived from the Hebrew word for *trouble*) has not passed away from the earth! The poet compares these hurtful words to "sharp arrows" and "burning coals" (4)—something to consider before (or even after) you utter any.

Then the psalmist compares his woe to sojourning in Meshech or dwelling among the tents of Kedar (5). Meshech was far to the north along the Black Sea (see Ezek. 39:1–2), while the tents of Kedar were far to the south in the Arabian desert (Ezek. 27:21; Kedar was one of the sons of Ishmael—see Gen. 25:13). Obviously, he wasn't literally dwelling in both places at the same time. More likely, he was comparing his plight with how it would feel to live so far outside his homeland. Alas, it's a plight that Jews have had to endure for thousands of years! On his journey up to the holy mountain, the pilgrim prays to experience God's *shalom*, yet all around him are people who are still plotting war (6–7). Israelis struggle with this dilemma still today! As we make our own pilgrimage to Zion in these psalms, let us pray that Israel's neighbors—and our neighbors too—would experience the *shalom* that passes all understanding that comes from knowing Messiah *Yeshua*.

❋❋❋❋❋❋ PSALM 121 ❋❋❋❋❋❋

He Watches over You

¹ A Song of Ascents.
> I will lift up my eyes to the mountains—
> from where does my help come?
² My help comes from ADONAI,
> Maker of heaven and earth.
³ He will not let your foot slip.
> Your Keeper will not slumber.
⁴ Behold, the Keeper of Israel
> neither slumbers nor sleeps.
⁵ ADONAI is your Keeper.
> ADONAI is your shadow at your right hand.
⁶ The sun will not strike you by day,
> nor the moon by night.
⁷ ADONAI will protect you from all evil.
> He will guard your life.
⁸ ADONAI will watch over your coming and your going
> from this time forth and forevermore.

Paul Wilbur

Here is another beautiful Song of Ascents, *ma-a-lot*. The Hebrew can also refer to steps, or even thoughts, that are ascending. If you have ever been to Jerusalem, then you know that you must "go up" to the city, since it is surrounded by steep hills. To these mountains the psalmist "will lift up" his eyes, from whence comes his help (1). Up there was the resting place of the ark of the covenant, so David's help came from ADONAI, the God of Israel who also made heaven and earth (2). Make sure you know the God you are calling on. Many gods are proclaimed and revered in the world today, but there is only one true living God—the God of Abraham, Isaac, and Israel!

Back in 1994, I was praying about the songs to include in my Integrity project, *Shalom Jerusalem*, when my friend Ed Kerr sent me a rendition of this psalm. I immediately loved it, and so it became the opening call to worship on the live recording performed right there on the mountain! "I lift up my eyes, I lift up my cry, to the hills around Jerusalem, to the God of all the earth. . . ." Today this song is recorded in English, Spanish, and Portuguese—the power and majesty of this ancient Song of Ascent lives on.

Next comes this well-known verse: *Hinei lo ya-noom v'lo yishan shomer Yisrael.* "Behold, the Keeper of Israel neither slumbers nor sleeps" (4). A שׁוֹמֵר, *shomer*, keeper or watchman, keeps vigilance while the city sleeps and rests. The safety of all the inhabitants depends on the watchman to stand guard, fight off the urge to sleep, and protect the people of the city. David assures us that the city and its people are safe and secure because it is no mere mortal who guards these gates and walls; it is ADONAI Himself! He will guard your going and coming, He will be your shade and protector, and He will be there "from this time forth and forevermore" (8). Praise ADONAI!

❈❈❈❈❈❈ PSALM 122 ❈❈❈❈❈❈❈

Pray for the Peace of Jerusalem

¹ A Song of Ascents. Of David.
    I rejoiced when they said to me,
    "Let us go to the House of ADONAI."
² Our feet are standing in your gates, Jerusalem—
³ Jerusalem, built as a city
    joined together.
⁴ There the tribes go up,
    the tribes of ADONAI
    —as a testimony to Israel—
    to praise the Name of ADONAI.
⁵ For there thrones for judgment are set up,
    the thrones of the house of David.

⁶ Pray for the peace of Jerusalem—
   "May those who love you be at peace!
⁷ May there be *shalom* within your walls—
   quietness within your palaces."
⁸ For the sake of my brothers and friends,
   I now say: "*Shalom* be within you."
⁹ For the sake of the House of ADONAI our God,
   I will seek your good.

Paul Wilbur

Another Song of Ascents, or steps, this psalm was used by ancient Israel when they came up the hills to worship the God of Israel in Jerusalem. It is also my setting of "Up to Jerusalem" on the *Shalom Jerusalem* project, recorded in Israel during Passover, 1995. For David, going to the House, בַּיִת, *beit*, of the Lord (1) was not a duty but the joy of his life. Today you can still stand in one of many gates (2) leading into the city of Jerusalem, just as the tribes of Israel (4) would pass through on their way up to the Temple and the presence of the living God. David longs for the *shalom* of His presence within Jerusalem's walls and palaces (7) as well as within his brothers and friends (8).

Verse 6 begins with the most well-known and quoted sentence in this song: *Sha-alu shalom Yerushalayim,* "Pray for the peace of Jerusalem." David gives two reasons to pray for the peace of Jerusalem: first for the good of the people of Israel (8), the apple of His eye, and second, "for the sake of the House of ADONAI our God" (9). May it be a House for praise and worship and a House of prayer for those from Israel and all nations who submit their lives to the King of the Jews, Messiah *Yeshua.*

 # PSALM 123

Be Gracious to Your Servants

¹ A Song of Ascents.
   To You I lift up my eyes—
   You enthroned in the heavens.

² Behold, as the eyes of slaves to the hand of their master,
  as the eyes of a slave-girl to the hand of her mistress—
  so our eyes look to ADONAI our God, till He shows us favor.
³ Show us favor, ADONAI, show us favor!
  For we have endured much contempt.
⁴ Our soul has had enough
  of the scorn of those at ease,
  the contempt of the proud.

Glenn Blank

When you have walked with Him awhile, *HaShem* may graciously call you His friend. So it was with Abraham (Isa. 41:8) and with the disciples of *Yeshua* after three years (John 15:15). But first we must relate to Him as a servant does to his master. For He is Almighty God, "enthroned in the heavens" (1). Especially for Americans fixated on "our rights," it is healthy to meditate on what it would be like to be a slave waiting on a master or mistress, looking to God "till He shows us favor" (2). Do you acknowledge Him as your Lord and Master? Are you willing to serve Him? Are you willing to wait on Him? Or do you get impatient with Him?

This poem was written during a time when our Jewish forebearers were enduring "much contempt" (3)—such as during the time of Nehemiah (2:19) when neighboring officials kept resisting his efforts to rebuild the city walls, so they kept the Jews weak. Have you ever had people use their power to abuse and ridicule you? Have you had "enough of the scorn" (4)? At such a time, all you can do is beseech God for His grace and aid. Can you take comfort knowing that the *Ruach* inspired this psalm for His people?

 # PSALM 124

Had He Not Been on Our Side

¹ A Song of Ascents. Of David.
  "Had ADONAI not been on our side"
  —let Israel now say—

[2] "Had *ADONAI* not been on our side,
    when men rose up against us,
[3] then they would have swallowed us alive,
    when their wrath burned against us.
[4] Then the waters would have engulfed us,
    the torrent would have swept over our soul,
[5] then the raging waters
    would have swept over our soul."

[6] Blessed be *ADONAI*, who has not given us
    as prey for their teeth.
[7] Our soul has escaped like a bird
    out of the snare of the trappers—
    the snare is broken, and we escaped!
[8] Our help is in the Name of *ADONAI*,
    Maker of heaven and earth.

Jeffrey Seif and Glenn Blank

The song "Amazing Grace" has long been a favorite. By the time John Newton composed it, he had lost his mother (at age seven), received a dozen lashes on a navy ship, been given as a slave in West Africa, become captain of a slave-trading ship, and just when it seemed like his ship would go down, finally called out to God for help. When Newton sang of having been "through many dangers, toils and snares," he knew whereof he spoke! God's amazing grace makes all the difference in life. "Had *ADONAI* not been on our side" (1–2), "they would have swallowed us alive" (3). Newton would have agreed—he survived as long as he did because God had a plan for his life. Otherwise, "the torrent would have swept over [his] soul" (4). Though you and I may not have experienced shipwreck or become "prey for their teeth" (6) (like those of a wild beast), you may have felt like you hit bottom. If that's you, give thanks to God that you "escaped like a bird" (7). Like the ancient psalmist and the eighteenth-century hymn writer, let's appreciate that "our help is in the Name of *ADONAI*" (8). God's amazing grace is not just reserved for songwriters. He gives it freely to all—including folks like you and me.

❉❉❉❉❉❉❉❉❉ PSALM 125 ❉❉❉❉❉❉❉❉❉

Like the Mountains around Jerusalem

¹ A Song of Ascents.
   Those who trust in ADONAI are like Mount Zion—
   it cannot be moved, but endures forever.
² As the mountains are around Jerusalem,
   so ADONAI is all around His people,
   both now and forever.
³ For a scepter of wickedness will not rest
   over the land of the righteous—
   lest the righteous set their hands to evil.
⁴ Do good, ADONAI, to the good,
   and to those upright in their hearts.
⁵ But as for those who turn aside to their crooked ways,
   ADONAI will lead them away with evildoers.
   Shalom be upon Israel.

Jeffrey Seif

People talk about security, marry for security, and hope to retire on Social Security. Despite all this investment in security, how much do most people really have in the end? Our psalmist found his security in God. He alone is a rock, solid as Mount Zion (1), immovable as the mountains around Jerusalem, only more so because "ADONAI is all around His people, both now and forever" (2). With that kind of confidence, he declares that "a scepter of wickedness will not rest over the land of the righteous" (3)—for all authority flows from God. God is just. He will "do good . . . to the good," but "as for those who turn aside to their crooked ways, ADONAI will lead them away with evildoers" (4–5). Though our works cannot save us, the Judge does consider them in deciding additional rewards or punishments, both in this world and the world to come. So let us consider how we may do good, so He may consider how He may do even more good to us, as well as to others whom He draws near.

⁕⁕⁕⁕⁕⁕⁕⁕ PSALM 126 ⁕⁕⁕⁕⁕⁕⁕⁕

Joyful Restoration of Zion

¹ A Song of Ascents.
>When ADONAI restored the captives of Zion,
>it was as if we were dreaming.
² Then our mouth was filled with laughter,
>and our tongue with a song of joy.
>Then they said among the nations,
>"ADONAI has done great things for them."
³ ADONAI has done great things for us
—we are joyful!
⁴ Restore us from captivity, ADONAI,
>like streams in the Negev.
⁵ Those who sow in tears
>will reap with a song of joy.
⁶ Whoever keeps going out weeping,
carrying his bag of seed,
>will surely come back with a song of joy,
carrying his sheaves.

Glenn Blank

After the devastating destruction of the Temple and exile in 586 BCE, Jews could only dream of the restoration of Zion. To be sure, they did dream, because the prophets had foretold it. Still, when this hope was fulfilled, it was astonishing—name another time when a people were allowed and encouraged to return to their homeland after many generations of exile. Since Ezra and tens of thousands of others began to return after seventy years, it has happened only once in all of human history—when millions returned to the same homeland after nearly nineteen hundred years! Is your jaw dropping yet? No wonder they were filled with laughter and singing songs of joy! You should see the fireworks in modern Israel on *Yom Ha-Atzma'ut*—the Day of Independence. It goes on for hours in every single community! The metaphor of sowing and reaping (5–6) has many applications in Scripture, but none more emotionally intense than the tears of Israel's captivity and the joy of Israel's restoration.

Do you know anyone who is still in a place of spiritual captivity, longing for streams in a dry land (4)? Pray now for that person to "reap with a song of joy" (5). Ask *Yeshua* to give you an opportunity to share the hope of restoration. If God can do it for Israel—not once but twice (as foretold in Isa. 11:11)—then surely He can do it for all who call on His Name. Soon Messiah will restore all things, wipe away all tears, and fill all with superabundant joy.

✳✳✳✳✳✳✳ PSALM 127 ✳✳✳✳✳✳✳

He Gives Sleep to His Children

¹ A Song of Ascents. Of Solomon.
    Unless ADONAI builds the house,
the builders labor in vain.
    Unless ADONAI watches over the city,
the watchman stands guard in vain.
² In vain you rise up early and stay up late,
eating the bread of toil—
    for He provides for His beloved ones even in their sleep.

³ Behold, children are a heritage of ADONAI
    —the fruit of the womb is a reward.
⁴ As arrows in the hand of a mighty man,
so are the children of one's youth.
⁵ Happy is the man whose quiver is full of them.
    They will not be put to shame
when they speak with their enemies at the gate.

Paul Wilbur

Here is a Song of Ascents traditionally attributed to Shlomo, the son of David, who would build "the house"—the Temple. King David's passion was to build a house for the Lord, but ADONAI told him no because of the blood on his hands. So, this psalm outlines the instructions and wise advice Solomon most likely received from his father on how to build God's House as well as how to protect it.

Doing things in our own strength is in vain and will come to nothing; protecting things in our own strength is also in vain (1). The root word for *watch*, שָׁמַר, *shamar*, from which we get *shomer*, watchman, also appears in Psalm 121:4: "The keeper of Israel neither slumbers nor sleeps."

It is also a waste of time to "rise up early and stay up late" (2), toiling and worrying. Why? Because *Adonai* gives sweet sleep to those He loves. In Psalm 4:9, David says he will "lie down and sleep in *shalom*" because the Lord keeps him safe. So it is not the toil of our labors nor the worrying of our souls that makes things prosper, but *Adonai*, the builder and protector, who takes good care of His beloved.

Now the psalmist seems to change course to tell us about the blessing of children. Or maybe it's no course change at all, but more about how *Adonai* watches over us as a good Father. For children are a "heritage" and "a reward" (3) from the Lord, demonstrating His protection "as arrows in the hand of a mighty man" (4). The blessings of the Lord are from generation to generation—He is the God of Abraham, and Isaac, and Jacob!

✴✴✴✴✴✴ PSALM 128 ✴✴✴✴✴✴

Blessing on Those Who Fear God

¹ A Song of Ascents.
>   Happy is everyone in awe of *Adonai*,
> who walks in His ways,
² for you will eat the labor of your hands.
>   You will be blessed
>   and it will be good for you.
³ Your wife will be like a fruitful vine within your house.
>   Your children will be like olive saplings around your table.
⁴ Behold, thus will the man be blessed
>   who fears *Adonai*.
⁵ May *Adonai* bless you out of Zion,
>   and may you see Jerusalem in prosperity
> all the days of your life,
⁶ and may you live to see your children's children.

>   *Shalom* be upon Israel!

Jeffrey Seif and Glenn Blank

Like Psalm 1, this psalm also promises that walking in God's ways will make us אַשְׁרֵי, *ashrei*—happy, blessed. We do life step-by-step. Those who seek God's will while taking these steps—guided by Scripture and the inner voice of God's Spirit in one's heart and conscience—will surely walk in His ways with confidence and contentment. The world is full of people pursuing happiness, yet many do not find it. Those who walk in God's ways, however, are called "happy" (1) and "blessed" (2)—both *ashrei*. There are both observable benefits and an interior sense of well-being, such as the satisfaction of eating "the labor of your hands" (2) and the pleasure of a secure and fruitful family gathering "around your table" for a *Shabbat* or holiday meal (3)—all the more when your children's children come to see you (6).

Every family has its times of trouble, so how do our families obtain the happy blessedness promised in this psalm? It begins and ends with a healthy "awe of ADONAI" (1), for the man "who fears ADONAI" will be blessed (4). We do not in blind terror run from danger or the unknown. Rather, with a wise awe we trust in His power and goodness—and this motivates us to keep on walking in His ways.

 PSALM 129

Haters Won't Prevail

¹ A Song of Ascents.
  "How many times they have been hostile to me,
      even from my youth"—let Israel now say—
² "How greatly they have been
      hostile to me, even from my youth.
    Yet they have not prevailed against me.
³ Plowmen plowed on my back—
      they made their furrows long!"
⁴ ADONAI is righteous—
      He has cut the ropes of the wicked.

⁵ May all who hate Zion
   be driven back in disgrace.
⁶ Let them be like grass on the roofs,
   which withers before it springs up—
⁷ with it a reaper cannot fill his hand,
   nor can a binder of sheaves fill his lap.
⁸ So the passersby may never say:
   "The blessing of ADONAI be upon you—
we bless you in the Name of ADONAI."

Glenn Blank

The problem of Zion haters is ancient and ceaseless. "How many times they have been hostile to me, even from my youth" (1)—this phenomenon still amazes Israelis and lovers of Zion. Why did the Edomites screech, "Strip her, strip her to her very foundation!" when the Chaldeans burned down the holy city (Ps. 137:7)? Why did the Romans raze it again, forbid Jews from entering it, and insult the Holy Land by renaming it Palaestina after our ancient, long-gone enemies? Why do Muslims throughout the world chant, "Death to the Jews," and some deny there was ever a Temple in Jerusalem?

Yet all the hostility has not prevailed against us (2), though their torment has been terrible (3). Why not? We can only point to *HaShem*, who has somehow "cut the ropes of the wicked" (4) meant to bind and enslave us. The Edomites and the Romans (during Roman times, the rabbis talked about Edomites as a code word for Romans) and the Chaldeans have long since been driven back (5), as shallow and rootless as "grass on the roofs" (6). All that is left of them is stones and shards for archaeologists.

Though cursing Zion's enemies seems hard to those who remember the message of love that fills these pages from Genesis through Revelation, these same pages are clear about the laws of blessings and curses, going back to Genesis 12:3, where *HaShem* promises "to bless those who bless you, but whoever curses you I will curse, and in you all the families of the earth will be blessed."

May many Zion haters heed the warning! And may many from all the families of the earth receive the blessing of those who bless her—and her coming King!

✳✳✳✳✳✳✳✳ PSALM 130 ✳✳✳✳✳✳✳✳✳

Forgiveness and Full Redemption

¹ A Song of Ascents.
  Out of the depths I cry to You, ADONAI!
² Lord, hear my voice!
  Let Your ears be attentive to the sound of my supplications.
³ If You, ADONAI, kept a record of iniquities—
  my Lord, who could stand?
⁴ For with You there is forgiveness,
  so You may be revered.
⁵ I wait for ADONAI, my soul waits,
  and in His word I hope.
⁶ My soul waits for my Lord,
  more than watchmen for the morning,
  watchmen for the morning.
⁷ O Israel, wait for ADONAI.
  For with ADONAI there is lovingkindness,
  and with Him is full redemption,
⁸ and He will redeem Israel
  from all its iniquities.

Paul Wilbur

The psalmist begins this song of ascending with a cry for help. The best place to run when you need help is the presence of ADONAI, hiding under His wings (Ps. 17:8) or in His strong tower of safety (Prov. 18:10). But we don't always do what is best when we are hurting.

Here the psalmist begins his cry for help from waters of great depths (1), feeling overwhelmed and drowning in his trials and entanglements of depression— not an enviable place, to be sure! When he asks the Lord to listen to his cry for help, he is aware of his own sin (3). Yet he is taking the right course; he is ascending the hill to ask forgiveness and mercy from ADONAI in the House of the Lord.

He continues his prayer by confessing that his soul longs for the presence of the Lord even more than a watchman (*shomer*) who waits for the dawn.

Imagine how a watchman would rejoice at the rising of the sun. The long, cold, lonely night watch is finally over; the sun chases away the shadows and the chill from the air. Even more than the exhilaration of a new day, "my soul waits" in anticipation for the coming of the Lord (5–6).

He finishes his song with the hope that all Israel will return to ADONAI and be saved, for only with the God of Israel is there forgiveness, mercy, and salvation (7–8). All other gods are cruel and their idols but sticks and stones with no eyes to see, or ears to hear, or arms to save. O that Israel would trust in the Lord and be saved!

✶✶✶✶✶✶✶✶ PSALM 131 ✶✶✶✶✶✶✶✶

Be Still My Soul

¹ A Song of Ascents. Of David.
   ADONAI, my heart is not proud,
      nor my eyes lofty,
      nor do I go after things too great
      or too difficult for me.
² But I have calmed and quieted my soul—
      like a weaned child with his mother,
      like a weaned child is my soul within me.
³ O Israel, put your hope in ADONAI
      from this time forth and forever.

Glenn Blank

In this Song of Ascents, the pilgrims continue to climb from the lowlands of humility up to high places of security and confident hope. The lowlands are a place where a "heart is not proud" (1) or vain about what one can do. The hills are a place of stillness in the presence of *HaShem*, where the soul is as secure as a toddler with his mother (2). The highest place is Israel's eternal hope of *HaShem* (3). Proverbs 3:34 and Jacob (James) 4:6 make this promise: God gives grace to the humble. Have you experienced this heavenly promise? It's not hard, if you are willing to let go of the pretense of pride. Humility is a gateway into His presence, where you find *Abba's* grace, intimacy, and eternal love.

✳✳✳✳✳✳✳✳✳ PSALM 132 ✳✳✳✳✳✳✳✳✳

Promise of *Ben-David*

¹ A Song of Ascents.
   Adonai, remember David,
   all his afflictions,
² and how he swore to Adonai,
   vowed to the Mighty One of Jacob:
³ "I will not enter the tent of my house
   nor lie on my bed,
⁴ nor will I give sleep to my eyes,
   nor slumber to my eyelids,
⁵ till I find a place for Adonai,
   a dwelling for the Mighty One of Jacob."

⁶ Behold, we heard of it in Ephratha,
   we found it in the fields of Joar.
⁷ Let us go into His dwelling place,
   let us bow at His footstool.
⁸ Arise, Adonai, to Your resting place—
   You, and the Ark of Your might.
⁹ Let Your *kohanim* wear righteousness,
   and let Your godly ones sing for joy.
¹⁰ For Your servant David's sake
   do not turn away the face of Your anointed.[a]

¹¹ Adonai has sworn to David
   a true promise He will not revoke:
   "From the fruit of your body
   I will set one upon your throne—[b]
¹² if your children keep My covenant
   and My law that I will teach them,
   then their sons will sit on your throne forever."

¹³ For Adonai has chosen Zion,
   He has desired it for His dwelling:
¹⁴ "This is My resting place forever.
   Here I dwell, for I have desired it.

a. 132:10. Or, *Messiah*.
b. 132:11. cf. Acts 2:29–35.

¹⁵ I will abundantly bless her food.
> I will satisfy her needy ones with bread.
¹⁶ I will clothe her *kohanim* with salvation,
> and her godly ones will sing aloud for joy.
¹⁷ There will I make a horn spring up for David,^c
> I have set up a lamp for My anointed.
¹⁸ His enemies I will clothe with shame,
> but upon himself his crown will shine."

Glenn Blank and Jeffrey Seif

Recall that ancient Jews probably chanted the fifteen Songs of Ascents as they made their way up to Jerusalem for a festival. In this one, they prayed that ADONAI "remember David" (1), the beloved king who had "vowed to the Mighty One" (2) that he would not rest until he found "a dwelling for the Mighty One of Jacob" (3–5). As sure as those Jews were making their way up to that holy House, they knew David had fulfilled that vow. Whether they were journeying from Ephratha to the south (where David was born) or Joar to the west (where David found the ark of the covenant, 1 Chron. 13:5–6), they must have been meditating on the dwelling place that the singing king had prepared for his God. They were looking forward to worshiping "at His footstool" there (7). Remembering how David brought "the Ark of Your might" to "Your resting place" (8) with his wonderful awe and dancing joy, they too looked forward to joining the Levites whose job it was to "sing for joy" (9). Verses 8–9 repeat Solomon's prayer when he dedicated the Temple in 2 Chronicles 6:41. It must have been awesome to see the ark brought into God's resting place in the Temple, the Levites leading all Israel in songs of exaltation, and the fire of God falling from heaven and His glory filling His House (2 Chron. 7:1)!

Now, generations later, the Jewish pilgrims are interceding, "for Your servant David's sake" (10). They remind God about the "true promise" that He swore to David: that He would set his descendants on the throne (11). This promise was conditional on his descendants keeping the covenant (12). Nevertheless, God has chosen Mount Zion as His dwelling and "resting place forever" (13–14). He promised to provide for the people and clothe their priests (15–16). He promised to make "a horn spring up for David" (17)—a

c. 132:17. cf. Luke 1:69.

horn was a symbol of strength, from which the *shofar* was made and anointing oil was poured. The promise to David looks forward to His "anointed"— מָשִׁיחַ, *Mashiach*, the Messiah. In Luke 1:69, Zechariah opened up his mouth in praise to God, "He has raised up a horn of salvation for us in the house of His servant David." Imperfect as David's descendants were, and unworthy of his throne, someone better was to come. Upon this son of David, "his crown will shine" (18). Imperfect as we are, and unworthy of God's favor, we can take heart in God's faithfulness to David fulfilled in his descendant *Yeshua.* The One who stuck it out with David will stand with us. Let's pray for the fire of His *Ruach* to fall and the glory of His presence to fill His House—and our hearts—again.

PSALM 133

Blessing of Unity

¹ A Song of Ascents. Of David.
  Behold, how good and how pleasant it is
  for brothers to dwell together in unity!
² It is like the precious oil upon the head,
  coming down upon the beard—Aaron's beard—
  coming down on the collar of his robes.
³ It is like the dew of Hermon,
  coming down upon the mountains of Zion.
  For there ADONAI commanded the blessing
  —life forevermore!

Paul Wilbur

If you ever have an opportunity to travel to Israel, or perhaps to join a Jewish wedding party, you will undoubtedly hear this song. It just might be the most-often sung and best-known traditional Jewish song. It is the next-to-last *Shir ha Ma a lot* or Song of Ascents that the children of Israel sang as they approached the House of the Lord in Jerusalem. Reaching their destination, they rejoiced together: *Hinei ma tov u ma na yim shevet achim gam yachad.*

"Behold, how good and how pleasant it is for brothers to dwell together in unity!" (1).

The word יַחַד, *yachad*, speaks of togetherness as when an army unites for battle. It carries the sense of "oneness," but it does not mean "one" as in single—one apple, one guitar, and so on. Nor does it denote uniformity or indivisibility; rather, it speaks of a composite unity. Huh? How about this illustration: a cluster of grapes is one cluster (*echad*) but many clusters grow together on the same vine (*yachad*). The clusters are all different, unique, and individual, but they are members in particular of that one vine. (I could get caught up here making more references to *Yeshua's* teaching in John 15, but I'll leave that adventure for you to enjoy on your own.)

David goes on to say that this unity is like the precious *shemen* or fragrant oil that was used to anoint kings and priests (2), the oil that was used to soothe and cleanse and promote healing. This *yachad* refreshes like the dew that falls on Mount Hermon and waters the mountains of Zion (3). What beautiful pictures of the blessing of dwelling together in unity. At Zion ADONAI commands a blessing. From my reading of Scripture, this blessing carried with it an ability to perform what was spoken over the person being blessed. So my own rendering of the key thoughts of Psalm 133 might go something like this:

> See how good it is when the people of ADONAI dwell
> together like a beautiful cluster of grapes.
> > It is as if a fragrant, healing oil
> > > has been poured out on the head,
> > like the smell of morning dew
> > > that falls on Mount Zion.
> > For it is there, in the beauty of unity,
> > > that ADONAI will command
> > > His power of favor and success,
> > > even everlasting life.

It is no wonder, then, that a major theme of the new covenant is that followers of Messiah should pursue unity. If we pursue Messiah and His righteousness, then unity and all its blessings will certainly pursue us!

✻✻✻✻✻✻✻✻✻✻ PSALM 134 ✻✻✻✻✻✻✻✻✻✻

Call to Evening Worship

¹ A Song of Ascents.
    Behold, bless ADONAI, all servants of ADONAI,
    who stand by night in the House of ADONAI.
² Lift up your hands to the Sanctuary
    and bless ADONAI.
³ May ADONAI bless you out of Zion—
    Maker of heaven and earth.

Glenn Blank

This psalm is the last Song of Ascents. The pilgrims have arrived "in the House of ADONAI" (1). Apparently they don't want to leave but stay up all night! If you've set your heart on worshiping Him, you too might want to linger and "lift up your hands to the Sanctuary" and just keep blessing the Lord (2). Didn't Paul Wilbur just write about how good it is to dwell there in unity? When you are there, in that holy place, you know that *HaShem* surely will "bless you out of Zion" (3). Come on in!

✻✻✻✻✻✻✻✻✻✻ PSALM 135 ✻✻✻✻✻✻✻✻✻✻

Jacob as His Treasure

¹ *Halleluyah!* Praise the Name of ADONAI.
    Give praise, O servants of ADONAI—
² standing in the House of ADONAI,
    in the courts of the House of our God.
³ Praise ADONAI, for ADONAI is good.
    Sing praises to His Name, for it is delightful.
⁴ For ADONAI has chosen Jacob for Himself,
    Israel as His treasured possession.[a]

a. 135:4. cf. 1 Pet. 2:9.

⁵ For I have known that ADONAI is great,
　　and that our Lord is above all gods.
⁶ Whatever ADONAI pleases, He does,
　　　in heaven and in earth,
　　　in the seas and in all deeps.
⁷ He makes clouds rise from the ends of the earth.
　　　He makes lightning for the rain.
　　　He brings wind out of His storehouses.

⁸ He struck down the firstborn of Egypt,
　　both man and beast.
⁹ He sent signs and wonders among you,
　　　O Egypt, on Pharaoh and all his servants.
¹⁰ He struck down many nations
　　and slew mighty kings:
¹¹ Sihon, king of the Amorites,
　　and Og, king of Bashan,
　　and all the kingdoms of Canaan,
¹² and gave their land as an inheritance,
　　　an inheritance to His people Israel.

¹³ ADONAI, Your Name endures forever,
　　　Your renown, ADONAI, from generation to generation.
¹⁴ For ADONAI will vindicate His people,
　　and have compassion on His servants.
¹⁵ The idols of the nations are silver and gold,
　　the work of human hands.
¹⁶ They have mouths, but cannot speak,
　　　eyes, but cannot see;
¹⁷ they have ears, but cannot hear,
　　　nor is there any breath in their mouths.
¹⁸ Those who make them will be like them—
　　so will all who keep trusting in them.

¹⁹ O house of Israel, bless ADONAI!
　　　O house of Aaron, bless ADONAI!
²⁰ O house of Levi, bless ADONAI!
　　　You who revere ADONAI, bless ADONAI!
²¹ Blessed be ADONAI out of Zion,
　　who dwells in Jerusalem. *Halleluyah!*

Jeffrey Seif and Glenn Blank

Chosen people? Throughout the Bible, people are called such, for example, "*ADONAI* has chosen Jacob for Himself" (4). What does this special status mean? Are the "chosen" supposed to be better than others? Or does it imply some special purpose or privilege? It may not always seem so. In *Fiddler on the Roof*, Tevye says to God, "I know, I know. We are Your chosen people. But once in a while, couldn't You choose someone else?"[1]

We begin with people called "servants of *ADONAI*," who have the privilege or task (depending on how they look at it) of standing in the courts of *ADONAI* and giving praise (1–2). Sounds like the Levites—David appointed them to sing joyfully and play musical instruments (1 Chron. 15:16). The modern equivalent would be the worship teams in many congregations. Are they the chosen people? Or are the chosen anyone with a recognized ministry and calling? When they sing praises, "it is delightful" (3)—so does chosenness imply that you should enjoy your ministry? You who stand in the House of *ADONAI*, do you?

It turns out that *HaShem* has "chosen Jacob" and "Israel as His treasured possession" (4). So the esteemed and valuable are not just a select worship team but a whole nation! Indeed, all Israel came to worship in the courts of *HaShem*—the Levites were there to lead them. That's something for musicians and worship leaders to remember—you are no more chosen than the congregation; your ministry is to lead them into His presence.

Why was Israel uniquely treasured? The other nations served many gods and idols, but Israel knows that *HaShem* alone is "Lord . . . above all gods" (5). Israel recognizes His authority over all creation (6–7) and over all nations (10)—as He demonstrated in Egypt (8–9) and with Sihon and Og who resisted Israel's approach to the Promised Land (11)—giving all the land of Canaan to Israel as an inheritance (12). For His Name's sake—consider how chosenness is connected with His Name—*HaShem* "will vindicate His people, and have compassion" on them (13–14). An inheritance and compassion are features of chosenness—so maybe we do want God to choose us, after all? The other nations have idols of silver and gold (15)—ominously "all who keep trusting in them" will be like them, that is, altogether powerless and helpless (16–18). God chose Israel to call people from all nations away from futile idols to the one true God.

The chosen nation is beckoned to "bless ADONAI" together with the house of Levi (19–20), because *HaShem* "dwells in Jerusalem" (21). So what more can we conclude about being "chosen"? Lacking is any arrogant superiority. Israel is not called to boast in themselves but only in God who chose them. To be chosen means to serve and praise the Lord and call others to join in. If you are ever inclined to think of yourself as better than others or to put a worship leader or minister on a pedestal, this psalm is a sober reminder that the chosen people are the servants of all. And by the way, as Moses found out in Exodus 4:13–14, it's definitely not a good idea to ask God to choose somebody else!

PSALM 136

His *Chesed* Endures Forever!

¹ Praise ADONAI, for He is good,
    for His lovingkindness endures forever.
² Praise the God of gods,
    for His lovingkindness endures forever.
³ Praise the Lord of lords,
    for His lovingkindness endures forever,
⁴ who alone did great wonders,
    for His lovingkindness endures forever,
⁵ who made the heavens by wisdom,
    for His lovingkindness endures forever,
⁶ who spread the earth on the waters,
    for His lovingkindness endures forever,
⁷ who made great lights,
    for His lovingkindness endures forever—
⁸ the sun to rule by day,
    for His lovingkindness endures forever,
⁹ the moon and stars to rule by night,
    for His lovingkindness endures forever,
¹⁰ who struck Egypt in their firstborn,
    for His lovingkindness endures forever,
¹¹ and led out Israel from among them,
    for His lovingkindness endures forever,

¹² with a strong hand and outstretched arm,
    for His lovingkindness endures forever,
¹³ who cut the Sea of Reeds into parts,
    for His lovingkindness endures forever,
¹⁴ and made Israel pass through the midst of it,
    for His lovingkindness endures forever,
¹⁵ but hurled Pharaoh and his army into the Sea of Reeds,
    for His lovingkindness endures forever,
¹⁶ who led His people through the desert,
    for His lovingkindness endures forever,
¹⁷ who struck down great kings,
    for His lovingkindness endures forever,
¹⁸ and slew mighty kings,
    for His lovingkindness endures forever,
¹⁹ Sihon, king of the Amorites,
    for His lovingkindness endures forever,
²⁰ and Og, king of Bashan,
    for His lovingkindness endures forever,
²¹ and gave their land for an inheritance,
    for His lovingkindness endures forever,
²² an inheritance for Israel His servant,
    for His lovingkindness endures forever.
²³ He remembered us in our lowly estate,
    for His lovingkindness endures forever,
²⁴ and separated between us
    and He delivered us from our adversaries,
    for His lovingkindness endures forever,
²⁵ who gives food to all flesh,
    for His lovingkindness endures forever.
²⁶ Praise the God of heaven,
    for His lovingkindness endures forever!

Jeffrey Seif and Glenn Blank

It's said, "If something is not worth saying a thousand times, it is not worth saying once." Though not a thousand times, the expression "for His loving-kindness endures forever" is repeated every time this psalmist put pen to paper. If there were a thousand verses here, the line would have been in every one! As it is, we have twenty-six reminders: כִּי לְעוֹלָם חַסְדּוֹ, *ki* (for) *l'olam* (forever) *chasdo* (His lovingkindness/mercy). The refrain is designed to make a deep impression in our souls—how true and meaningful it is. Amen?

The first half of each verse backs up the claim. God is "good" (1)—that's our way of returning the favor of His pronouncement over all of creation seven times in Genesis 1 alone, טוֹב, *tov*! He is "the God of gods" and "the Lord of lords" (2–3)—repeating a word is a Hebrew idiom of superlative emphasis, picked up to exalt Messiah *Yeshua* in 1 Timothy 6:15 and Revelation 19:16. He is a wonder-worker (4), the Creator (5–9)—let's never take for granted the miracle of creation!—and miracle-doer for Israel's redemption from Egypt (10–15) and passage into the Promised Land (16–22). How easy it is to take what God has done in the past for granted and wonder what He's done lately. But how will we recognize what He does now if we do not call to mind what He has done already?

God's goodness further translates into His remembering "us in our lowly estate" (23). Where would any of us be without His lovingkindness? His *chesed* "separated between us and . . . our adversaries" (24). Are you glad that He has come between you and your ageless adversary? If you're not sure, consider how in Zechariah 3, *satan* was standing by and ready to accuse the *kohen gadol* (high priest) Joshua because of the filth of his sin. Then the angel of *HaShem* Himself stood there between them and rebuked the adversary! Now put yourself in Joshua's shoes. Is God good, or what? (And who was that angel?)

Let's not forget that God "gives food to all flesh" (25)—have you thanked Him for our daily bread today? When we add it all up, surely He's a good God on record doing good things for His people. "Praise the God of heaven" (26). What has He done for you lately? Why not take an inventory right now and make a list of God's goodness in your own affairs? And don't forget to say, over and over again, *ki l'olam chasdo*!

PSALM 137

By the Rivers of Babylon

¹ By the rivers of Babylon,
    we sat down and wept,
        when we remembered Zion.

² On the willows there
>   we hung up our harps.
³ For there our captors demanded songs
>   and our tormentors asked for joy:
>   "Sing us one of the songs of Zion."
⁴ How can we sing a song of *ADONAI* in a foreign land?
⁵ If I forget you, O Jerusalem,
>   let my right hand wither.
⁶ May my tongue cling to the roof of my mouth
>   if I cease to remember you,
>   if I do not set Jerusalem above my chief joy.
⁷ Remember, *ADONAI*, the children of Edom,
>   what they said on the day Jerusalem fell:
>   "Strip her, strip her to her very foundation!"
⁸ O daughter of Babylon, the devastated one,
>   happy is the one who repays you
>   as you have paid us.
⁹ Happy is the one who seizes your little ones
>   and dashes them upon the rock.

Jeffrey Seif and Glenn Blank

This poem is a tough one. For openers, the psalmist is extremely discouraged. It's more than just a bad day at the office. He has lost his home. He is a refugee. He has barely survived the fall of the Davidic dynasty, the ravaging of Jerusalem and the Temple—and who knows what else in his personal life. As if that is not bad enough, while he is being dragged off in chains (possibly in a slave market), his captors are tormenting him and his comrades and demanding they "sing us one of the songs of Zion" (3). The songs of Zion tell of God's greatness, power, and love for His people. "Let's hear some of those now," taunt their captors. The singers of Zion respond: "How can we sing a song of *ADONAI* in a foreign land?" (4).

Some of us have wondered: "How can I sing a song of God's goodness in a world full of such badness?" But the psalmist promises that he will never forget Jerusalem, that he will keep the memory alive even in a hellish world. Such determination was crucial to his survival, and the survival of the Jewish people as well. Never forget. Next year in Jerusalem!

Difficult as it is to read of the captives' depression, what comes next in the psalm is even tougher. God knows about depression; here it is in His book. Though depression can be clinically defined as "anger turned inward," now the anger turns outward, and the psalmist curses his enemies. It has shocked Bible readers ever since it was penned. After recalling how the Edomites gloated when the Babylonians devastated Jerusalem (7–8a), he exclaims: "Happy is the one who repays you as you have paid us. Happy is the one who seizes your little ones and dashes them upon the rock" (8b–9). Talk of killing babies—even of our hateful enemies—does not exactly comport with Judeo-Christian sensibilities, does it? Must it? Do distressed persons say things they don't necessarily mean? Yes, all the time. Holocaust survivors cannot be expected to have kind things to say about the Nazis. (Rose Price was an amazing exception, and that only by the power of God's grace.) Disturbing as the hyperbole is, we do well to make room for venting and allow people to do so as needed. After the *shiva* (time of mourning), we can remind them that it's time to forgive and to sing one of the songs of Zion.

PSALM 138

Your Right Hand Delivers Me

¹ Of David.
 I praise You with all my heart.
 In the presence of the mighty I will sing praises to You.
² I bow down toward Your holy Temple
 and praise Your Name for Your love and Your faithfulness.
 For You—magnified above all Your Name and Your word.
³ On the day I called, You answered me.
 You made me bold with strength in my soul.
⁴ All the kings of the earth will praise You, ADONAI,
 when they hear Your mouth's speech.
⁵ So they will sing of the ways of ADONAI,
 for great is the glory of ADONAI.
⁶ For though ADONAI is exalted,
 yet He looks upon the lowly,
 but the haughty He knows from afar.

⁷ Though I walk amid trouble,
>   You revive me.
>   You stretch out Your hand against the wrath of my enemies,
>   and Your right hand delivers me.
⁸ ADONAI will fulfill His purpose for me.
>   Your lovingkindness, ADONAI, endures forever.
>   Do not abandon the work of Your hands.

Jeffrey Seif and Glenn Blank

In the previous psalm, the writer has a picture of the burning Temple in his rearview mirror. His world has fallen apart, and he is leaving Jerusalem in chains. Then we read this one, with a psalmist worshiping God in His holy Temple. He praises God with all his heart "in the presence of the mighty" (1). God is so good (all the time!), and the poet delights to "bow down toward Your holy Temple" (2). To this day, Orthodox Jews *daven* or bow slightly in the direction of the Temple Mount. Where He is, it is good. Circumstances change, moods change. Unlike the depressed and uncertain exile of the previous poem, this one affirms: "On the day I called, You answered me. You made me bold with strength in my soul" (3). From depths of despair to God's pastoral care—how can it be? It can be, because life is precarious, and human feelings are fickle. The next chapter of your life has not been written (even if God can peek ahead), because you have to live it. Yet God is always faithful. Though He is "exalted," God "looks upon the lowly" (6), and when "I walk amid trouble," He revives me (7). Whatever unfolds in your next chapter, God "will fulfill His purpose" (8) for you.

Glenn Blank remembers a time when it looked like he was going to fail, and he started thinking that would be the end of God's plan for him. Then a friend stopped by and recommended that he take a break and pray. Sure enough, the next morning, relief came. When you're in a place of trouble or lowliness, take a break and pray. *HaShem* is your deliverer. He does not abandon the work of His hands. He will fulfill His purpose for you.

✳✳✳✳✳✳✳✳✳ PSALM 139 ✳✳✳✳✳✳✳✳✳✳

How Precious Your Thoughts!

¹ For the music director: a psalm of David.
    ADONAI, You searched me and know me.
² Whenever I sit down or stand up, You know it.
    You discern my thinking from afar.
³ You observe my journeying and my resting
    and You are familiar with all my ways.
⁴ Even before a word is on my tongue,
    behold, *ADONAI*, You know all about it.
⁵ You hemmed me in behind and before,
    and laid Your hand upon me.
⁶ Such knowledge is too wonderful for me,
    too lofty for me to attain.
⁷ Where can I go from Your *Ruach?*
    Where can I flee from Your presence?
⁸ If I go up to heaven, You are there,
    and if I make my bed in *Sheol*,
    look, You are there too.
⁹ If I take the wings of the dawn
    and settle on the other side of the sea,
¹⁰ even there Your hand will lead me,
    and Your right hand will lay hold of me.
¹¹ If I say: "Surely darkness covers me,
    night keeps light at a distance from me,"
¹² even darkness is not dark for You,
    and night is as bright as day—
    darkness and light are alike.
¹³ For You have created my conscience.
    You knit me together in my mother's womb.
¹⁴ I praise You, for I am awesomely, wonderfully made!
    Wonderful are Your works—
    and my soul knows that very well.
¹⁵ My frame was not hidden from You
    when I was made in the secret place,
    when I was woven together in the depths of the earth.

¹⁶ Your eyes saw me when I was unformed,
    and in Your book were written the days that were formed—
    when not one of them had come to be.
¹⁷ How precious are Your thoughts, O God!
    How great is the sum of them!
¹⁸ Were I to count them,
    they would outnumber the grains of sand!
    When I awake, I am still with You.

¹⁹ If only You would slay the wicked, O God!
    Away from me, you bloody men!
²⁰ For they speak about You with wicked intent.
    Your enemies reproach You in vain.
²¹ Do I not hate those who hate You, ADONAI?
    Do I not loathe those who rise against You?
²² I hate them with total hatred—
    I consider them my enemies.

²³ Search me, O God, and know my heart.
    Examine me, and know my anxious thoughts,
²⁴ and see if there be any offensive way within me,
    and lead me in the way everlasting.

Glenn Blank

Once upon a time, I was a liberal, secular Jew. Nevertheless, O God, "You searched me and know me" (1). I learned some Hebrew and had my *bar mitzvah*, but the God of Israel seemed distant to me. Yet "You discern my thinking from afar" (2). I went to Penn State to study literature—"You are familiar with all my ways" (3). As I was composing a paper, suddenly *Yeshua* appeared to me in a vision—You "laid Your hand upon me" (5). I had no idea what to make of it—"such knowledge is too wonderful for me" (6).

So I started studying the religions of the world, unconsciously seeking anything but Jesus. But "where can I flee from Your presence?" (7). A professor at this large secular university required that his students buy a Bible (as background for seventeenth-century literature), for "even there Your hand will lead me" (10). Though as a young man I struggled with depression and loneliness, "even darkness is not dark for You" (12). I came to appreciate that Your book is the foundation of all Western literature and the greatest book ever written. I hungered more and more to know You, "for You have created my conscience" (13); You created my soul to seek You and find You. You showed me, in a vision of mist rising and falling in a valley, how "wonderful are Your works" (14). When I surrendered my life to You, I still barely understood You and had no idea what You had written "in Your book" for me (16)!

When I began to follow You, I still had the thoughts of a liberal, secular Jew. I thought the world would too soon overpopulate. Then Your Spirit led me to this psalm. I contemplated how You saw me "when I was made in the secret place" (15), how "Your eyes saw me when I was unformed" (16). Your gracious Spirit helped me to understand the connection between Your great love for every human being and Your precious thoughts toward each one of us (17).

When I first began to follow You, I wondered if I should really "hate those who hate You" (21). For haven't You taught us even to love our enemies? Nevertheless, I was convinced that I must stand with You and what You stand for, no matter what it costs. Then I learned that my real struggle is not with flesh and blood, but spiritual powers (Eph. 6:12)—"I consider *them* my enemies" (22, emphasis added).

As I continue to walk with You, I continually pray, "Search me, O God, . . . and know my anxious thoughts" (23), for I know that I can still be distracted by thoughts within and disturbances without. So I keep asking God to remove "any offensive way within me," because I still need His Spirit to lead me "in the way everlasting" (24).

☀☀☀☀☀☀☀ PSALM 140 ☀☀☀☀☀☀☀

Protection from the Wicked

¹ For the music director: a psalm of David.
² Rescue me, ADONAI, from the evil man.
　　Protect me from the violent men—
³ who devise evil in their heart—
　every day they stir up wars.
⁴ They sharpen their tongue like a serpent's
　　—viper's venom is under their lips.ᵃ *Selah*

a. 140:4. cf. Rom. 3:13.

[5] Keep me safe, ADONAI, from the clutches of the wicked.
> Protect me from the man of violence who planned to push me off my
> feet.

[6] The proud have hidden a trap and cords for me.
> They spread out a net by the path.
> They set snares for me. *Selah*

[7] I said to ADONAI: "You are my God!"
> Hear, ADONAI, the sound of my supplications.

[8] God my Lord, the strength of my deliverance,
> You shield my head in the day of battle.

[9] Grant not, ADONAI, the desires of the wicked.
> Do not let their evil plan succeed,
> or they will exalt themselves. *Selah*

[10] As for the head of those surrounding me,
> may the mischief of their lips overwhelm them.

[11] Let burning coals fall upon them.
> May they be cast into the fire, into deep pits,
> never to rise again.[a]

[12] May a slanderer not endure in the land.
> May calamity hunt down a violent man.

[13] I know ADONAI will vindicate the poor,
> and secure justice for the needy.

[14] Surely, the righteous ones will praise Your Name.
> The upright will dwell in Your presence.

Jeffrey Seif

Life comes replete with many challenges, not least of which are challenging people who impose themselves upon our lives. Though it would be better if we could reform them all, it seems the best we can often do is seek the Lord for protection. The psalmist beseeches *HaShem* to "rescue" him "from the evil man" (2). There are some folks who just seem forever determined to "stir up wars" (3). If that's your experience, you're not alone. Cops see it all the time. So do saints—such as Paul getting beaten up pretty good a few times. Though I sincerely hope it does not describe anyone you know, well, there's this enemy who sharpens his tongue "like a serpent's" (4). You know about him? He's the kind who tries to "push me off my feet" (5), hide a "trap" as if

a. 140:11. cf. John 15:6; Rev. 20:15.

a person were an animal, or "spread out a net" as if a person were a helpless bird (6). That's when all you can do is raise the sound of your supplications to the Lord (7), seeking Him as "the strength" of your deliverance (8) and beseeching Him to "not let their evil plan succeed" (9).

The psalmist is not looking to take matters into his own hands. He prays, "Let burning coals fall upon them"—he is seeking justice only God can render, including the ultimate justice of "deep pits, never to rise again" (11). As Paul recommends in Romans 12:19–20, "Never take your own revenge, loved ones, but give room for God's wrath—for it is written, 'Vengeance is Mine; I will repay,' says ADONAI. Rather, 'If your enemy is hungry, feed him; if he is thirsty, give him a drink. For by doing so you will heap coals of fire upon his head.'" *HaShem* has His own ways of bringing mischief on the lips of a slanderer (10) or calamity on a violent man (12)—unless or until he repents. Though the psalmist is in trouble, he is confident: "I know ADONAI will vindicate the poor" (13)—the last word could also be translated as "the afflicted." Moreover, "the upright will dwell in Your presence" (14). Though aware of his problems at the present, he looks beyond the present and to *HaShem* who provides His presence.

 # PSALM 141

Evening Petition for Protection

¹ A psalm of David.
> ADONAI, I call to You—come quickly to me!
> Hear my voice when I call to You.
² May my prayer be set before You like incense.
> May the lifting up of my hands be like the evening sacrifice.
³ Set a guard, ADONAI, over my mouth.
> Keep watch over the door of my lips.
⁴ Let not my heart turn to any evil thing,
> to practice deeds of wickedness
> with men that work iniquity,
> nor let me eat of their delicacies.

⁵ Let the righteous strike me—it is kindness.

    Let him correct me—it is oil on my head

    —my head will not refuse it.

    Yet still my prayer is against their wickedness.

⁶ Their judges are thrown down from a cliff.

    Then they will hear my words, since they are sweet.

⁷ As when one plows and breaks open the earth,

    so our bones are scattered at the mouth of *Sheol*.

⁸ For my eyes are toward You, God my Lord.

    In You I have taken refuge—do not expose my soul.

⁹ Keep me from the jaws of the trap they have laid for me,

    and from the snares of the evildoers.

¹⁰ Let the wicked fall into their own nets,

    while I pass by safely.

Glenn Blank and Jeffrey Seif

"Help!" Many a prayer has been just this one word or launched by this word. Yet David understands that the help he most urgently needs is knowing *how* to pray. Sure, he needs God to "come quickly to me" when he lifts up his voice (1). But his next request is about how he prays, that it would somehow be as acceptable to God as the incense and the evening sacrifice offered in the tabernacle of the Lord (2). Though he might have asked for angels to protect him from danger, instead he requests "a guard . . . over my mouth" (3), to avoid saying anything unworthy before *HaShem*. Then he realizes that he may need help with more than just his lips. Acceptable prayer must come from the heart, which must not "turn to any evil thing" or even the "delicacies" that wicked men eat (4). If his prayer is to be truly righteous, he must be willing to "let the righteous strike" him, accepting correction as oil poured on his head (5). As Proverbs 15:31 says, "One whose ear heeds a life-giving reproof dwells among the wise." With righteous prayer, the psalmist will have vindication against "their judges" (or rulers), and they will finally hear his words as "sweet" (6). They will recognize how he has suffered as if his back were the earth under a plow, as near death as "the mouth of *Sheol*" (7). But rather than focus on his enemies, his "eyes are toward . . . God," the refuge of his soul (8). Only God can protect him from traps, snares, and nets that he cannot see, so that he can "pass by safely" (9–10).

What can we learn from how David prays? You don't need to be perfect to ask God for help. Crying out "Help!" is a good start. You can ask *HaShem* to show you how to pray, and you can learn from David's model. You can be humble, teachable, open to correction, and willing to learn from adversity. You can keep turning your eyes toward *Elohim*, trusting that He will surely work all things together for good for those who love Him (Rom. 8:28) and will safely deliver you out of "the jaws of the trap" (9).

✴✴✴✴✴✴✴✴✴✴ PSALM 142 ✴✴✴✴✴✴✴✴✴✴

A Refuge from Trouble

¹ A contemplative poem of David, when he was in the cave, a prayer.
² I cry aloud with my voice to *ADONAI*.
    With my voice I seek favor from *ADONAI*.
³ I pour out my complaint before Him,
    before Him I tell my trouble.
⁴ When my spirit grows faint within me,
    You know my path.
    In the way where I walk they have hidden a trap for me.
⁵ Look at my right hand and see,
    for no one cares about me.
    I have no refuge—
    no one cares for my soul.
⁶ I have cried out to You, *ADONAI*.
    I said: "You are my refuge,
  my portion in the land of the living."
⁷ Listen to my cry,
  for I am brought very low.
    Rescue me from my persecutors,
  for they are too strong for me.
⁸ Bring my soul out of prison,
  so I may praise Your Name.
    The righteous will triumph through me,
  for You will reward me.

Jeffrey Seif and Glenn Blank

A popular Beatles song suggests that we go to "Mother Mary" when we are in trouble. People do need someone to turn to when life's troubles hit. Hiding from Saul and his army in a cave in the cliffs above Ein Gedi—where the caves can still be seen—David desperately cries aloud to *HaShem* (1–2). He admits his prayer is a complaint about his troubles (3), especially about traps hidden to catch him (4). When it seems as if "no one cares for" his soul (5), when there is no other refuge, where does David turn? Where would you turn?

Maybe you've never hidden in a cave, but we've all had troubles to *kvetch* or complain about. Unlike some who see faith in God as fire insurance for the other side of the grave, David sees God as the One who cares about him when nobody else does "in the land of the living" (6). Disconsolate and feeling weak compared to his persecutors, he knows where to turn for rescue (7). From that deep, dark place, he cries out yet again, "Bring my soul out of prison, so I may praise Your Name" (8).

Do you know what it's like to be that desperate? When David cries out to God, he trusts that God "will reward" him. When you find yourself in what seems like a prison for your soul (8), do what David did—praise His Name, turn to the One who came to set the captives free (Luke 4:18). When you do, *Abba* Father will come and whisper in your ear: "I am here. I am here for you."

 # PSALM 143

Hide Not Your Face from Me

¹ A psalm of David.
> Hear my prayer, ADONAI,
> give ear to my petitions.
> In Your faithfulness and Your righteousness,
> answer me!
² Do not bring Your servant into judgment,
> for in Your eyes no one living is righteous.
³ For an enemy pursues my soul.
> He crushes my life down to the ground.
> He makes me dwell in darkness, like those long dead.

⁴ So my spirit grows faint within me.
  My heart is shocked within me.
⁵ I remember the days of old.
  I meditate on all You have done.
  I ponder the work of Your hands.
⁶ I spread forth my hands to You.
  My soul longs for You as a parched land. *Selah*
⁷ Answer me speedily, ADONAI—my spirit fails.
  Hide not Your face from me,
  lest I become like those who go down into the Pit.
⁸ Make me hear Your lovingkindness in the morning,
  for in You I trust.
  Show me the way I should go,
  for to You I lift up my soul.
⁹ Deliver me from my enemies, ADONAI.
  I hide myself in You.
¹⁰ Teach me to do Your will, for You are my God.
  Let Your good *Ruach* lead me on level ground.
¹¹ For Your Name's sake, ADONAI, revive me.
  In Your justice bring my soul out of trouble.
¹² In Your mercy cut off my enemies
  and destroy all who harass my soul,
  for I am Your servant.

Glenn Blank

As you meditate on this psalm, ponder all that David went through, all that *Yeshua* went through, all that the children of Israel have gone through, all that someone you know is going through now. Then intercede as David did, asking *HaShem* to "hear" his prayer, to "give ear" to his petitions (1). Pray that *HaShem* not bring His "servant into judgment" (2a). Recall that Isaiah repeatedly called Israel His servant (41:8; 44:1, 21; 45:4; 49:3–7), with whom the Suffering Servant identifies completely.

O Lord, "in Your eyes no one living is righteous" (2b)—until Messiah came to avert the evil decree against us. Save Your people Israel and deliver the one You know whose soul the enemy pursues, relentlessly crushing him into the ground (3). We remember and meditate on how You delivered Israel from bondage and rescued David from his oppressors; we ponder what *Yeshua* endured for our sake (5). We join David and the Son of David in spreading forth our hands in intercession (6). Though You hide Your face from our sin, ADONAI, You have been gracious to send a deliverer so that we would not go down into the Pit (7) without hope. May the one who has not experienced your salvation "hear Your lovingkindness in the morning" (8). Deliver Israel from her enemies, ADONAI (9). Teach the one who is going in every direction but the right one how to walk in Your *Ruach* as on level ground (10). Do justice, O Lord (11) and cut off the enemies "who harass my soul" (12), "for I am Your servant"—David, Israel, *Yeshua*, and you, dear intercessor.

✳✳✳✳✳✳ PSALM 144 ✳✳✳✳✳✳✳

Rescue from Battle

¹ Of David.
　　Blessed be ADONAI my Rock—
　　who trains my hands for war,
　　my fingers for battle.
² He is my lovingkindness, my fortress,
　　my strong tower, and my deliverer,
　　my shield, in whom I take refuge,
　　who subdues my people under me.
³ ADONAI, what is man, that You take note of him?
　　Or the son of man, that You consider him?[a]
⁴ Man is like a breath—
　　his days are like a passing shadow.
⁵ ADONAI, part Your heavens and come down.
　　Touch the mountains, so they smoke.
⁶ Flash forth lightning and scatter them.
　　Send out Your arrows and confuse them.
⁷ Stretch forth Your hands from on high.
　　Snatch me, deliver me out of deep waters,
　　out of the hand of foreigners,
⁸ whose mouth speaks falsehood,
　　whose right hand is a right hand of deceit.

a. 144:3. cf. Heb. 2:6.

⁹ God, I sing a new song to You, on a ten-string harp
    I sing praises to You—
¹⁰ who gives salvation to kings,
    who rescues Your servant David from the evil sword.
¹¹ Snatch me, deliver me
    out of the hand of foreigners,
    whose mouth speaks falsehood,
    whose right hand is a right hand of deceit.
¹² Then our sons will be like plants nurtured in their youth,
    our daughters like corner pillars carved for the construction of a
      palace.
¹³ Our storehouses are full,
    supplying every kind of produce.
    Our flocks increase by thousands
    and ten thousands in our fields.
¹⁴ Our oxen bear a heavy load.
    There is no breach,
    no going into captivity,
    no outcry in our streets.
¹⁵ Happy are such a people!
    Blessed are the people whose God is ADONAI!

Jeffrey Seif and Glenn Blank

What do we make of David blessing God, "who trains my hands for war" and "my fingers for battle" (1)? Though pacifists may read "my strong tower" and "my shield" as metaphors, for David the chieftain of mighty men, they describe strategic assets. Perched precariously in the middle of the Fertile Crescent, David knew it was God "who subdues my people under me" (2). Though in Psalm 8:4–5 it is the grandeur of creation that provokes David's amazement—"What is man, that You are mindful of him?"—here it is his utter dependence on God as his defense. Why should the Eternal One "take note" of a man (3), whose days "are like a passing shadow" (4)? Armies march to and fro, wreaking havoc, and people need to see God parting the heavens to come down for them (5), flashing lightning like arrows to scatter their enemies (6), and so these images have been recorded for them. People need help from heaven while here on earth. That's why David has written, "Stretch forth Your hands from on high. Snatch me, deliver me . . . out of the hand of foreigners" (7). Though wars are ancient and ongoing, David lifts up "a new song" to God (9)—new because it is always good news that God "gives salvation to kings" and "rescues" His servants (10).

After fighting through to victory, David turns to the blessings of peace—of children nurtured in palaces (12), of full storehouses and abundant flocks (13), of the real satisfaction of "no breach, no going into captivity, no outcry in our streets" (14). Yes, happy or blessed (both are *ashrei*) are such a people (15)! So, is God a therapist to vent at or a deliverer who helps us win in war? Counseling is a fine way to get things off our chest. Sometimes, though, we need to put on a breastplate and go fight. Can God be counted on out there, on the battlefields of life? David the warrior-king reassures us, with resounding praises, yes!

❋❋❋❋❋❋❋❋ PSALM 145 ❋❋❋❋❋❋❋❋❋

Glory of the Kingdom

¹ A psalm of praise. Of David.
  I will exalt You, my God, the King,
    and I will bless Your Name forever and ever.
² Every day I will bless You,
    and praise Your Name forever and ever!
³ Great is ADONAI, and greatly to be praised
    —His greatness is unsearchable.
⁴ One generation will praise Your works
    to another and declare Your mighty acts.
⁵ I will meditate on the glorious splendor
    of Your majesty and Your wonders.
⁶ They will speak of the might of Your awesome deeds,
    and I will proclaim Your greatness.
⁷ They will pour out the renown of Your great goodness,
    and sing joyfully of Your righteousness.
⁸ ADONAI is gracious and compassionate,
    slow to anger and great in lovingkindness.
⁹ ADONAI is good to all.
    He has compassion on all His creatures.

¹⁰ All Your works praise You, ADONAI,
  and Your *kedoshim* bless You.
¹¹ They declare the glory of Your kingdom
  and speak of Your might,
¹² to make known to the sons of men His mighty acts
  and the glory of the majesty of His kingdom.
¹³ Your kingdom is a kingdom for all ages,
  and Your dominion endures from generation to generation.

¹⁴ ADONAI upholds all who fall
  and raises up all who are bowed down.
¹⁵ The eyes of all look to You
  and You give them their food on time.
¹⁶ You open Your hand
  and satisfy every living thing with favor.
¹⁷ ADONAI is righteous in all His ways
  and kind in all His deeds.
¹⁸ ADONAI is near to all who call on Him,
  to all who call on Him in truth.
¹⁹ He will fulfill the desire of those who fear Him.
  He will hear their cry and save them.
²⁰ ADONAI watches over all who love Him,
  but all the wicked He will destroy.
²¹ My mouth declares the praise of ADONAI.
  Let all flesh bless His holy Name forever and ever!

Glenn Blank

Many psalms are prayers for earthly kings, who may serve as stand-ins for the King of kings. This acrostic poem (one verse for each letter of the Hebrew: *aleph*, *bet*, and so on) exalts "my God, the King" (1). Moreover, David's goal is to "bless" and "praise" His Name "forever and ever" (1–2). So we're not talking about temporal kingdoms, like Solomon's or Nebuchadnezzar's, which had their day and then got buried in archaeological mounds. We're talking—or rather we're exalting and praising—the One who rules over an eternal kingdom! His "greatness is unsearchable" (3), for it is far greater than what you can see with your natural eyes or comprehend with your natural mind. Ever since the original Passover—how many generations ago was that?—"one generation will praise Your works to another" (4). Would that all our families would meditate on "the glorious splendor of Your majesty" (5) and "the might of Your awesome deeds" (6) at our Seders and Thanksgiving dinners! Then we would "sing joyfully" about "Your great goodness" (7), as the righteous surely do in eternity! When the glory of God's kingdom touches mortal life, creatures feel His compassion (8), people become *kedoshim* and long to "make known . . . the majesty of His kingdom" (9–12). Just to be absolutely clear, we're talking about a "kingdom for all ages" (13).

The eternal kingdom is not just by-and-by. As it draws near, it transforms this world. So *Yeshua* proclaimed, "The kingdom of heaven is near" (Matt. 4:17)—in other words, at hand, available, ready to deal. *HaShem* demonstrates its reality when He "upholds all who fall" (14). For as *Yeshua* said, "Blessed are the poor in spirit, for theirs is the kingdom of heaven" (Matt. 5:3). *HaShem* provides food for all who look to Him (15), for "those who hunger and thirst for righteousness . . . shall be satisfied" (Matt. 5:6). He shows kindness (or mercy, *chesed*, 17) by giving mercy to the merciful. He is "near to all who call on Him" (18), for the pure in heart shall see God. He will "fulfill the desire of those who fear Him" (19)—such as those who are persecuted for the sake of righteousness. He will save them, and "theirs is the kingdom of heaven" (Matt. 5:10). When the kingdom of heaven draws near enough to touch the earth—when the King Himself returns to restore all things (Acts 1:6; 3:21)—He will save all "who call on Him in truth" (18–19), while the wicked will fall into ruins (20). Blessed are those who open their mouths to bless His holy Name (21).

How about you? Are you ready for the coming of His kingdom? Then pray for the establishment of His kingdom order in your life today.

 # PSALM 146

Justice of the Kingdom

¹ *Halleluyah!* Praise A DONAI, O my soul!
² I will praise A DONAI all my life.
    I will praise my God yet again.
³ Do not put your trust in princes—
    in man, in whom there is no salvation.

[4] His breath departs,
　　he returns to his dust.
　　In that very day his plans perish.
[5] Happy is he whose help is the God of Jacob,
　　whose hope is in ADONAI his God,
[6] who made heaven and earth, the sea, and all that is in them,
　　who keeps truth forever,
[7] who executes justice for the oppressed,
　　who gives bread to the hungry.
　　ADONAI sets the prisoners free.
[8] ADONAI opens the eyes of the blind.[a]
　　ADONAI raises up those who are bowed down.
　　ADONAI loves the righteous.
[9] ADONAI protects outsiders,
　　upholds the fatherless and the widow,
　　but thwarts the way of the wicked.
[10] ADONAI will reign forever,
　　your God, O Zion, from generation to generation.
　　Halleluyah!

Jeffrey Seif and Glenn Blank

Powerful people employ people to keep people from them. Bosses expect secretaries to protect them from the incessant demands of others. Bodyguards protect rock stars. Presidents and potential presidents have special agents to protect them from the press of the crowd and potentially dangerous people. The psalmist has God. He figures that trusting in God is better than trusting in princes or other persons—they may offer protection, but can they offer salvation (3)? What happens after a human "returns to his dust"? Ever since Adam, people breathe their last, and their "plans perish" (4). Better to look for help from the One who "made heaven and earth" (5–6).

Powerful people may not see it this way—especially those who cannot see Him at all. But the psalmist sees His power, which "executes justice for the oppressed" (7). Have you ever noticed that the power of oppressors doesn't last? Somehow the God of justice "raises up those who are bowed down" (8) and sends His compassion to the powerless (9). For so He announced in

a. 146:8. cf. Matt. 9:27–30.

Torah, "He enacts justice for the orphan and widow, and loves the outsider, giving him food and clothing" (Deut. 10:18). The Eternal One is all about justice and compassion. The kingdoms of powerful people rise and fall. But the kingdom of God endures forever (10).

Need evidence? Consider how *HaShem* has preserved the children of Israel "from generation to generation" (10). For thousands of years and against all odds, He restored Israel to Zion—in spite of the murderous schemes of Haman, Hadrian, and Hitler. History demonstrates that *HaShem* ultimately "thwarts the way of the wicked" (9). Need more evidence? Consider the influence of a man who was flogged and executed on a Roman stake, yet who now claims the allegiance of multiplying myriads around the globe? Consider how Jews in Israel and around the world who have experienced the reality of *Yeshua* firsthand have become a growing movement. Together, Jews and gentiles are proclaiming *Yeshua* as the coming King of Israel in Zion. One who seemed so powerless has become the most powerful of all! *Baruch HaShem!*

PSALM 147

He Builds Up Jerusalem

¹ *Halleluyah!*
    How good it is to sing praises to our God.
    How pleasant and fitting is praise.
² ADONAI builds up Jerusalem.
    He gathers together the exiles of Israel.
³ He heals the brokenhearted
    and binds up their wounds.
⁴ He determines the number of the stars.
    He gives them all their names.
⁵ Great is our Lord and mighty in power—
    His understanding is infinite!
⁶ ADONAI upholds the humble.
    He brings the wicked to the ground.
⁷ Sing to ADONAI with thanksgiving.
    Sing praises to our God on the harp.

⁸ He covers the sky with clouds.
    He provides rain for the earth.
    He makes grass sprout on the hills.
⁹ He gives food to the cattle
    and to the young ravens which cry.
¹⁰ He delights not in the horse's strength,
    nor takes pleasure in a man's legs.
¹¹ ADONAI delights in those who revere Him,
    in those who trust in His lovingkindness.

¹² Exalt ADONAI, O Jerusalem!
    Praise your God, O Zion!
¹³ For He strengthens the bars of your gates.
    He blesses your children within you.
¹⁴ He puts *shalom* within your borders.
    He satisfies you with the finest wheat.
¹⁵ He sends earth His command—
    His word runs swiftly.
¹⁶ He gives snow like wool.
    He scatters frost like ashes.
¹⁷ He hurls down His hail like pebbles—
who can stand before His cold?
¹⁸ He sends forth His word and melts them.
    He makes His wind blow and waters flow.
¹⁹ He declares His word to Jacob,
    His decrees and His rulings to Israel.
²⁰ He has not done so with any other nation.
    They have not known His judgments.
    Halleluyah!

Glenn Blank

This "pleasant and fitting" song of praise (1) was probably written after the exiles returned to the land and were rebuilding Jerusalem (2). Indeed, the ancient Septuagint translation into Greek added a preface attributing this psalm to the postexilic prophets Haggai and Zechariah. Those who suffered exile now agree that *HaShem* "heals the brokenhearted and binds up their wounds" (3). By working through the Persian kings and the Hebrew prophets to encourage the rebuilding of the Temple and the repopulation of Jerusalem and Judea, God demonstrated His authority as well as His compassion. His power is seen in the heavens, where He "determines the number of the stars" (4), and on the earth, where He "upholds the humble" (6). Though all living things depend on Him for rain and food (8–9), He especially exalts Himself through the praises of singers (7) and those who revere and trust Him (11).

The second half of the poem focuses on Jerusalem (12). The prophets and Levitical singers encourage people to return by celebrating how God "strengthens the bars of your gates" (13)—probably an allusion to Nehemiah's successful reconstruction project restoring Jerusalem's walls and gates. As a result, Jews could be confident that "He puts *shalom* within your borders" (14). The promised prosperity goes outside the city to the countryside of Judea, where "He satisfies you with the finest wheat" (14). He "gives snow" and "hurls down . . . hail," then sends "His word and melts them." He causes wind to blow and waters to flow (16–18). These things are not just meteorological coincidences. They follow from God's Word (15). Through Moses and the prophets, *HaShem* had promised that He would restore His people in the land when they called upon His Name. Thus history and nature confirm that God is faithful to His word. The exile confirmed the righteousness of "His judgments," and the restoration confirmed His mercy and faithfulness to His covenant promises, distinguishing Israel from "any other nation" (20). O Zion and those who love Zion, step back and see the big picture of history and nature, and praise *ADONAI*!

 # PSALM 148

Praise Him, All Creation!

¹ *Halleluyah!*
  Praise *ADONAI* from the heavens!
  Praise Him in the highest!
² Praise Him all His angels!
  Praise Him all His armies.
³ Praise Him, sun and moon!
  Praise Him, all stars of light.

⁴ Praise Him, highest heavens,
    and waters above the heavens.
⁵ Let them praise the Name of ADONAI,
    for He commanded and they were created.
⁶ He set them in place forever and ever.
    He made a decree that will never pass away.
⁷ Praise ADONAI from the earth,
    sea monsters and all depths,
⁸ fire and hail, snow and vapor,
    storm wind doing His bidding,
⁹ mountains and all hills,
    fruit trees and all cedars,
¹⁰ beasts and all cattle,
    crawling things and winged birds,
¹¹ kings of the earth and all peoples,
    princes and all rulers of earth,
¹² both young men and maidens,
    old men and children.
¹³ Let them praise the Name of ADONAI,
    for His Name alone is exalted.
    His glory is above earth and heaven.
¹⁴ He has raised up a horn for His people,
    a praise for all His *kedoshim*,[a]
    for the children of Israel—
    a people near to Him.
    Halleluyah!

Jeffrey Seif and Glenn Blank

The scroll of the Psalter nears its end with a chorus of praise for the Creator. "His angels" and "His armies" lead off, because they are "in the highest"—the eternal heavens (1–2). In case you're wondering about those armies, take a look at 2 Kings 6:17, where *HaShem* opened "the servant's eyes, and he looked and saw the hills full of horses and chariots of fire all around Elisha." If you're wondering if those horses and chariots can contend with nukes and missiles, don't. We're talking chariots of supernatural fire. *Cheruvim*, seraphim, and armies of angels worship the Eternal One. Heavenly bodies join the choir,

a. 148:14. Heb. *kedoshim*; *righteous* or *holy ones*.

including sun, moon, and stars (3–4)—everything He created by His command (5). The very way they move in their celestial places praises Him (6). "Sea monsters" and extreme weather phenomena with all their force (7–8), mountains and trees with their soaring height (9), beasts and birds (10) with their lumbering or soaring life—all praise Him. Finally, even humans will join in—all kings and rulers, young and old (11–12)—when the glory of God explodes into consciousness. Quite a cast! Everyone and everything is called to "praise the Name of ADONAI" (13).

The climax of this praise is found in verse 14: "He has raised up a horn for His people." Perhaps you're thinking the horn is a *shofar.* That's a good thought, but it's more than that. The horn is a symbol of the One whom the *shofar* heralds: the King of kings, may His Name be exalted forever! At the outset, back in Genesis, all creation was connected to God. At the end, ahead in Revelation, all will be reconnected to Him. Living in between Genesis and Revelation, here we are in a world of disconnection, everything and everyone falling apart from each other and from God. Look up. The One who created all living things for His praise is invisibly but surely pulling all things together again. If you are "saved," you have been pulled into God's kingdom already. So get up and join the choir now! All creation has been waiting (Rom. 8:19) to hear you sing, or to at least make a joyful noise!

PSALM 149

Praise with Singing and Dancing

¹ *Halleluyah!* Sing to ADONAI a new song,
    His praise in the assembly of the *kedoshim.*
² Let Israel rejoice in its Maker.
    Let the children of Zion be glad in their King.
³ Let them praise His Name with dancing.
    Let them sing praises to Him with tambourine and harp.
⁴ For ADONAI takes pleasure in His people.
    He crowns the humble with salvation.
⁵ Let the *kedoshim* exult in glory.
    Let them sing for joy on their beds.

⁶ Let God's high praises be in their mouth
   and a two-edged sword in their hand—
⁷ to execute vengeance upon the nations
   and rebukes on the peoples,
⁸ to bind their kings with chains
   and their nobles with fetters of iron,
⁹ to carry out the sentence decreed—
   this is the glory of all His *kedoshim*.
   Halleluyah!

Paul Wilbur

This psalm invites us in with the very opening word . . . Halleluyah! Praise *Adonai*! No matter where I travel in the world, this word always elicits the same response whether the audience is Hispanic, Asian, Middle Eastern, or Canadian. Whenever I stand before a crowd and proclaim, "Halleluyah!" they always shout it right back to me. After opening with the word that every nation around the world knows in Hebrew, the psalmist tells us to sing to the Lord a שִׁיר חָדָשׁ, *shir chadash*, a new song. It not only means to sing something fresh, but also something out of a freshness of the new spirit given you from *Adonai*. So we are invited to sing and prophesy in the sanctuary as we minister to the living God.

Israel is now urged to boast "in its Maker"; the children of Zion—the fortress city of God—are to "be glad in their King" (2). They are to praise Him with dancing (in ancient and modern Israel, a circle dance) and with songs accompanied by tambourines and harps (3). The entire congregation is encouraged to open their mouths, lift their hands, take up the instruments, and bless the Lord from a heart of thanksgiving. Why? Because the Lord takes great delight and "pleasure in His people" (4), and He inhabits the *tehillim* of His flock. Let the people of *Adonai* be joyful in the abundance of the glory of the presence of their King, and may they even "sing for joy on their beds" (5). Have you ever experienced the manifest presence of God so fully that you simply could not keep your mouth shut? Have you ever been so taken with the glory of *Adonai* that you couldn't fall asleep and just continued to sing to Him a song never heard before? Such praise-filled joy is His desire for you!

When God arises on our praise, His enemies will scatter. But look what else happens when the high praise of God is in our mouths and the two-edged sword of the Word of God is in our hands (6): ADONAI executes vengeance and punishment. He binds kings, principalities, and powers with chains and fetters of iron, and He carries out the sentence decreed for them (7–9). All we do is praise the Lord! In 2 Chronicles 20, a prophet speaks to a frightened people who think they are about to be annihilated by three foreign armies. What does he tell them? Do not be afraid or discouraged, for the battle belongs to the Lord! So they went out to battle equipped with . . . a *shir chadash* . . . and the Lord did the rest! Halleluyah!

PSALM 150

Praise with *Shofar* and Cymbals

¹ *Halleluyah!* Praise God in His Sanctuary!
   Praise Him in His mighty expanse.
² Praise Him for His acts of power.
   Praise Him for His enormous greatness.
³ Praise Him with the blast of the *shofar*.
   Praise Him with harp and lyre.
⁴ Praise Him with tambourine and dance.
   Praise Him with stringed instruments and flute.
⁵ Praise Him with clash of cymbals.
   Praise Him with resounding cymbals.
⁶ Let every thing that has breath
   praise ADONAI. *Halleluyah!*

Paul Wilbur

Hallelu et ADONAI! Praise the Lord! So we have come to the last song of this beloved book of *Tehillim*, praise songs. In my humble opinion this one is a glorious outburst from a heart completely in love! I can imagine David singing this in several different keys, with more verses than are scribed here, as the ark of the covenant was being carried on the shoulders of the Levites up to Jerusalem. Maybe he shouted it as he held high the head of Goliath, or maybe a choir at his coronation sang it.

My friend Ted Pearce set this psalm to music, and I liked it so much I sang it on a recording we made in the desert of Ein Gedi on the first night of Sukkot in 2009. Ted used all the instruments in his setting that David listed here. I thought it would be nice to add to the list of "who" and "what" should *hallel* ADONAI, and so I wrote another verse that you will never read in the Scriptures:

> Praise Him in the heavens,
> Praise Him moon and stars!
> Praise Him for His glory and pow'r,
> Praise Him with guitars!
> Praise Him in the battle,
> Praise Him in the storm,
> Praise Him for the victories won,
> Praise Him with this song![1]

One of the highest intentions of ADONAI for His people Israel is to be the worship leader of the nations. Certainly one of the tasks of the sons of Jacob was to reveal the one true God of Abraham, Isaac, and Jacob to the world: to be a priestly nation among the nations and so reveal the salvation of ADONAI, His faithfulness and lovingkindness, to every tribe and every tongue; to make known His power and His covenant; to demonstrate His goodness; and to sing of His great love forever. Happy is the people whose God is the Lord.

And so this great book of praise comes to a close, as it should, by inviting everything and everyone from everywhere that has breath to *hallel* ADONAI, praise the Lord. . . . *Halleluyah!*

Notes

Psalm 44

1. *Newsweek*, January 25, 2012.
2. *Third Guttman-Avi Chai Report*, January 2012.

Psalm 49

1. http://psalms.schechter.edu, accessed September 2011.

Psalm 55

1. "In Memorium A.H.H.," in *Alfred Lord Tennyson: In Memorium*, ed. Robert H. Ross (New York: W. W. Norton, 1973).

Psalm 65

1. Israel's Hope, *Introducing Israel's Hope* © 1985 Integrity's Hosanna! Music.

Psalm 109

1. C. S. Lewis, *Reflections on the Psalms* (New York: Harcourt, Brace, 1958), chap. 3.

Psalm 135

1. *Fiddler on the Roof*, directed by Norman Jewison (Beverly Hills, CA: United Artists, 1971).

Psalm 150

1. Paul Wilbur, *Desert Rain* © 2010 Integrity Media.

About the Authors

Professor Jeffrey Seif teaches at a variety of Bible colleges and seminaries in the United States and Israel. In addition to his twenty-four years in higher education, Jeff pastors and presently leads Sar Shalom, a Messianic synagogue in Dallas, Texas. He is a sought-after congregational speaker and conference speaker. Jeff is a graduate of the North Texas Regional Police Academy and has earned a master's degree and doctorate from Southern Methodist University, Dallas. He has many books and articles to his credit. Among other things, Jeff is the chief theologian and vice president of the Messianic Jewish Family Bible Society, which has produced the Tree of Life Version of the Holy Scriptures. Learn more about him at www.familybiblesociety.org.

Messianic Rabbi Glenn David Blank leads Beit Simcha (www.beitsimcha .org), a Messianic Jewish congregation in Allentown, Pennsylvania. His ordination as Messianic Rabbi is through IAMCS. He also serves as the conference chair and member of the Tikkun America Apostolic Team (www.TikkunAmerica .org) and as the literary editor of the Tree of Life Version of the Holy Scriptures. Glenn earned his doctorate in cognitive science and an MS degree in computer science from the University of Wisconsin–Madison. He earned an MA degree in English from the University of Michigan and a BA degree in English from Pennsylvania State University. After twenty-seven years, he retired as professor emeritus from Lehigh University in 2011 to pursue full-time ministry. Glenn has two children and currently helps his wife with day care for his granddaughter. His testimony is viewable on YouTube or www.beitsimcha.org.

Paul Wilbur was on his way to the opera houses and synagogues of the world when he met a young singer at Indiana University graduate school of music who would alter his life plans forever. Paul was determined to follow the footsteps of Metropolitan Opera star Richard Tucker, until he fell in love with Israel's Messiah back in March of 1977 on a fishing trip with his friend Jerry Williams. From the very first day, Paul knew his destiny was to sing, but the subject matter was to undergo a radical transformation. For more than thirty-five years, Paul has traversed the globe with guitar in hand, singing and declaring the praises of *Yeshua* (Jesus) the Messiah who set him free so many years ago. He has recorded too many projects to list here, performs them in multiple languages in nearly one hundred nations, has served for years on Messianic and church staffs, is a published writer, records with Integrity Music, has been married to the love of his life for more than thirty-three years, and has two sons and two daughters-in-law and a grandson who all serve in the ministry together. Paul and his entire tribe live in Jacksonville, Florida, and can be reached through www.wilburministries.com.

 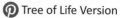